The Invention and Decline of Israeliness

The Invention and Decline of Israeliness

State, Society, and the Military

Baruch Kimmerling

UNIVERSITY OF CALIFORNIA PRESS
Berkeley · *Los Angeles* · *London*

The publisher
gratefully acknowledges
the generous contribution
to this book provided by
the S. Mark Taper Foundation

University of California Press
Berkeley and Los Angeles, California

University of California Press, Ltd.
London, England

First paperback printing 2005
© 2001 by the Regents of the University of California

Library of Congress Cataloging-in-Publication Data

Kimmerling, Baruch.
   The invention and decline of Israeliness : state,
society, and the military / Baruch Kimmerling.
       p.   cm.
   Includes bibliographical references and index.
   ISBN 978-0-520-24672-0 (pbk : alk. paper)
   1. National characteristics, Israeli.   2. Jews—
Israel—Identity.   3. Israel—Social conditions—
20th century.   4. Israel—Ethnic relations.
5. Religion and state—Israel.   I. Title.

DS113.3.K56 2001
306'.095694—dc21   00-067238

Manufactured in the United States of America
13   12   11   10   09   08
10   9   8   7   6   5   4   3   2

The paper used in this publication is both acid-free
and totally chlorine-free (TCF). It meets the
minimum requirements of ANSI/NISO
Z39.48-1992 (R 1997) (Permanence of Paper). ♾

To Diana—
Without whose lifelong support I would
have had nothing

Contents

Acknowledgments

This book is a summary of an approximately ten-year process of professional and intellectual discussions, debates, and sometimes bitter controversies with friends, colleagues, students, and rivals. I have been fortunate enough to be surrounded by highly stimulating intellectual environments in the offices, faculty clubs, and corridors of the Hebrew University and the University of Washington at Seattle. I have also been supported and spoiled by a vivid global exchange through the wonders of the Internet and the electronic mail system. The names of those who have contributed to these environments are so innumerable that, with the exception of the late Dan Horowitz, I shall refrain from listing them. The final version was rewritten following very thoughtful, wise, and constructive comments of three anonymous peer reviewers of the University of California Press.

I would like to thank my devoted students and assistants who have aided me throughout all these years and made possible the implementation of this mission: Jon Simons, Matthew Diamond, Lauren Erdreich, Michal Laron, Hagit Schwartz, and Keren-Or Schlesinger. I also am pleasantly indebted to the Eshkol Center of Israel Studies and to the Silbert Center for Research of Israeli Society and Director Arieh Schachar for their generous support in funding the research demanded by the present volume. I am deeply grateful to Malcom Reed and Cindy Fulton of the University of California Press, who handled the manuscript so carefully, and special thanks to Peter Dreyer for his excellent editorial work.

Parts of this volume are based on previously published material. Chapter 2 is based on "State Building, State Autonomy, and the Identity of Society: The Case of the Israeli State," published in the *Journal of Historical Sociology* 6, 4 (1993): 397–429. Chapter 4 partially relies on "Between Hegemony and Dormant *Kulturkampf* in Israel," published in *Israel Affairs* 4, 3–4 (1998): 49–72. Part of chapter 5 derives from "The New Israelis: Plurality of Cultures without Multiculturalism," *Alpayim* 16 (1998): 264–308 (in Hebrew). Chapter 6 is adapted from "Religion, Nationalism and Democracy in Israel," published in *Constellations* 6, 3 (1999): 339–63. Finally, chapter 7's main source is an essay titled "Political Subcultures and Civilian Militarism in a Settler-Immigrant Society," published in *Security Concerns: Insights from the Israeli Experience*, edited by Daniel Bar-Tal, Dan Jacobson, and Aharon Klieman (Stamford, Conn.: JAI Press, 1998), pp. 395–416.

I am grateful to all the publishers who so generously granted me the right to use the material. Nonetheless, all these papers served only as foundations for the present chapters of this volume. Most were completely rewritten to include (or sometimes exclude) new material and ideas and to present a coherent narrative.

Introduction

This book offers an overview and analysis of the construction and deconstruction of hegemonic, secular Zionist Israeli national identity from the early years of the Zionist movement to the present. Today, for better or for worse, Israel is a very different polity than was envisioned by any of the streams of Zionism, or even by the builders of the Israeli state and society. During the past two decades, changes have accelerated, and few earlier assumptions about Israel's demographic composition, political and social boundaries, cultural character, or social and economic structures remain valid. In addition, Israel is undergoing processes of change in position and location on both the international and regional planes—processes that are strongly interlinked with domestic developments.

Nevertheless, the changes in rhetoric and social roles have left some of Israel's core characteristics and social institutions unaltered. Israel is still an active immigrant settler society, domestically and externally a relatively strong state (even if less stable than in the past), based on two deep cultural codes, common at least to its Jewish citizens—militarism and "Jewishness." The increasing Jewish sentiment—a mixture of secular nationalism and mainly popular-fundamentalist religiousness—is at the same time a partial continuation of the initial social order and a consequence of its decline.

Perhaps the most dramatic changes that have occurred in Israel are the evaporation of the image of a single, unified Israeli society, the decline of a unique Israeli identity (notwithstanding excluded and marginal groups, such as the Arabs and Orthodox Jews), and the diminishment of hegemonic secular Hebrew culture. Within the Israeli state, a system of cultural and social plurality is emerging, but in the absence of a concept or ideology of multiculturalism. Today, Israel is undergoing an accelerated process of invention, creation, and institution-building by about seven different cultures and countercultures, without an accepted hierarchy among them. These cultures are based on and reinforced by ethnic, class, and religious components and differ in the sharpness of their social boundaries, the level of their organization, and their consciousness of the degree to which they are separate.

This process is being complemented by another trend, the subdivision of Israeli identity, nationalism, and collective memory into many versions, with only a soft common core. The result has been not only a process of reshaping collective identity but also a continuous conflict over the meaning of what might be called Israeliness, the rules of the game, and the criteria for distribution and redistribution of common goods.

The seven cultures, which are each presently in different stages of crystallization, are the previously hegemonic secular Ashkenazi upper middle class, the national religious, the traditionalist Mizrahim (Orientals), the Orthodox religious, the Arabs, the new Russian immigrants, and the Ethiopians. Although none of these social groups is homogeneous, and most of them harbor deep political and ideological divergences (e.g., "hawks" vs. "doves"), each still holds on to a separate collective identity and also wages an open cultural war against the others.

It seems that two contradictory phenomena have occurred within the Israeli state. The first phenomenon entails the decomposition of the original Zionist hegemony into many conflicting ideological and institutional segments, which have created a kind of diverse degree of separatist civil society or societies, as was mentioned above. The second phenomenon entails the persistence of the state's strength and centrality—in terms of both monopolizing regulation of the common good and passing legislation, as well as playing a key role in the continuous interrelations between the cultural sphere and the might and myth of the state's military.

The multidimensional relationships of this second phenomenon make for an almost total lack of boundaries between the military and social (public and private) spheres. This is not just a matter of military world-views (sometimes called the "military mind") influencing civilian institutions, and neither is Israel the kind of besieged and completely mobilized "Jewish Sparta" it is often depicted as. Rather, the situation is one in which military and other social problems are so highly intermingled that social and political issues become construed as "existential security" issues and vice versa, making it almost impossible to differentiate between them. The Israeli military-industrial complex, which is well described by the professional literature, is merely a particular case of the wider military-cultural complex.

What is the historical background of this situation? How and why has it occurred, and what are the practical consequences for Israel? These are the major issues dealt with in this volume. The book attempts to provide a kaleidoscopic and multifarious picture of Israeli state and society by combining historical evidence, sociological analysis, and cultural paradigms.

In addition, I am arguing that the strength and capability of the Israeli military to penetrate society is predicated by the military's all-embracing and civilian nature. For this reason, the state and its extension through the military institution has been a major actor in the Zionist story. Nevertheless, because the state is not in a zero-sum situation vis-à-vis other actors of civil society (or semi-autonomous spheres of activity), a process of partial "normalization" and individualization has occurred, and nonstatist bodies based on diverse organizational principles have appeared.

I also share my late friend and colleague Dan Horowitz's view that Israeli civilians are "partially militarized" and the military is "partially civilianized." In this volume, I go further in analyzing just how partial this "partially" is, which parts have been militarized and which civilianized, how this was done, and, most important, why. Today, Israel is considered one of the most powerful medium-sized nation-states in the world. The Israeli state's internal strength is demonstrated by its high capacity to recruit internal human and material resources for collective goals, while its external strength is demonstrated by its formidable military might and its salient influence on global, economic, and political agendas. Nonetheless, the Israeli state and society still constitute an active immigrant settler sociopolitical entity (perhaps the last of its kind in the world), lacking a finalized and consensual geopolitical and social identity, boundaries, and location in the political and cultural environment of the Middle East. These traits create a strong sense of vulnerability and weakness, which continues to endanger the state's very existence in the region, as well as the stability and continuity of its original internal social fabric and structure.

As an immigrant settler society, Israel has not only faced violent resistance on the part of the hostile local population of the country and other nations of the region, but has also made confrontation with them a source of internal strength for its settler elites and leadership and a tool for material and human resource mobilization. As a society espousing an ideology of immigration, it has not only imported human and material capital, but has also been obliged to use the tools of "human engineering" in order to homogenize immigrants by imposing newly invented identities on existing ideologies, symbols, and identity codes.

The Israeli state came to being in the context of incremental Jewish immigration from many countries and continents, against the will of the local population, and in the face of both passive and active resistance. Unlike most other immigrant settler societies—in North and South America, Australia, Africa, and Asia—the Zionist colonizers did not choose their destination because of an abundance of natural resources, fertile free land, water, mines, oil, forests, or a comfortable climate. Nor did the immigrants to the so-called "Land of Israel" represent an imperial power. Rather, the target land was chosen because of a national ideology, Zionism, based on symbols and codes borrowed from the nineteenth-century European version of Jewish religion and ethnicity. The secular (liberal- or socialist-oriented) founding fathers and the inventors of modern Jewish nationalism borrowed the religiously preserved collective memory of the ancient Holy Land, *Zion,* as the territorial base for their nation- and state-building efforts. These reinterpretations of religious notions and myths were intended to serve as a powerful recruitment engine for Jewish immigration to Zion by proffering a collective form of salvation from persecution and oppression suffered in Europe and, to a lesser degree, in other parts of the world. At the same time, religious symbols and especially biblical texts, constructed and reinterpreted as "history," were considered a very useful tool for generating internal and external legitimacy for the Zionist colonization venture.

In the beginning, Zionism was only a marginal idea among Occidental (so-called Ashkenazi) Jewry. About 150 years before the triumph of Zionism, the traditional form of European Jewish community (or ghetto) had been slowly dismantled by a series of internal and external events and processes (see chapter 1). The political and social emancipation granted to Jewish citizens by several European states, and accelerated by the French and American revolutions, produced a small, but very influential Jewish cultural enlightenment movement, which was highly ambivalent about Jewish religion and ethnicity. More important results of political emancipation included large waves of secularization, both in conjunction with, and separate from, attempts at complete assimilation of the Jews into local non-Jewish society. In addition, emigration from the Jewish settlements of eastern Europe to North America and to a lesser degree to western Europe increased during this period. The countereffect of these processes was the appearance of Jewish Orthodoxy, which attempted to rebuild and redraw the boundaries of the religious community by increasing the severity of social control over its members and the surveillance of daily-life practices.

The idea of a Jewish polity in Palestine as a viable and perhaps the sole option for those Jews who did not succeed in immigrating to the United States became relevant as other options seemed to close. The riots and pogroms of 1881 and 1903–5 in eastern Europe sufficed only to bring a handful of Jews to Palestine. The vast majority preferred the option of individual (or familial) redemption, and migrated to America. In the meantime, a tiny World Zionist Organization was created by a handful of assimilated Jewish intellectuals, who were very disappointed by the failure of emancipation, but had been inspired by European nationalistic movements.

Despite the small size of its formal organization and active resistance on the part of the local Arab population, the Zionist organization succeeded in establishing a viable bridgehead in Palestine under the British colonial umbrella. After the Holocaust and World War II, the existence of this bridgehead made possible the establishment of the Jewish nation-state. Establishment of the state also, however, required that a considerable portion of British Palestine be ethnically cleansed of its Arab inhabitants (see chapter 1). This clearance made possible the establishment of a state more nationally homogenous, with more territory, and, from the Jewish nationalist point of view, with more "rational" borders than originally allocated by United Nations Resolution 181 and the territorial partition plan.

The vast amount of abandoned and expropriated Arab lands and properties were nationally expropriated and used to strengthen the state in two ways. Reallocation of lands ameliorated the physical problem of accommodating the first waves of nonselective mass immigration. At the same time, expropriation empowered the fledgling state by making it the supreme source of resource allocation.

From the very beginning, the veteran Zionist elite detected and perceived two major threats: the external threat of being militarily defeated by the surrounding Arab states, and the internal threat of the decomposition and alteration of the original characteristics of the state by mass immigration. These two different kinds of threats were perceived as interconnected (see chapter 3). On the one hand, "lowering" the human quality and the cultural level of society and redirecting social resources for the "healing" and reeducation of large quantities of new immigrants posed a danger to the security of the state by destabilizing its social fabric. This existential, or security threat, could be avoided by encouraging "higher quality [Jewish] elements" to immigrate to the country, and by limiting emigration. On the other hand, the external threat was also regarded as implicitly "functional" for the cohesion and social integration of "Jewish society."

Three complementary institutions were designed to meet these threats: the state bureaucracy, the educational system, and the military. The building of an efficient bureaucratic apparatus was a necessary condition for the creation of a highly centralized, strong state, sustained by a hegemonic culture. As with the educational system and the military, however, this bureaucratization not accomplished easily or without harsh internal struggles (see chapter 2). The schools were, of course, the backbone of the educational system, but a substantial portion of the veteran population was also recruited for the informal education of children, youth, and adults. The most salient institution, however, was the military and the policy of compulsory conscription, designed both to safeguard the existence of the state and to resocialize immigrants by serving as the central and preferred "melting pot." Within this framework, the new Israeli man and woman were to be created.

Zionism was an almost unbelievable success, from both internal and external points of view. In the 1940s and 1950s, the consolidation of a Jewish immigrant settler state in the middle of the Arab Middle East was perceived as against all odds. In retrospect, however, Israel's establishment and evolution into a potent political and military entity came to seem self-evident. Only later, when its initial identity and structure had decomposed and fragmented, and many kinds of Israeliness appeared, did it become clearer that these successes contained the seeds of internal contradiction.

Many contemporary observers have been so impressed by these rapid changes in the relative power of various groups within the Israeli state, and its transformation from a monocultural system into a plurality, that they have proclaimed the start of a "post-Zionist era." This term is problematic and unhelpful, however, because such fashionable "end-ism" is overloaded with either strong negative or positive sentiments (depending on ideological bias) and lacks explanatory power.

The present volume is a third-generation sociohistorical analysis of Israel. Shmuel N. Eisenstadt's *Israeli Society,* published in Hebrew and English in 1967, was the first pioneering analysis and description of Israel, and in many ways fixed paradigmatically the study of this society for a generation in Israel and abroad. The book became the standard textbook about Israel. It was written under the heavy influence of two streams of interwoven thinking: functionalism and hegemonic Labor party Zionism. Israel was depicted as a heroic, modern (i.e., Western) immigrant country striving to attain two complementary goals: to "absorb" and modernize a vast number of new immigrants from underdeveloped countries and to defend the state from its enemies, who inexplicably sought to destroy it. The most intriguing aspect of Eisenstadt's approach is its mixture of sociology, ideology, and mythology. By mixing historical and societal analysis, Eisenstadt reinforced and reproduced the official myths created by the dominant stratum of the Palestine Jewish community, the so-called Yishuv. The use of weighty professional sociological terminology served him well, giving his work high scientific credibility and an appearance of being "value-free." The story he told took place within an almost exclusively "Jewish bubble," or environmental vacuum. Moreover, mainly young, Ashkenazi, socialist male workers of the land (but not peasants) were credited with building the Jewish nation, with little room accorded other Jewish participants in this heroic venture. Eisenstadt presented a linear-developmental perception of Israel's social history, from an embryonic newly founded pioneering community toward a modern, highly developed Western country. A successfully created "Israeli" man, whose identity was the final product of a masterful melting pot, populated this country.

Eisenstadt's linear social historiography and sociography culminated in his second book on Israel, *The Transformation of Israeli Society: An Essay in Interpretation,* published in 1985. Here Israeli society was encapsulated within a great Jewish civilization and tradition, beginning with the Jewish nation's founding fathers—Abraham, Isaac, and Jacob—-

and coming to a logical end in the Israeli and American Jewish centers, with an obvious preference for the former. With this, Eisenstadt, the secularist and moderate socialist, adopted (probably unconsciously) the fundamental Jewish religious paradigm of the nature and roots of Israel—as a Jewish state.

The second generation of Israeli sociological projects is mainly identified with the names of Dan Horowitz, Moshe Lissak, Yonathan Shapiro, and Eva Etzioni-Halevy, and with pure political sociology. Etzioni-Halevy's *Political Culture in Israel: Cleavage and Integration among Israeli Jews,* published in 1977, was the first to anticipate fundamental changes in the Israeli political arena. Horowitz and Lissak, lifelong collaborators, divided Israeli sociography into two periods, and consecrated a book to each. The first is the period of the Yishuv, the politically organized Jewish ethno-community in Palestine prior to sovereignty. The second period extends from the constitution of the independent Israeli state to the mid 1980s. The first book, *Origins of the Israeli Polity: Palestine under the Mandate* (published in Hebrew in 1977 and in an abridged English version in 1978), departed very little from the path established by Eisenstadt, yet focused on the building of political institutions and on political quarrels among the Jews in Palestine (the Hebrew version going into encyclopedic detail). Horowitz and Lissak's second volume, *Trouble in Utopia: The Overburdened Polity of Israel* (published in English in 1989 and in Hebrew in 1990), was, in part, a paradigmatic breakthrough. It included the internal and external Jewish-Arab conflict within its conceptual framework. Internal Jewish-Arab relations were conceptualized as yet another among the many "cleavages" in a deeply divided society. All these "cleavages"—ethnic (Ashkenazim vs. Mizrahim), religious-secular, and political ("doves" vs. "hawks")— were considered destructive. The desired society was conflict-free and harmonious. Horowitz and Lissak argued that the Israeli political system functions improperly owing to too many simultaneous demands to fulfill internal and external goals. The major thesis thus remained highly influenced by Eisenstadt's and Horowitz and Lissak's previous neofunctionalist approach (softened by some ingredients from the conflict-oriented paradigm). Zionist ideology and terminology were interchangeable with sociological theorization and problematization: Israel was considered the only successful materialization of utopia in the world, despite some difficulties in implementation because of "overload." Israel was regarded as self-evidently a democracy, albeit with minor imperfections.

Yonathan Shapiro challenged the self-satisfaction of the "Jerusalem School" (consisting of Eisenstadt, Lissak, Horowitz, and others). Although he never wrote a single comprehensive book on Israeli society and history, Shapiro analyzed internal party politics and mechanisms in a series of monographs, coming to the conclusion that Israel is democratic only in a very formal and narrow sense of the term. He depicted the Israeli political scene as a Bolshevik-type regime, in which a very small old-timer elite group rules the state under the premise of democracy. Fearful even of their own young colleagues and disciples, this oligarchy actively limited the political skills of their successors so as to survive politically throughout their own lifetimes.

Despite Shapiro's highly critical approach to Israeli sociology and political science and his analysis of the ruling elite (very much resembling C. Wright Mills's critiques of American sociology), Shapiro himself was distinctly myopic when it came to other characteristics of Israeli society and its sociology. For example, very much like Eisenstadt, Shapiro completely ignored the impact of the Jewish-Arab conflict. He almost completely overlooked the cultural, religious, gender, ethnic, and national tensions and rifts built into the Israeli state. The Jewish-Arab conflict, wars, and the militarization of society were exogenous factors in his sociology. Shapiro's students (such as Gershon Shafir, Uri Ben-Eliezer, and Hanna Herzog) added major correctives to his work, but also in monographic studies and not in comprehensive, paradigmatically oriented books.

Although Alan Dowty's *The Jewish State: A Century Later,* published in 1998, includes the most up-to-date data and literature on the Israeli state and society, it should be considered as belonging to the second-generation approach to Israel. Although aware of the growing trend of critical scholarship on the Israeli state and society represented by the first two generations of sociologists and political scientists, Dowty produced an apologetic overview of the Israeli case. Dowty asserted that Israel is a consociational democracy rooted in the "democratic manners" of the Diaspora Jewish community (Kehila). Equating Israeli citizens with the public members of an ethno-religious nonsovereign community (Kahal), Dowty made at least two major errors. He confused rule over a civil sovereign state with decision-making within a community. He also failed to detect the mechanisms and institutional arrangements of consociationalism that traditionally excluded Arabs from the system (a mistake that Horowitz and Lissak had already partially avoided).

To the second-generation books, one may add two "dissident" analyses of Israeli society. While Horowitz and Lissak perceived social, cultural, and ideological heterogeneity as destructive "cleavages," in his 1978 *Israel: Pluralism and Conflict*, Sammy Smooha proffers the paradigm of "pluralism." Heterogeneity is seen as given, natural, and possibly a precondition for a liberal democratic regime. Influenced by the seminal work of Nathan Glazer and Daniel Patrick Moynihan, *Beyond the Melting Pot: The Negroes, Puerto Ricans, Jews, Italians, and Irish of New York City* (1963), Smooha regrouped Israeli society into the dominant Ashkenazi group, the dominated Mizrahi and religious groups, and the exploited and collectively excluded Arab and Palestinian groups. Smooha emphasized the contrast between formal civic equality and the ethnic cultural and stratificational dominance of a secular Ashkenazi minority over all other social components of the state. Smooha was also the first Israeli sociologist to observe the tension between Israel as a Jewish nation-state and its pretension to be an open democratic state. In a way, the present volume follows the approach begun by Smooha, but takes it into different directions and conclusions.

Elia Zuriek also contributed a highly critical description of the Israeli system in his 1979 book, *The Palestinians in Israel: A Study in Internal Colonialism*. This was the first Palestinian critique of the Israeli-Zionist state, and was based on the theoretical concept of internal colonization developed by Michael Hechter in his analysis of the Celtic ethnic role in the British state-building process. Both Smooha's and Zuriek's books remained unrecognized by the majority of professional communities in Israel and the world. The Israeli and the American social science and history communities were not yet ripe to analyze the Israeli polity as a real, concrete entity; instead, they were stuck with and enchanted by its mythological and idealistic image.

Despite their heavy ideological biases and their consistent tendency to interchange sociological theory with ideology and terminology, these two generations of sociological streams laid the foundation for a very rich, viable, diverse, and important body of empirical and theoretical knowledge about Israel. In fact, these approaches well reflected the internal sociological process that society was undergoing. This was well analyzed by Uri Ram in his book *The Changing Agenda of Israeli Sociology: Theory, Ideology and Identity*, published in 1995.

As for myself, I am a sociologist of politics in the wider sense of the term, interested in both the institutional and cultural dynamics of the political foundations of social life and its historical background. I consider myself as acting mainly within the Weberian tradition. The original foci of my research and theoretical, as well as intellectual, interests have been mainly the impact of the Jewish-Arab (and Israeli-Palestinian) conflict on Israeli and Palestinian societies, sociology of war and the military, and later, the development of collective consciousness and emerging nationalism.

The study of military institutions and culture was carried out, not only in terms of the direct outcome of the Jewish-Arab conflict, but also as a central phenomenon penetrating most of the Israeli state's and society's institutional spheres, such as the economy, class stratification, ethnicity, and ideology (including religion and civil religion). This leads me to ask questions about collective identities (including nationalism) in general and identities in Israel (Jewish and Arab) in particular. In this context, the Gordian knot linking secular nationalism and its religious foundations in past and present has captured my sociological imagination. I have analyzed all these societal phenomena in the context of Jewish-Arab relations (but without relating to the conflict as a single or deterministic variable), while challenging the conventional wisdom that constructs the "realities" of most of social, cultural, and economic spheres as "conflict-free" regions and activities.

In 1975, I concluded a Ph.D. thesis that dealt with the territorial factors of Jewish state- and nation-building and introduced me straight into the problematic heart of the Jewish-Arab conflict. This "opening" was the basis for my book *Zionism and Territory* (1983), which is now generally accepted—even by its critics—as the beginning of a new approach to the analysis of Israeli society and social history. Prior to this book, the conflict was, as indicated above, considered by social scientists mainly as a residual category, and it appeared and disappeared in their works on Israel in a deus ex machina fashion. In *Zionism and Territory* and other writings, I instead conceptualize the conflict as an inherent characteristic of Israeli society and culture, and hence as an unavoidable variable in their sociological analysis.

Such an analysis located the Israeli collectivity in comparative perspective in the context of immigrant settler societies such as those of North and South America, Australia, New Zealand, South Africa, Rhodesia, and French Algeria, emphasizing both its similarities and uniqueness. The amount of the available "free land" (conceptualized as different degrees of "frontierity") was considered as one of the central variables, which determined many ingredients of ideological value systems, as well as the institutional and economic structures and practices.

This analysis is also central to my book *Zionism and Economy* (1983), which treats Zionism not just as an ideology and an idea but more as a set of social, political, and economic practices, which helps explain the creation of a highly centralized statist system (in Hebrew, *mamlachtiut*) during the first two decades of Israel's existence (e.g., the monopoly over land and its distribution between various societal segments).

At the same time, I engaged in a series of independent and collaborative empirical and theoretical studies of the impact of the military and wars on Israeli society. The major outcome of these studies was the book *The Interrupted System: Israeli Civilians in War and Routine Times* (published in 1985), in addition to various papers about Israeli militarism. This book provided an analytical and empirical study of direct and indirect impacts of wars on Israeli civilian society.

During the early 1990s, I revisited my own and others' research in these fields and reached some additional and different conclusions. At this stage, I was influenced by the collection of Peter Evans, Dietrich Rueschemeyer, and Theda Skocpol, *Bringing the State Back In* (1985), by the historical sociology of Charles Tilly, and later by Joel Migdal's *Strong Societies and Weak States* (1985, 1988). The Israeli state was reanalyzed within the context of two external circles (in addition to "the conflict"): the mobilized Jewish Diaspora and the changing world order. Adopting a less institutional, more culture-oriented approach, I reinterpreted past findings, supported by new evidence, leading me to characterize the Israeli state as a special (but not unique) type of militaristic society. This "civilian militarism" was found to be not only a basic cultural code but also an organizational principle around which large segments of the society are "arranged." This type of militarism, contrasted, for example, with the "classic" praetorian type, is much subtler and is mainly a consequence of the intrusion of "military-mindedness" into civilian institutions and cultures. This situation led me to analyze the "peace process" from both sides in terms of the militaristic culture and power game.

This series of works, and others that followed, also led me to doubt the ability of some producers of mainstream Israeli social science and historiography to free themselves from Zionist ideologies, Jewish ethnocentrism, and "nation-building" approaches in their conceptual and theoretical dealings with the existence of "others" and "the conflict" within so-called Israeli society. These arguments triggered a series of controversies within academic and intellectual communities and were interpreted as a part of the debate over "post-Zionism." The controversy is well described and analyzed by Laurence Silberstein's *The Postzionism*

Debates: Knowledge and Power in Israeli Culture (1999). Two additional important studies heralded a third generation of new critical approaches to Israeli society. Gershon Shafir studied the first period of Zionist colonization efforts and extrapolated from that limited period to the entire Zionist venture in his *Land, Labor, and the Origins of the Israeli-Palestinian Conflict, 1882–1914* published in 1989. Shafir mixed Zuriek's colonization approach with Edna Bonacich's ethnically split labor market theory. Michal Shalev's volume *Labour and the Political Economy of Israel* (published in 1992) analyzed the complex relationships between the state, the all-embracing labor union Histadrut, and the dominant Labor party.

The next major step was the formulation of a more coherent and developed sociohistorical conceptual framework for "the conflict" (or, better yet, the whole spectrum of Jewish-Arab relations). This major step was rooted in my conclusion (mainly following Georg Simmel and Lewis Coser) that a conflict (any conflict) is an integral social system, that in order to be fully analyzed and understood, knowledge of all parties involved must be included. In other words, in order to achieve a more accurate picture of the "Jewish side" of relations, the "Arab and Palestinian side" must be analyzed with the same tools. As previously mentioned, the Arabs of Palestine were not traditionally incorporated conceptually and theoretically in the analysis and research of Israeli state and society. Moreover, despite the abundance of monographic works on Palestinian society, there existed no single comprehensive social and sociohistorical study of this collectivity. Thus, together with Joel Migdal, I undertook extensive research on the society-building process of Palestinians from a sociological-historical perspective, both on institution-formation and identity-formation levels. This research was published in a co-authored volume, *Palestinians: The Making of a People* (1993). This sociohistorical research presented a "case study" of a stateless society divided between different internal segments and facing many external forces (e.g., Ottoman Turks, Egyptians, Zionist colonization, colonial powers, world market, and Arab and Islamic societies, states, and cultures). The work was built on the basic assumption of a refined version of the world systems approach. The Hebrew and Arabic versions of the book have been extended through the constitution of the Palestinian National Authority.

I should like to make my readers aware that, in addition to my professional activities, I am deeply involved in Israeli public discourse, both intellectually and politically. For the past thirty years, I have written freelance for different sections of the Hebrew daily newspaper *Ha'aretz*, from its literary and cultural supplements to the op-ed page. A polemical book entitled *The End of the Israeli WASP's Hegemony* is soon to be published in Hebrew.

Finally, I should like to say something about the structure of this book. Chapter 1 is a selective descriptive presentation of Israeli and, to a lesser extent, Palestinian historiography, serving a double aim. The first purpose is to shed light on events, "heroes," and processes mentioned or hinted at throughout this volume for the reader, without giving overly detailed explanations. The second and more substantial aim of the chapter is to provide the reader with the sources of Zionist and Palestinian historiography, iconography, and mythology which are the cornerstones of Israeli and Palestinian collective identity and nationalism. The author of this volume strongly insists that it is impossible to understand the history of one without understanding the motives and the practices of the other.

Chapter 2 deals with the processes of building the Israeli state and the state's struggles over supremacy within and among its various agencies and pre-sovereignty institutions. Chapter 3 presents and analyzes the invention and imposition of Israeli Zionist hegemonic collective identity and nationalism, the beginning of its partial decomposition and decline, and the built-in causes of that decline.

Chapters 4 and 5 are dedicated to the analysis of a new societal reality and its crystallization in the aftermath of the decline of hegemonic culture and the subsequent regrouping of the Israeli system into seven cultures and countercultures. These chapters explore the relations between these cultures and the appearance of a civil society in the making. In chapter 6, Israeli collective identity, political regime, and nationalism and their connection to religion, gender, and ethnocentrism are reanalyzed, but this time in historical and ideological context, as well as in interconnection with the regime, or what usually is referred to as "Israeli democracy." Despite the end of the cultural hegemony of one group, however, "Jewishness" and a consensual militaristic ethos have remained central pillars of the Israeli state and its institutional arrangements. In this new, highly fragmented social situation, the role of the state has changed, but its centrality and strength have remained.

Finally, chapter 7 sharpens the analysis of how power-oriented, security-related, and constructed social codes have penetrated the entire Israeli political culture, in such a way that war-making has not only become the state's ethos and the central binding code of a fragmented, pluralistic, cultural system, but even incorporates peace-making as part and parcel of itself.

CHAPTER I

The Mythological-Historical Origins of the Israeli State

An Overview

In Israel, even more than in any other society, the past, present, and future are intermingled; collective memory is considered objective history, and history is a powerful weapon, used both in domestic struggles and external conflict. On the domestic terrain, the past is used in order to determine who is entitled to full membership in the collectivity and according to what criteria, the type of laws and regime, and the desired borders of the state. Different pasts and their interpretations are also a central component in the construction of conflicting identities and identity politics.

In the foreign sphere, and to some degree the domestic, the distant past, in the form of ancient or recently invented and cultivated Jewish myths, archeology, and history, is used and abused to grant legitimacy to the very existence of the Jewish polity in the region. The ultimate weapon of the Jewish claim against the recently reconstructed Palestinian people, in their battle over the land, is the simple axiom "We were here from time immemorial," suggesting that the Palestinians are at best newcomers. As a direct response to this meta-historical argument, the Palestinians invented their own "time immemorial," alluding to their Canaanite roots, preceding the Jewish tribes who conquered the land according to the biblical description. This weird argument about "who preceded whom" is a daily and routine issue within the ongoing Israeli-Arab cultural dimension of the conflict.

Without knowledge of this complex of mythology, collective memory and history, and historical facts constructed and reinterpreted from context to context (or what Yael Zerubavel calls meta-narratives), the "Israeli story" is completely incomprehensible.

FROM BIBLICAL PALESTINE TO ISLAMIC CONQUEST

Hebrew mythology tells us that thirty years before the destruction of Troy, about 1200 B.C., the Israelite tribes, led by Joshua, conquered part of the Land of Canaan. Through conquest, the ancient Israelis annihilated most of the inhabitants of the country and established the territorial base for a semi-monotheistic religion and civilization, as well as a regional empire. No wonder that the Book of Joshua became central to the Israeli secular civil religion and later to the national religious movement's theology. This empire was then supposedly built up during the reigns of King David and King Solomon, following the collapse of the Assyrian world power in 1075 B.C.[1]

This nascent Jewish civilization was based on, among other symbols, a mythology surrounding the "patriarchs" Abraham, Isaac, and Jacob and the prophet Moses; even today, Jews still consider themselves descendants of one common father. Recently, there have been many "scientific" efforts to "prove" genetically the continuity of the Jewish people. Moses is believed to have codified the "laws of Yahweh" into the texts known as the Bible during the exodus from slavery in Egypt and before Joshua's conquest of Canaan. According to these myths, however, Yahweh had even earlier designated Canaan to the first patriarch, Abraham, as the "Promised Land." This land later became known as "Palestine," named after the Philistines, who supposedly settled the coastal plain of the country in 1190 B.C., and were annihilated by King David in a series of bitter battles. These semi-historical and semi-mythological occurrences, which occurred 3,000 to 3,500 years ago, are still used and abused in the "historiography" of the present struggle over the land of Palestine.

In 587 B.C., the Chaldean king Nebuchadnezzar II destroyed Jerusalem, the capital of Judea, and deported a considerable part of the Judean population—mainly the elite and artisans—to Babylon. The dream of the Judeans there was to return to "Zion" (a synonym both for Jerusalem and for the "Land of Israel"), which they were finally able to do when Cyrus of Persia gained control over the ancient Middle East,

---

1. On the Old Testament as mythology, see Thompson, *Mythic Past*.

and in 550 B.C., the Temple of Yahweh, which Nebuchadnezzar had destroyed, was rebuilt. The Judean polity rose again when struggles between rival candidates for the Jerusalem priesthood and attempts to Hellenize the religious cult led, in 168 B.C., to a peasant revolt against the Jerusalemite elite and their Seleucid Hellenistic patrons. The military leader of the revolt, Judah the Maccabee, turned it into a guerrilla civil war, which was eventually won. His family took over the Jerusalem priesthood and, in alliance with the Roman Empire, conquered large territories, converting their populations to Judaism. Quarrels among the Maccabean dynasty subsequently led Rome to crown Herod as king of Judea. The story of the Maccabean revolt was absorbed into ethno-religious mythology as part of the struggle for the purification of idolatrous cults from the Jewish religion and the restoration of the "true faith," and it is commemorated today by the Hanukkah holiday.

After a series of Judean rebellions against the region's Hellenistic and Roman rulers, the Romans destroyed Jerusalem and the Second Temple in A.D. 70. In A.D. 135, following another rebellion, the Jewish elite were again exiled, effectively destroying the Jewish polity, and the province was renamed Syria Palaestina by the Romans. It was subsequently known as "Palestine," a title officially adopted in the twentieth century by the British colonial state, and, later, by the local Arab population as their own ethno-national identity.

Two constitutive myths of Zionism are connected to this period—the fall of Masada and the failure of the Bar-Kochba rebellion against the Roman Empire. Masada was a fortress in the Judean desert built by Herod the Great (73–74 B.C.). During the great Jewish revolt of A.D. 66–73 against the Romans, a group of Jewish rebels took over the fortress. During the siege of the city, an extremist sect called the Sicarii, who had waged internal terror against other Jews, were driven out of Jerusalem. The Sicarii fled to Masada, where they assailed the Jewish villages in the vicinity for food and support. Having burned Jerusalem in A.D. 70, the Romans went on to besiege Masada in A.D. 73. After a siege lasting four to eight months, the 960 Jews at Masada committed suicide in order to avoid being enslaved by the Romans.[2] Despite the highly ambiguous story (including questions about the very identity of

2. The suicide story is told by the Jewish-Roman historian Josephus Flavius. Nachman Ben-Yehuda convincingly argues in his book *The Masada Myth* that the supposed group suicide was, in fact, mass murder. A small number of men, he claims, actually slaughtered all the others, including children and women. For a more comprehensive analysis of the Zionist meta-narrative, see Zerubavel, *Recovered Roots.*

the Sicarii, their doubtful involvement in the battle against the Romans, the act of suicide or mass murder), Zionist myth makers, hungry for epic narratives, reconstructed the Masada events as a story of Jewish heroism and a Jewish "fight for freedom."

A second revolt against the Roman Empire in A.D. 131–35, led by a strongman and false messiah called Bar-Kochba,[3] and supported by a zealous religious figure, Rabbi Akiba, ended in catastrophe and the elimination of the organized Jewish community from the country. Bar-Kochba and Rabbi Akiba were elevated by the Zionist mythology to the degree of saints and national heroes.[4]

During these turbulent times, many Jewish religious sects appeared and disappeared in Judea. This history of turbulence in the Jewish world, and of Hellenistic and Roman religious oppression, included the crucifixion of Jesus (around A.D. 29–33) and St. Paul's trial in Rome (A.D. 60). After Rabbi Yohanan Ben Zakai established a new center in the town of Yavneh (A.D. 70), Judaism itself underwent a major transformation, which defined it in the first place as a religion, as opposed to the earlier proto-nationalist emphasis. Over the next 130 years, Rabbi Judah ("the Prince") and his successors developed the Mishna, a codification of Jewish religious law in the Diaspora that spread through the Greco-Roman world. Like the previous "culture of return," the Mishna was also based on the premise that the Jews would eventually return to their homeland, but at the same time it also laid the foundations for rabbinical Judaism by providing for the possibility of an ethno-religious Jewish existence without political-territorial foundations. At this time, too, Christianity separated itself from Judaism and spread among the Roman underclass and slave populations. By A.D. 391, Christianity had survived countless persecutions to become the dominant religion of the Roman Empire.

Several hundred years later, in the deserts of Arabia, a new culture and religion, Islam, came into being when mythic Muhammad defeated the city of Mecca at the battle of Badr (A.D. 630) and made it the center of the new religion, with himself as prophet. His successors, the caliphs Abū Bakr and 'Umar, conquered the Fertile Crescent and the Middle East (A.D. 630–43). Arabized and Islamized, Palestine now became *Jund*

---

3. Bar-Kochba, or "Son of the Star," as his followers called him, was also called Bar Koziba, or "The Liar," by his opponents.

4. Only during the 1980s was an attempt made to equate this rebellion with the insane politics that led to national disaster. See Harkabi, *Bar Kokhba Syndrome*.

Filastin, the military district of Palestine, which included parts of Africa, eventually reaching as far as Spain.

Beginning in 1099, the Crusaders, under the leadership of European Christian kings, succeeded for a relatively short time in conquering the Holy Land and establishing the Latin kingdom of Jerusalem. In 1187, Saladin, a legendary Kurdish-born general and the founder of the Ayyubid Dynasty, started to take the Holy Land back for the Muslims by defeating the Crusaders at the battle of Hittin.

Saladin has since become a contemporary Palestinian hero, symbolizing the Arab hope for liberation of Palestine after a lengthy period of colonization and the establishment of the Jewish-Zionist state. For their part, the Zionists also drew a lesson from the demise of the Latin kingdom. By identifying the major "mistake" of the Christian settlers—their failure to maintain their cultural, technological, and military links with their countries of origin and their openness to the local Levantine culture—the Zionists hope to avoid it.

THE SEEDS OF ZIONISM IN EUROPE

About 150 years before the triumph of Zionism, traditional Jewish communities in western Europe slowly began to be dismantled. The political and social emancipation granted to Jewish citizens by several European states following the French and American revolutions produced a small but very influential Jewish cultural enlightenment movement, the Haskala, which was highly ambivalent about Jewish religion and ethnicity. More important results of the political emancipation included large waves of secularization, both in conjunction with and separate from attempts at complete assimilation of the Jews into local non-Jewish society. In addition, emigration increased from eastern Europe to North America and to a lesser degree to South America.[5] The countereffect of these processes was the appearance of Jewish Orthodoxy, which attempted to rebuild and redraw the boundaries of the religious community by imposing stricter social control on its members and overseeing their daily lives.

The ideological and lifestyle opportunities and options presented to

---

5. Among the 65 million Europeans who migrated to the New World between 1800 and 1850, there were more than 4 million Jews, or 6 percent of the total, compared with their 1.5 percent representation in the total population of Europe. During the first quarter of the twentieth century, about 20 percent of European Jewry migrated to the Americas.

Jews by the brave new world of sociopolitical emancipation and inter-continental mobility were immense. Even nationalism opened up new horizons for Jews, who could now choose to adopt a new collective identity and become loyal solely to their French, German, Dutch, or English citizenship. Alternatively, they could choose to divide themselves between private and public spheres, between religion and nationalism, and to be Jewish by religion at home and German, say, by nationality in public. In the context of European nationalisms, Zionism had no place. Other ideas also captured imaginations. A radical transformation of the entire world order, based on socialist, communist, or some other universalistic ideology, would also, it was thought, include personal or collective salvation for Jews. Later, the historian Simon Dubnow fused nationalism, internationalism, and secular Jewishness into a non-Zionist cultural nationalism.

At the beginning of the nineteenth century, there were about 2.5 to 3 million Jews in the world. By the end of the century, their number had grown to close to 13 million—one of the most unprecedented demo-graphic increases known to history. About four-fifths of the world's Jews lived in eastern Europe, including the "Pale of Settlement," a frontier zone of the Russian Empire designated by the government in 1794 as permitted territory for Jewish settlement. Here Jewish semi-autonomous communal life flourished in the absence of the newly created Western dichotomies between religion and secularism, private and public spheres, citizens' rights and oppression and persecution. During this pe-riod, the Jews rapidly transformed themselves from a semi-rural popu-lation into an urbanized people, socially organized around the almost exclusively Jewish ghetto, or *shtetl,* in which local leadership was able to exercise control over the members and boundaries of the community.

In 1881–82, a wave of pogroms directed at Jews broke out along the western frontier of the Russian Empire. At the same time, the Romanian government reduced many of the rights accorded to its Jewish subjects. Many of the Jews affected by these events immigrated to America, while a much smaller percentage established associations to prepare for their return to what Jews had always considered their utopian fatherland and patrimony—Palestine/Eretz Israel (the Land of Israel), the Holy Land. The best known of these movements was a small group of high school students in Kraków known as the Bilu association, which was supported by a larger organization called the Lovers of Zion, established in Ka-towice (Silesia) in 1884. Envoys were sent to buy land in Palestine and to establish agricultural colonies there. A striking similarity exists between this group's motives and those of the first Protestant immigrants to North America, as seen in the mixture of articulated religious convictions strengthened by a history of persecution. This movement founded colonies such as Zichron Yaakov, Hadera, Gadera, and Mishmar Hayarden. In addition, and unrelated to the Bilu movement, an agricultural school (Mikve Israel) was founded in 1870 for Jewish students by a French-Jewish philanthropist organization, the Alliance Israélite universelle, and an agricultural settlement was set up by Orthodox Jews who had left Jerusalem in 1878. Later, in Zionist historiography, this immigration came to be considered the "first wave" of Zionist immigration and as such was linked to other, subsequent "waves," despite the fact that it was not politically driven and that the newcomers did not possess a coherent ideological vision.

All the lands on which these colonies were established were purchased from major landowners, and, in many cases, the Arab peasants who had previously leased the land, and often considered it to be their own property, were driven away. The Jewish colonists tried to be self-sufficient, but economic necessity soon forced them to employ hired labor. In many cases, the seasonal and permanent laborers they employed were the Arab peasants previously expelled from the same lands. This caused friction between the colonists and the local population and even led to attacks on colonial settlements, such as that by Bedouin tribal warriors on Petach Tikva. A circumstance that allowed for these frictions was the general weakness of the Ottoman Empire and the poor state of law and order outside urban areas and military garrisons. One response of the Jewish colonists was to adapt to the common pattern of cooperation at the time and hire protection from local Arab strongmen and chiefs.

On several occasions, the Ottoman authorities tried to bar Jewish immigration and impede the transfer of land to foreign ownership, as evidenced by a law to this effect promulgated in 1893. Support from the local Sephardi Jewish community, who all held Ottoman citizenship, and bribes to Turkish officials cleared many of these obstacles, but not all the Ottoman clerks were corruptible. A Tiberias district officer, Amin Arsalan, bitterly opposed the registration of extensive Jewish land purchases, because he saw it as part of the Arab "denationalization" of the district. This episode ended when, following Jewish intervention in Istanbul, Arsalan was fired. From 1892 onward, Arab notables sporadically resisted Jewish colonization. In Jerusalem, for example, they petitioned the Ottoman government, demanding an end to Jewish immigration and land purchases. In general, however, they never posed much trouble for Jewish immigration, mainly because the scope of immigration was very small and never amounted to a real threat to the interests of local notables. On the contrary, their lands actually rose in value.

THE BIRTH OF THE ZIONIST IDEA

In 1894, an assimilated Jew, Captain Alfred Dreyfus, was found guilty of treason by a French military court and sentenced to degradation and deportation for life (he was subsequently fully exonerated in 1906, reinstated as a major, and decorated with the Legion of Honor). The Dreyfus Affair, which was exposed by Émile Zola's article "J'accuse" in 1898, shocked the Jewish world, especially Western assimilated Jews. It seemed to provide evidence that even a completely assimilated Jew with a brilliant military career in an enlightened and free country such as France could not escape the clutches of anti-Semitism. Among the journalists covering the trial was Theodor Herzl, a young correspondent representing the famous Viennese newspaper *Neue Freie Presse*. According to Zionist myth, the Dreyfus Affair was the trigger to Herzl's search for a solution to the "Jewish Problem." Herzl, born in a Budapest ghetto in 1860, was, like Dreyfus, a completely assimilated Jew who had never been particularly concerned by his ethnic origins. He held a doctorate in law, but was preoccupied with writing theatrical plays and newspaper articles. The Dreyfus trial and subsequent outbreaks of anti-Semitism changed his life.

Herzl's first thought was a collective and honorable conversion of world Jewry to Christianity. His second was to find a place in the world for an ingathering of Jews and establish an independent Jewish state. Inasmuch as he was a completely secular product of the late European colonial world, he envisaged this state in political, social, and economic terms. Among other places, he considered Argentina, with its abundance of free land, natural resources, and good climate. Later, he also considered the British protectorate of Uganda in East Africa, which was politically convenient. Initially, he thought Palestine inappropriate owing to its lack of resources and harsh climate. However, as Herzl grew closer to his fellow Jews, he discovered the sentimental and symbolic appeal of Jerusalem and Eretz Israel, which most Jews continued to regard as their fatherland.

At the time, most Jews still believed in a miraculous messianic return to the Holy Land at the apocalyptic "end of days." The strength of

messianic belief had been evidenced in 1665, when a self-appointed messiah named Shabbtai Zvi made his appearance. Backed by a noted
scholar of Jewish mysticism (Kabbalah), Abraham Nathan Ben Elisha
Haim Ashkenazi, Shabbtai Zvi managed to provoke mass hysteria
among hundreds of thousands of Jews, from the territories of the Ottoman Empire to Poland and eastern and western Europe, by proclaim-
ing the Day of Redemption to be June 18, 1666. Despite the opposition
of several rabbis, Jews were ready to march as a mighty army and restore
the godly kingdom of David on earth. Eventually, the Ottomans interpreted the millenarian movement as a rebellion and put the "messiah"
in jail, where he converted to Islam. The affair was an enormous disaster
and has remained traumatic in Jewish collective memory. Nonetheless,
the hope for the coming of the messiah has never ceased. In 1755, Jacob
Frank, a Polish cloth dealer, declared himself to be the reincarnation of
Shabbtai Zvi and the messiah. More recently, a similar phenomenon
broke out among the followers of the late Brooklyn Hassidic Rabbi
Menachem Schneerson. The supposed redemption is linked with a miraculous inclusion of Greater Israel (i.e., the territories occupied in the
1967 war) into the Israeli state and the transformation of Jewish Israeli
society into a holy, moral community (see chapter 3).

Despite Orthodox Jewry's denunciation of him as a new Shabbatean,
Theodor Herzl was a practical politician. He concentrated his efforts in
three main directions. First and foremost, he raised financial support for
the establishment of a national loan fund from great Jewish bankers and
philanthropists such as Maurice de Hirsch and the Rothschild family.
Second, but no less important, he garnered political support and recognition by the great world powers of the right of the Jewish people to
establish a national commonwealth in Palestine. Third, he organized the
spread of Jewish associations and individuals who shared Zionist views
into a viable political and social movement. In 1896, Herzl published
his manifesto *Der Judenstaat* ("The State of the Jews"—Herzl was fully
aware of the implications of not calling it "The Jewish State"). In this,
Herzl argued that assimilation was not a cure, but rather a disease of
the Jews. The Jewish people needed to reestablish their own patrimony,
with well-to-do western European Jews financing the proletarian Jews
threatened by pogroms in eastern Europe. Herzl's preferred regime, in
this utopian pamphlet, was modeled on the enlightened and liberal
Austro-Hungarian monarchy, and, if not at a monarchy, he aimed at
least at an aristocratic republic. In the state of the Jews, everyone would
be equal before the law, free in his faith or disbelief, and enjoy mild

social security rights, regardless of his nationality. This pamphlet was followed in 1902 by the utopian novel *Altneuland* ("Old-New Country"), in which several Arab characters enjoy full rights of citizenship, indicating that, contrary to the usual assertions, Herzl was well aware that the Holy Land was not "empty."

Herzl called delegations from all European Jewish communities to attend a convention at Basel in 1897 in order to establish the World Zionist Organization (WZO). This convention, which became known as the First Zionist Congress, adopted a program for "the creation of a home for the Jewish people in Palestine, to be secured by public law." In his diary, Herzl wrote, "in Basel I founded the Jewish state." Today, Herzl has become a Zionist icon, and his memory is used and abused on festive occasions to give Zionism respectability as a liberal, humanistic movement.

The most important tools created by the new organization were a bank, established in 1899, and the Jewish National Fund (JNF), established in 1901, whose aim was to raise funds for the purchase of land in Palestine and later to subsidize settlers and settlements. The land acquired by the JNF was considered inalienable "Jewish public" land, never to be sold to or cultivated by non-Jews. Until 1948, the JNF was the major orchestrator of the Jewish-Arab conflict in Palestine, converting money into "nationalized territory."

The term "Zionism" was coined to label the Jewish national movement, whose declared aim was the establishment of a Jewish nation-state in Palestine, and the return of stateless and persecuted Jews to the political stage of history. "Zion," a biblical term for Jerusalem, as well as for the entire Holy Land, refers to the ancient patrimony of the Jews, which, according to Jewish mythology, was "promised" by Yahweh to Abraham and his descendants, the Children of Israel.

In order to attain this goal, it was necessary to establish a systematic and efficient immigration and colonization movement, which was supposed to accomplish the mass transfer of European Jewish populations to Palestine and create an immigrant settler society—all without the firm political and military support and vested interests of a colonial power. Until 1948, these tasks were carried out under the military and political umbrella of the British colonial superpower. Colonial authority was beginning to fade in Palestine, however, and Zionism was something of an anachronism in the context of worldwide postcolonial political culture. What were the Zionists' goals in Palestine, and how were they implemented against the will of local and foreign Arab leaders and

peoples,[6] as well as in the face of strong Jewish opposition? The struggle
with the former of these two oppositions is now known as the "Jewish-
Arab conflict." The narrative and history of this conflict, its context,
and its symbols date back to the beginning of human civilization. The
Jewish immigrants and settlers in Palestine never regarded themselves as
colonists, or their movement as a part of the world colonial system;
rather, they saw themselves as a people "returning to their homeland"
after two thousand years of forced exile. From the point of view of the
local Arab population, however, the Jews were strangers, Europeans,
whites, and representatives of alien powers and foreign cultures. The
Jews were confident that their historical and religious "rights" entitled
them to purchase the land, and later to conquer it by the sword. Like
other colonizers, they were convinced that their presence signaled material, social, and cultural progress and the liberation of the native inhabitants from ignorance. The Arab inhabitants of the area, and of the
entire region, saw the Jews as a source of corruption of their moral,
traditional society and as agents of the Western colonial world order.
Thus, while the Zionists considered their "return" to be a solution to
the "Jewish problem," the Arabs saw themselves as victims, paying the
price for injustices committed by European Christianity.

LAYING THE FOUNDATIONS OF A STATE— THE SECOND AND THIRD WAVES

The newly created Zionist organization would have been an empty shell
without Jews ready to emigrate to Palestine, instead of to North America, the preferred destination for most of the Jews in the Russian Pale
of Settlement. Immigration to Palestine demanded placing the almost
utopian goal of the creation of a new society, culture, and polity from
the ground up above more immediate and concrete personal interests.
Of the Jews emigrating from Russia between 1904 and 1914, only a
small fraction (about 40,000) went to Palestine. This influx was especially high after the failure of the 1905 Russian rebellion.

In contrast to the "first *aliya*" (ascension or pilgrimage) of relatively
wealthy, family-oriented, apolitical immigrants, the "second wave" consisted of young, secular, educated singles, who were highly ideologized
and politicized. They felt that in order to create a viable economic infrastructure, a local Jewish labor market was needed. To this end, they

---

6. See Kimmerling and Migdal, *Palestinians.*

originated the principle of "pure Jewish labor." Their success led to an ethnically and nationally segregated labor market in Palestine, with the Jewish half safely protected from competition from the cheaper labor of Arab peasants (*fellaheen*).[7]

Socialist and communist ideas combined with nationalist goals to formulate the Zionist strategy for establishment of an exclusively Jewish communal society that would later become the basis for a state. To further this goal, part of the Zionist community in Palestine set up a quasi-military security organization, Hashomer ("The Guard"), to take over responsibility for the defense of the Jewish colonies from local Arab strongmen. This organization is considered to be the basis of later Jewish military and militaristic organizations, and some of its major figures were later incorporated into Zionist mythology.

This second wave of immigrants, reinforced in 1919–23 by a third wave with a similar sociopolitical profile, not only created sharper distinctions between Arabs and Jews, but also introduced an overt power dynamic into the relationship, and for the first time explicitly stated the goal of establishment of a separate Jewish polity. The term "state," however, was not used or even mentioned for many years by most of the local leaders of the newly established Jewish polity, as they did not want to be too explicit about their intentions vis-à-vis the local inhabitants or the British colonial regime. Later, the "Revisionist" party, established in 1925 and led by Vladimir Jabotinsky, split from the Zionist movement and demanded a more aggressive and overtly Zionist policy of establishing a Jewish state in the territorial framework of Greater Palestine (including Transjordan, which had been outside of Palestine's borders since 1922).

The immigrants of the second and third waves thought of themselves as "practical Zionists" and believed that the way to gain control over the land was not through politics and diplomacy, such as by securing a charter from a great power (as Herzl and later Jabotinsky demanded), but rather through work, immigration, land purchases, and the establishment of new settlements as territorial faits accomplis. Their slogan "One more *dunum* [of purchased land],[8] one more goat" became the cornerstone of the Zionist strategy of a gradual and incremental process of institution-, state-, and society-building. Supported by funds from the

---

7. Shafir, *Land, Labor, and the Origins of the Israeli-Palestinian Conflict*.
8. A dunum is a Turkish measure of land commonly used in the Middle East. An acre is equal to about 4.5 dunums.

World Zionist Organization, the socialist immigrants created new patterns of social institutions (such as the *kibbutz,* or agrarian communal settlement). Their labor union became a large-scale economic entrepreneur, establishing health care funds, schools, a bank, a publishing house, newspapers and periodicals, and canteens for laborers and the unemployed. They also took responsibility for the security of the whole Jewish community in Palestine.[9] Most important, they created a centralized institutional structure that gained hegemonic rule over the entire immigrant settler community (see chapters 2 and 3).

THE ZIONIST COLONIZERS IN PALESTINE

World War I, and the subsequent transformation of the world order, altered the fate of Palestine. With the final collapse of the Ottoman Empire, and following previous British-French understanding, the League of Nations put Palestine under British colonial rule in July 1922. This "mandate" made the British responsible for creating the political, administrative, and political conditions to "secure the establishment of the Jewish national home and the development of self-governing institutions, and also to safeguard the civil and religious rights of all the inhabitants of Palestine, irrespective of race and religion" (article 2 of the Charter). The mandatory charter also granted official representational status of the Jewish community in Palestine to the Zionist organizations and their local branch, the Jewish Agency.

The most dramatic event had, however, occurred several years earlier, on November 2, 1917, when the British government issued the well-known Balfour Declaration (named for Arthur Balfour, then foreign secretary), which stated that "His Majesty's Government views with favor the establishment in Palestine of a national home for the Jewish people and will use their best endeavors to facilitate the achievement of this objective. It being clearly understood that nothing shall be done which may prejudice the civil and religious rights of existing non-Jewish communities in Palestine or the rights and political status enjoyed by Jews in any other country." The earlier version of the declaration, favored by the Zionist leader Chaim Weizmann, included the words "reconstruction of Palestine as a Jewish State." Some sources argue that the declaration was redrafted under pressure from Edwin Montague, a Jewish minister in the British cabinet, who was concerned that a declaration

9. Horowitz and Lissak, *Origins of the Israeli Polity.*

supporting a Jewish state would redefine the Jews as a separate nation, threaten their recently achieved rights of citizenship in Europe, and even fuel anti-Semitism.

British commitment to the Jewish people resulted from a mixture of traditional religious feelings toward the "People of the Bible," British imperial interests vis-à-vis French aspirations in the region, and the expectation that Jewish immigrants would play the white settlers' role in the territory. Zionist leaders spoke in terms of three to five million Jews arriving in Palestine and transforming the small Jewish minority there into a firm majority. The Balfour Declaration was the first major triumph of Zionist diplomacy and the first real threat to the Arabs of Palestine. As such, it provided the impetus for a countrywide protest movement and the establishment of local political institutions, such as the Muslim-Christian Association, various nationalist clubs, and, later, the Arab Executive Committee, the first central Palestinian national authority.

The second Zionist triumph was the appointment of Sir Herbert Samuel, a declared Jewish Zionist, to the office of high commissioner on July 20, 1920. The Jews celebrated his arrival in Jerusalem in terms equivalent to the coming of the messiah, a king, or a descendant of David's dynasty. Samuel, however, put British interests first. He and the local British administration understood that the Zionists could not supply the several million Jewish immigrant settlers that they had promised. Postwar Jewish immigration (the third "wave") to Palestine hardly succeeded in drawing 40,000 people in its first four years. Moreover, after the 1917 Bolshevik revolution, and the stabilization of the Soviet regime in 1922, one of the major reservoirs of potential Jewish immigration was almost completely cut off. The majority of eastern European Jews still able to migrate chose the North American option over the Zionist vision as long as U.S. immigration policy allowed them to do so.

The British understood that the demographic and ethnic composition of Palestine would not change in the near future, and that they would have to deal with Arab unrest if they did not alter their pro-Zionist policy and take Palestinian Arab interests into consideration. With this in mind, Samuel initiated the establishment of a Supreme Muslim Council to fill the vacuum left by the demise of Islamic Ottoman rule. He appointed a young militant Palestinian, Amin al-Husseini, a member of a prominent Jerusalem family, as president of the council and later to the position of Mufti (Muslim priest) of Jerusalem—the highest Islamic authority of the country. Al-Husseini combined his religious position

with nationalistic and anti-Zionist rhetoric to become the most prominent leader among the local Arabs and one of the creators of the emerging Palestinian collective identity. In Zionist demonology, "the Mufti"
is a central figure even today, especially after his flight from Palestine
and alliance with Nazi Germany.

OPPOSITION TO BRITISH RULE

The era of British colonial rule is considered the formative period of
both the Jewish Zionist and Palestinian Arab polities. The colonial government functioned as a minimalistic state, providing basic services for
its subjects: law and order, justice (courts), an educational system, basic
social and health care systems, a financial and monetary system, and an
infrastructure (such as roads, railroads, electricity, ports, and postal and
broadcasting services). Moreover, on the symbolic level, the colonial
state made an additional and crucial contribution by constituting "Palestine" as a geographic, economic, social, and political entity distinct
from the surrounding lands and peoples.

The Zionists were fully aware of the implications of the colonial state-
building effort, and made the control of this process their highest priority. They feared that the "natural development" of the decolonization
process and continuing Jewish demographic inferiority would lead to
transference of control over the country to the majority Arab population
of Palestine. This forced the Zionists to withdraw from the mandatory
state and to establish their own parallel autonomous institutions, including a quasi-underground, paramilitary organization—the Haganah
("Defense" in Hebrew). It is characteristic that in its first stage, the Haganah was a sectarian "army," affiliated with and under the command
of the labor movement and its highly centralized labor union, the Histadrut. Only following the Arab revolt in 1936 was control over the
Haganah passed to the Jewish Agency, in response to its need for funding from the entire community. Zionist historiography considers the
present Israeli military force a direct continuation of the Haganah militia.

The British authorities were well aware of the Haganah's existence,
and, with the exception of a short period after World War II when the
Haganah launched operations against the British administration, a tacit
agreement allowed for its maintenance in exchange for keeping a low
profile, self-imposed restraint, and agreement essentially to act as
backup to the British military and police forces. From time to time, for

example, during the last stage of the Arab rebellion of 1938–39 and several times during World War II, the British military even cooperated with the Jewish militia.

THE INTERCOMMUNAL WAR

The Haganah replaced Hashomer, which had dissolved as a result of its sectarian and exclusive tendencies. The Haganah held a more universal concept of recruitment, which was extended to all eligible members of the Jewish community, and envisioned itself as the nucleus of a future Jewish armed force. From the Zionist point of view, the Haganah was not only the basis for a future Jewish military but also met the immediate defense needs of Jewish settlements and protected Jews in the face of countrywide Arab violence. The British colonial state was supposed to provide security for the Jewish and Palestinian Arab communities, but the local British security forces were not large enough to cover the entire country. The Haganah aimed to use local recruits from every Jewish settlement or neighborhood to provide security until the British police or military could arrive. Jews were trained in the use of weapons, taught how to coordinate regional and even countrywide resistance, including moving members, weapons, and ammunition from place to place, and to retaliate if necessary against Arab (and later British) targets. Apart from its security function, the Haganah also played an important role in maintaining the predominance of the socialist segment of the Jewish community.

The importance of the Haganah became apparent in the early days of the British period. In February 1920, a small Jewish settlement, Tel-Hai, located in the northern area of the country, was attacked by Bedouin tribes as part of the rebellion against French rule in Syria led by Faisal I, who had declared himself king of Greater Syria, including Palestine. Tel-Hai was located in a no-man's-land between the British- and French-controlled areas that had great political importance for both the British and the Zionists in determining the northern boundaries of Palestine. The isolated settlers, led by Joseph Trumpeldor, a former Jewish officer in the Russian military, asked permission to withdraw. The Zionist leadership refused and instead tried to send them reinforcements. The settlement fell, and most of the settlers, including Trumpeldor, were killed, becoming the first national heroes and martyrs in Zionist mythology (see chapter 3). The "Tel-Hai Affair" had almost nothing to do with Jewish-Arab relations in Palestine, but it served to emphasize the need for a strong Jewish military and to reinforce the view that the Arabs could be met only with force.

From time to time, the Palestinian Arabs reacted with violence to the perceived Jewish threat and in accordance with their own aspirations. The first major outbreak occurred in the wake of the enthusiasm surrounding King Faisal's temporary success in Syria and rumors that the British had agreed to support not only his regime there but also his rule over Palestine. After the festival of Nabi Musa (established as a national holiday on April 5, 1920) at the supposed tomb of Moses, Muslims attacked the Jewish quarter in Jerusalem. Before the British could intervene, five Jews and four Arabs had been killed, and about two hundred Jews and thirty Arabs had been wounded. On May Day, 1921, the declaration of a "Soviet Palestine" in Tel Aviv by Jewish socialists and communists attracted Arabs from Jaffa. In the riots that developed, forty-five Jews and fourteen Arabs were killed, and about two hundred were wounded. Shortly afterward, during the 1921 Nabi Musa celebrations, Arabs attacked several Jewish settlements, killing forty-eight Jews. In the resulting British intervention, forty-eight Arabs were also killed.

The most emotional issue for both sides has been and remains the status of the Western (Wailing) Wall. The Wall is considered by Jews to be the last remnant of the Temple, the most sanctified space of ancient Israel and, even for secular Jews, a symbol linking the modern Jewish nation with the land. For Muslims, the wall is the outer rim of Haram al-Sharif, the third holiest site in the Islamic world, where, according to Islamic legend, the Prophet Muhammad tethered his horse during his Night Journey. On Haram al-Sharif, the Jewish Temple Mount, Muslims built the Al-Aqsa Mosque and the Dome of the Rock in the seventh century. Religious Jews, as well as several nationalist groups, believe that Jewish redemption will be accompanied by the rebuilding of the Temple on the site of the mosque. Fear of destruction of the holy mosque was, and remains, a major concern for local Muslim Arabs and the entire Muslim world. This anxiety adds an additional religious dimension to the Jewish-Arab conflict.

On Friday, August 23, 1929, rumors spread among the Muslims that the Jews were planning to attack Haram al-Sharif. Large crowds went out to defend the holy place and attacked the Jewish quarter of Jerusalem, as well as Jewish quarters in the ancient cities of Tiberias, Safed, and Hebron. In Hebron, there was a massacre of Jews, and the ancient Jewish community had to be completely evacuated. Jews retaliated by killing seven Muslims in a Jaffa mosque. The irony was that most of those who suffered in the 1929 riots were Orthodox Jews who had preceded the Zionist immigrations and opposed them, rejecting the whole Zionist enterprise as Shabbateanism. After a week-long delay, British troops suppressed the riots, but not before 133 Jews and 116 Arabs had been killed. When a Jewish settler entered the Ibrahami Mosque ("The Tomb of the Patriarchs") in Hebron on February 25, 1994, and in a desperate attempt to halt the Oslo Accords massacred about 30 Palestinian worshippers in the middle of the Ramadan fast, certain elements in the Jewish population considered it vengeance for the 1929 massacre. Such massacres (as well as those in Deir Yassin and Kafr Qassim) sharpened for each side the demonic character of the other in the interethnic conflict and were considered final "evidence" of their "real intentions."[10]

THE ARAB REVOLTS

Restrictions on immigration to the United States in the mid 1920s and the rise of Nazism in Europe had an immediate impact on both Jewish and Arab communities in Palestine. Between 1932 and 1944, about 265,000 new Jewish immigrants arrived in the country. This was a new type of Jewish immigration. Most of the newcomers were from Poland and Germany, and they were mainly well-to-do families of the educated Jewish bourgeoisie. They had a major impact on the local economy, shifting the orientation of the Jewish community from rural to urban. New Jewish neighborhoods and towns appeared, and relatively large and technologically advanced industrial enterprises were established in a short period of time. By the mid 1930s, the Jewish population exceeded one quarter of the total population of Palestine and had taken on the look of a completely viable, self-sufficient, and self-confident society. The Jews spoke their own language, a revitalized and modernized ancient biblical Hebrew, and built up a new national social identity, which emphasized the differences between them and Diaspora Jewry.

The strengthening of the Zionist Jewish community and the emergence of a local Jewish nationalism had a twofold effect on Palestinian Arabs. First, their own collective identity became more salient and clearcut: the "Palestinian" appeared as a counterclaim to Zionism, arguing for the unalienable right of the local Arab population to rule all the

10. For an excellent overview of the political ingredients in the Jewish-Palestinian conflict, see Morris, *Righteous Victims*.

territory of the mandatory state. The second effect of the rapidly growing Jewish entity upon the Palestinians was a feeling of immediate threat
and an urgent need to confront the Jews before they grew into a powerful community with allies among the imperialist powers, and before
they came to represent world Judaism's claim to full control over the
territory. By this time about 5 percent of the total land (but about 10
percent of cultivable land) had been bought by Jews (see table 1). These
lands included Lake Tiberias (the Sea of Galilee), the country's main
reservoir, and the most fertile parts of the great valleys and coastal plain,
constituting a continuum of "Jewish territory."

In 1936, the Palestinian Arabs revolted with fury against British colonial rule, the Jewish settlers, strangers, and their own leadership, middle and upper classes, and townsmen. The first stage of the rebellion
was a 175-day strike, during which the Arabs tried to paralyze the country's economy, transport, and transportation. Most Arab workers and
merchandise disappeared from the markets. Bus, truck, and cab drivers
turned off their engines, the railroad ground to a virtual halt, and the
main port at Jaffa was shut down. What remained of traffic on the
roads—that of the British and Jews—became the target of rebel attacks,
forcing all vehicles to move in convoy. The British and the Jews were
taken by surprise. The British arrested and exiled the Arab leadership,
which until this very day has not been allowed to return to the country.
Only after the Oslo Accords had been implemented, and autonomy for
most of the Palestinian population in the occupied territories (first in
Gaza and Jericho in 1995) was granted, were some of the Palestinian
leadership repatriated.

By 1936, however, the Jewish economy was strong enough, not only
to survive the Arab boycott and economic warfare, but even to prosper
by using the opportunity to strengthen and diversify its production. Arab
laborers were replaced by new Jewish immigrants, and a new Jewish
port, a longtime demand of the Jewish community, was established by
the British authorities in Tel Aviv—now a rapidly growing city alongside
Jaffa. Vegetables, chickens, and dairy products, which had previously
been an almost exclusively Arab domain, were replaced in the markets
by Jewish-supplied products.

The Palestinian general strike ended with the appointment of a Royal
Committee of Inquiry, known as the Peel Commission. Several inquiries
had been made by different British commissions since the establishment
of British rule over Palestine, particularly after riots. Most found Jewish
land purchases and immigration to be the major reason for Arab unrest.

TABLE I

JEWISH POPULATION AND ESTIMATED LAND
OWNERSHIP IN PALESTINE (1880–1947)

Year	Jews	Arabs	% of Jewish population	Jewish land ownership (in dunums)*	Cumulative percentage
1880	25,000	300,000	6	22,000	0.3
1917	56,000	500,000	10	650,000	3.0
1922	84,000	666,000	11	750,000	3.2
1931	174,000	850,000	17	1,172,000	4.0
1936	384,000	916,000	28	1,381,000	5.0
1945	608,000	1,242,000	31	1,588,000	6.0
1947	640,000	1,300,000	33	1,900,000	7.0

SOURCE: Kimmerling, *Zionism and Territory.*
*1 acre = approximately 4.5 dunums.

After each report was published, new regulations and laws were issued to restrict the purchase of land and to limit immigration to the "absorption capacity" of the country (usually quantified by the rate of unemployment).

This time, however, the Peel Commission went further, recommending partition of the territory between the Arabs and Jews and the establishment of a Jewish state, an Arab state (linked with Transjordan), and an international enclave—a corridor between Jaffa and Jerusalem that included Bethlehem. Both the Arabs and the Jews rejected the partition proposal. Since then the idea of partition as the basis of a solution to the Jewish-Palestinian conflict has often reappeared in one form or another. The most recent agreements to grant autonomy to the Palestinian people in (a still disputed) part of the country as an interim stage toward what will probably be a tiny state with limited sovereignty, supervised and controlled by the Israeli state, is yet another manifestation of the partition solution.

After the publication of the Peel Commission report, the Arab revolt was resumed by rebellious peasant groups (or "gangs," as the British and Jews called them) with even more violence. It was a cruel war against all "foreigners"—Jews, British, and all those not perceived as in line with the rebels, including Arab collaborators or suspected collaborators with the British and the Zionists. For a while, the British authorities lost control over most of the country, and parts of it were declared "liberated" by Palestinian rebels. The Jews sank their resources into defending their settlements, neighborhoods, and the roads connecting them. For their part, the British flooded the country with troops drawn from all parts of the empire and turned the 1939 revolt into a bloodbath. Most of the Palestinian leaders fled (including Hajj Amin al-Husseini) or were exiled or jailed. Some of the upper and middle class fled to Beirut and Alexandria. Palestinian Arabs have marked this as a glorious point in their history, one of the biggest anti-colonial revolts of the time. The social outcome of the revolt was, however, disastrous for the Palestinians. The dismantlement of several generations of leadership and the dispersal of a large segment of the middle and educated classes are still felt today.

After the brutal suppression of the revolt, the British made diplomatic efforts to reach a Jewish-Arab agreement involving the other Arab states (e.g., the St. James Conference in February 1939). In fact, the British withdrew from the basic orientation outlined in the Balfour Declaration and issued a White Paper on May 17, 1939, in which they redefined the mandatory obligation to guarantee an independent Palestine, ruled by the Arab majority of its population. Severe restrictions were imposed on Jewish immigration and land purchases. The British knew, however, that the Jews would remain loyal to Britain in the coming conflict with Nazi Germany, and the White Paper was aimed at securing Arab support in the war effort.

PALESTINE AND WORLD WAR II

During World War II, the Jewish-Arab conflict reached an almost complete stalemate. During the first part of the war, the country was turned into a large military base for British and Allied troops, contributing to the economic rehabilitation of both communities after the catastrophic years of the Arab revolt. Each community knew that the war was an interim period before the decisive struggle over control of the land resumed. During the war, President Roosevelt promised self-determination for all people, and the Arabs and Jews each understood this promise in terms of their own claims and aspirations.

During the war, however, Jewish claims became much more vigorous as a result of the dreadful years of the Holocaust, in which the Nazis and their collaborators managed systematically to exterminate about six million European and North African Jews. In the postbellum years, the international community felt a strong obligation to compensate the Jewish people for the horrors of the Nazi genocide, and for the fact that the Allies had done little to avoid or reduce the extermination of the Jews. The Palestinians meanwhile resented having to pay for crimes committed by Europeans.

As a result of the war, both sides were forced to reconsider their basic positions. Feeling vulnerable, the Palestinian Arabs turned to the patronage of the Arab countries, which had just established the Arab League. For their part, the Zionists changed from a British to an American orientation. As early as May 1942, David Ben-Gurion, the leader of the Jewish community of Palestine since 1933, convened a meeting of Zionists in the United States to urge that after the war "Palestine be established as a Jewish Commonwealth [code for "state"] integrated in the structure of the new [postwar] democratic world." This declaration, commonly known as the "Biltmore [Hotel] Declaration," also called for the financial and political mobilization of American Jewry on behalf of the Zionist cause.

In the meantime anti-British Jewish resistance increased. Alongside the semi-official Jewish militia, the Haganah, two additional underground organizations had gradually developed. The National Military Organization (known by its Hebrew acronym EZEL, or "Irgun"), which was affiliated with the Zionist Revisionist party, was established in 1931. The "Israel Freedom Fighters" (the LEHI, or "Stern Gang"), which espoused a more radical orientation, split from EZEL in 1940. Between 1944 and 1947, these two radical organizations conducted a full-scale guerrilla war against British and Arab targets, including the use of terror tactics aimed at individuals. For a short period, they cooperated with the Haganah. For the most part, however, the Haganah actively operated against these two underground groups, perceiving the intra-Jewish fight as a prelude to the upcoming battle for political dominance in the soon to be established Jewish state.

When World War II ended, and the British colonial state in Palestine terminated its mandate, the question remained of who would rule Palestine—the Arab majority or the Jewish minority. A third option was partition. A fourth option, a binational state, was completely rejected by all parties.[11]

11. Small groups within the Jewish community, such as Brit-Shalom, Ichud, and later Mapam, the left-wing Zionist-Socialist party, supported the idea in the late 1930s and 1940s. The vast majority, however, rejected it. The main disseminators of binationalism were intellectuals at the Hebrew University such as Martin Buber and Yehuda Leib Magnes. They met with very hostile reactions by the majority of their compatriots.

A JEWISH STATE IS DECLARED

On April 30, 1946, the report of an Anglo-American Committee of Inquiry was published. It called for immediate permission for the entry of 100,000 Jewish refugees and the suspension of the severe restrictions on buying land imposed by the 1939 White Paper. In long-range terms, the committee envisaged a binational state based on vague political mechanisms, presumed to ensure that neither the Jews nor the Arabs could dominate the other population. On the day the committee's conclusions were published, U.S. President Harry Truman declared his support for the issuing of 100,000 certificates of immigration to Jewish immigrants to Palestine and the lifting of land purchase restrictions, but without committing himself to the other parts of the recommendations. This was the first direct American involvement in the Palestinian conflict. The fact is that the Americans were concerned with the fate of the Jewish survivors of the Holocaust, but not to the point that they were willing to change American immigration laws and permit increased entrance to the United States.

A year later, the United Nations nominated another committee to investigate the Palestinian problem and offer recommendations to the General Assembly. The majority of the committee called for an end to the mandate and the creation of a Jewish state and an Arab state (with Jerusalem as an international city). These recommendations served as the basis for the November 29, 1947, partition decision adopted by the UN General Assembly (Resolution 181). The Zionist Organization accepted the resolution, regarding it as the realization of the Zionist vision of the establishment of an independent Jewish state in part of "the Land of Israel." The Palestinian Arabs rejected the resolution, considering it an unacceptable transfer of their lands to European immigrants and settlers. The entire Arab and Islamic world supported them. With the UN decision, the British prepared to leave the territory, in expectation of chaos.

The Jews proclaimed an independent state on May 14, 1948 (the Fifth of Iyyar in the Jewish calendar), the day that the mandate was terminated, and established this date as Israel's Independence Day (see chapter 3), a historical counterpoint to the Holocaust. A day later, troops of several Arab states (mainly Egypt, Syria, Transjordan, and Iraq) began their invasion of Palestine, with the aim of nullifying the partition resolution and the establishment of the Jewish state and rescuing their Palestinian brethren. Yet, even before this point, from December 1947 to

May 1948, a bitter intercommunal war had broken out between the
Palestinian Arab community and the Jewish community. Jews still made
up only about 30 percent of the population, but because they were a
self- and politically selected immigrant population, they had about a 1.5
to 1 advantage over the Palestinian population in the decisive age group
of 20- to 45-year-old men.

THE WAR OF 1948

The first stage of the intercommunal war was marked by the initiative
and relative superiority of local Palestinian forces, reinforced by volunteers, mainly from Syria and Egypt. Some of these volunteers were
absorbed into the Arab League–sponsored "Arab Liberation Army."
The Arab forces attacked Jewish traffic between the settlements and
struck at some Jewish urban centers. Through January 1948, about 400
Jews were killed. Jewish convoys seeking to reinforce and supply the
Hebrew University in Jerusalem and some of the rural and urban settlements (Yihiam, Hartuv, the Etzion Bloc, and even Jerusalem) were destroyed. From April on, however, Jewish forces regained the initiative.
On April 8, the most charismatic and promising of the Palestinian military commanders, Abd al-Qadir al-Husseini, was killed in the battle for
the road to Jewish Jerusalem. On April 18 and 22, Jewish military forces
overran the Arab neighborhoods of Haifa and Tiberias. The most decisive event was the capture of the center of Palestinian society—the
proud city of Jaffa—on May 13. In fact, the entire intercommunal war
can be seen as the battle between Jewish Tel Aviv and the older city of
Jaffa. It was almost self-evident that if Tel Aviv should fall, the entire
Jewish will would collapse, and if Jaffa surrendered, the modern and
urban part of Palestinian society would disappear.

The Jewish military forces operated according to the so-called Plan
D, whose major aim was to ensure control over the territories designated
by the United Nations for the Jewish state and over free movement between Jewish settlements on the roads controlled by Arab villages. The
plan also took into consideration the inability of the Jews to spread their
forces among hundreds of Arab villages, the logical consequence of
which was the destruction of almost all conquered Arab villages and the
banishment of their inhabitants beyond the borders of the presumed
Jewish state. The conquered Arab villages were often found empty, or
half empty, because Arabs had fled after hearing news and rumors of
Jewish atrocities (such as the massacre of about 125 villagers of Deir

Yassin on April 9). Once Arabs had left the country, they were not permitted to return. Thus, a de facto ethnic cleansing was carried out. At the end of the 1948 war, the number of Palestinian refugees was estimated to be between seven and nine hundred thousand.[12] Most of their villages, towns, and neighborhoods had been destroyed or were repopulated by veteran or newly immigrated Jews. Refugee camps were established in all of the surrounding Arab lands, slowly creating a Palestinian exile, or *ghurba*. In Palestinian historiography, the events of 1947 and 1948 came to be called al-Nakba, the Catastrophe (or even Holocaust). Palestinian society ceased to exist for many years as a distinct social, economic, and political entity. The Jews called this war the War of Independence.

In the aftermath of the war of 1948, the remaining local Arab community was mostly rural, located in the central mountain area—in what later became known as the West Bank (of the Jordan River) or "Judea and Samaria." The next and subsequent Arab-Israeli wars, excluding the 1982 war in Lebanon, were conducted without the independent participation of the Palestinians. In fact, tacit agreements existed between Israel and several Arab countries, especially the Hashemite kingdom of Transjordan, based on mutual interest, to "de-Palestinianize" the Palestinians. Transjordan's King Abdullah ibn Hussein wanted to incorporate the remaining territory and Arab population of Palestine into his country and to present himself as the inheritor of the Arab Palestinian state never established following the UN resolution. Both countries inherited substantial portions of the territories of Arab Palestine. Whereas the Jewish state was to have received only 5,000 square kilometers under the 1937 partition plan, and 14,000 square kilometers under the UN partition proposal, 21,000 square kilometers fell under the state of Israel's control after the signature of all the armistice agreements in 1949. In the narrow and overpopulated Gaza Strip, which remained under Egyptian control, Amin al-Husseini launched a failed attempt to establish an independent Palestinian government.

The war of 1948 was a relatively costly one for Jewish Israelis in terms of casualties, with about 1 percent of the total Jewish civilian and military population killed. Military units from Egypt, Syria, Iraq, Lebanon, Saudi Arabia, and Yemen took part in the war, but the best-trained and equipped Arab military force, the Transjordanian Arab Legion, hardly participated. When it did, Transjordan's role was mainly

12. See Morris, *Birth of the Palestinian Refugee Problem, 1947–1949.*

passive, with the defensive aim of preventing Jewish occupation of important regions designated by the partition resolution as Arab or international. Only the eastern neighborhoods of Jerusalem and the Etzion Bloc, the sole Jewish enclave in the central mountain area, were captured by the Arab Legion. The relative passivity of the Arab Legion in the war of 1948 reinforced the tacit agreement between Abdullah and the Zionist leadership to share the territory of Arab Palestine.

After several initial successes, the relatively small and poorly equipped Arab forces were defeated on the northern front (in an offensive lasting from November 9 to July 19). In October, the newly created Israeli army conquered the Negev desert, driving southward to the Gulf of Aqaba, and gained an outlet to the Dead Sea, an area that contains the country's largest concentrations of potassium and uranium. Several generals tried to persuade Ben-Gurion to conquer the whole of Palestine (as was done in 1967); however, he resisted, arguing that the world would not allow Israel to hold on to such an excessive amount of territorial gain. In addition, he argued that with the remaining Arab territory, the country would include "too many Arabs." Indeed, when the Israelis took over the Sinai Peninsula, they were forced to withdraw, mainly as the result of U.S. pressure. Between January and July 1949, on the island of Rhodes, armistice negotiations were conducted and concluded between Israel and all its immediate Arab neighbors.

THE ISRAELI STATE AND PALESTINIAN NATIONALISM: THE EARLY YEARS

Already during the war of 1948, the Israeli state opened its gates to Jewish immigration. One of the most important laws passed by the Knesset, the Israeli parliament, was the Law of Return (see chapter 6), which almost indiscriminately allowed every Jew in the world to immigrate to Israel without restriction (see chapter 3). This law was considered the true embodiment of Zionism—the creation of a Jewish nation-state that would be a *terre d'asile* for any Jew in the world, whether persecuted or not. By 1954, the Jewish population of Israel more than tripled, reaching approximately two million. Jewish refugees flooded the country from Europe, Iraq, Kurdistan, Yemen, Egypt, Libya, Morocco, Tunisia, and Algeria. Often Jewish emigration from these countries was sparked by pogroms and other oppressive actions taken against Jews as the result of frustration engendered by the Arab defeat in Palestine.

On the other side of the demographic coin, the Palestinians were
segmented into four major groupings:

1. In Israel, there remained approximately 150,000 Palestinians,
    who received Israeli citizenship and, at least formally, equal
    rights as a recognized minority.
2. On the West Bank, the Palestinians received Jordanian citizen-
    ship. This group was divided into two major classes—the original
    population of the region, living in villages and towns such as
    Nablus, Hebron, and Bethlehem, and the refugees who settled in
    the camps. Segments of these groups eventually moved to the East
    Bank of the Jordan, and part of them, mainly the old notable
    families, were absorbed into the Jordanian ruling oligarchy, mer-
    chant class, and newly established civil service. In all cases, they
    were kept far away from the most important power focus of the
    country, the military, which remained intact as representative of
    the Bedouin warrior class.
3. In the Gaza Strip, the Palestinians received neither citizenship nor
    any other type of citizens' rights and lived in camps alongside the
    original inhabitants of Gaza's coastal area.
4. Other Palestinians were dispersed among other Arab and non-
    Arab countries. During the 1950s and 1960s, a major Palestinian
    center developed in the oil-rich desert emirate of Kuwait, which
    welcomed skilled and educated young Palestinians, who contrib-
    uted to its development.

The Arab-Israeli conflict, reinforced by the developing Cold War,
took on an international dimension once the surrounding Arab states
were drawn in. As a condition for recognition of the Jewish state, the
Arab states demanded that Israel withdraw to the 1947 partition-
resolution border (which they had previously rejected), and that all Palestinian refugees be returned to their homes. Perceiving these demands
as another attempt to annihilate the Jewish state, the Israelis rejected
them outright. Israel argued that the Arab countries should absorb the
refugees, just as the Jews had absorbed their own refugee brethren. In
the meantime, a *petite guerre* developed along the armistice lines. Palestinian infiltrators from the refugee camps in the Gaza Strip and the
West Bank harassed the new border settlements, trying to reappropriate
property or just to take revenge by killing Israelis. The Israeli govern-

ment developed a retaliation policy against the host Arab countries, arguing that they should take responsibility for the infiltrations and killings.

In the years after the war, part of the Arab world was riven by internal turmoil and a series of coups d'état; while, at the same time, the world witnessed the rise of a pan-Arab ideology, whose spokesman was the young Egyptian leader Gamal Abdel Nasser. Pan-Arabism urged the unification of the Arab world and its transformation into a military, political, economic, and cultural world power in collaboration with Nehru's India and Tito's Yugoslavia. Pan-Arabism viewed its place to be in the "neutral third world," which was supposed to emerge as a balancing power between the Western and Eastern blocs. Within this ideological framework, the problem of Palestine was marginalized, its solution being postponed until all the Arab states were united. A group of young Palestinian intellectuals and students, key members of which attended Cairo University and belonged to its student union, challenged this approach. Yasser Arafat, a young engineering student, was elected chairman of this group, which later became the kernel of the Fatah organization.

In the 1950s and early 1960s, the "Palestine First" approach, in opposition to Pan-Arabism, was still a weak and persecuted voice in the Arab world. In semi-underground periodicals such as *Filastinuna* (Our Palestine), edited by Khalil al-Wazir (better known as "Abu Jihad") and published in Lebanon, a new Palestinian strategy and identity were developing. The liberation of Palestine was perceived as a precondition for Arab unity, to be implemented by the Palestinians themselves through "armed struggle." The new Palestinian political thinking was deeply influenced by the Algerian and Vietnamese revolutions, and figures such as Che Guevara, General Vo Nguyen Giap, and Jomo Kenyatta became heroes of the new revolutionary movement. Franz Fanon's *The Wretched of the Earth* and similar works were translated into Arabic and became standard textbooks in some Palestinian refugee camps.

During the late 1950s, many Palestinian associations, organizations, and groups were established, among them al-Fatah, headed by Yasser Arafat (since 1959) and the Arab Nationalist Movement, which developed into the Popular Front for the Liberation of Palestine, headed by Dr. George Habash. In January 1964, the first Arab summit in Cairo issued a general statement on the need to organize the Palestinian people and enable them to play a role in the liberation of their country and achieve "self-determination." In May of the same year, following the declaration, the veteran diplomat Ahmad Shukayri succeeded in convening the first Palestinian National Council (the PNC), which adopted the Palestinian National Charter of the Palestine Liberation Organization (PLO). While the convention, which was held in East Jerusalem, was attended by delegations from the entire Palestinian community in exile and the territories occupied by the Jordanians and the Egyptians, it was still dominated by representatives of the old notable families. The PLO's charter adopted a very radical position vis-à-vis the right of the Jewish polity to exist in the Middle East. In January 1965, al-Fatah launched its "armed struggle" for the liberation of Palestine by trying to blow up the main Israeli water pipeline.

THE END OF THE "ALL OR NOTHING" STRATEGY

In 1937, testifying before the Royal Commission, the Palestinian leader Jamal al-Husseini observed, "Every Jew's entrance into Palestine means an Arab leaving Palestine." This summarized perceptions on both sides of the conflict as a zero-sum game, in which any social, political, material, or cultural gain on the part of one side meant an equivalent loss for the other side. The central resources in the conflict were land and people—both tangible, measurable, and easily quantifiable. From the outset, ideological, religious, and primordial cleavages were secondary issues, and they only entered into the conflict at a later point. The conflict was also total, because it touched every member of both communities, who were all potential victims of and recruits for battle. This totalization of the conflict referred to the immediate relationship between the immigrant Jewish settlers and the native population, and to the intercommunal conflict taking place in the Middle Eastern arena.

In other cases of conflict between immigrant settlers and local populations of settled land, different patterns developed:

· In North America, Australia, and New Zealand, settlers brought exclusive orientations and enough power to destroy the local social fabric and political structures and to largely annihilate the indigenous population.

· In Central and South America, settlers brought some inclusive orientations, gradually absorbing the local population and being absorbed by them (mainly through intermarriage). Thus, in the newly formed nations, the descendants of settlers formed the upper and ruling classes, while the descendants of the indigenous population constituted the lower classes.

In South Africa, Rhodesia, Algeria, Palestine, and Ireland, settler and indigenous communities developed simultaneously, keeping their social, religious, and racial boundaries intact. In most of these cases, the settlers developed highly advanced and viable societies. However, they were not strong enough to secure hegemonic rule over the overwhelming indigenous majority. French Algeria and Rhodesia disappeared. South Africa is currently in the midst of a unique experiment of transformation into a multiracial state, governed by a black majority. The Irish problem still remains unresolved, and traditional Balkan ethnic clashes have been rekindled by the disintegration of the Yugoslavian federation. Israel has arrived at the conclusion that a territorially small, relatively homogeneous Jewish state will be more secure and defendable than a larger state that includes a large minority of Palestinians who do not want to be ruled by Jews. The Palestinians seem to have arrived at a similar conclusion: that accepting a smaller but autonomous—and later independent—entity is better than bargaining for "all or nothing."

SETTING AND SETTLING BOUNDARIES

Popular Palestinian historiography usually links the change in the fate of the Palestinian people to the establishment of the PLO and the institutionalization of "armed struggle" against Israeli targets and interests. These events are described as the birth of a new generation of Palestinians—the generation of revolution (as opposed to the generation of the Catastrophe). However, no Palestinian political or guerrilla organization could have had as great an influence on the reappearance of the Palestinian problem on the world agenda as the consequences of the 1967 war. After 1967, "original Palestine" reappeared, this time under total Jewish control. Moreover, three of the abovementioned Palestinian communities found themselves living under a common (Jewish) political system. Palestinian status under "Arab control"—in Jordan and Egypt—had been ambiguous. These Palestinians could not openly declare themselves to be oppressed (by an alien force), even if that was the reality; and, they could not develop or rebuild a separate identity. They were considered "part and parcel of the Arab world," or were thought of as

"Jordanians," whether they accepted that identity or not. Only under the control of their enemy—the Jewish Zionist state—could they "re-Palestinianize" themselves and build a separate identity and communal institutions.

For Israel, conquering the entire territory of mandatory Palestine, as well as the Sinai Peninsula (prior to its return to Egypt as the first part of the deal for "peace in exchange for territory") and the Syrian (Golan) Heights, was an opportunity to revitalize its character as an immigrant settler society. New lands were opened up for Jewish settlement, especially the core territories of the ancient Jewish kingdoms of David and Solomon, an essential component of Jewish mythic consciousness. The capture of many holy places of the Jewish religion, which had been controlled by the Jordanians until 1967, served to strengthen religious and messianic sentiments, chauvinistic orientations, and the settlement drive within Jewish Israeli society. The scope, the ease, and the speed of the 1967 victory were perceived as a sign of divine grace and the supremacy of the Jewish presence in the region. Only the fear of the demographic effects of incorporating a massive and rapidly growing Arab population within the Jewish state prevented the full de jure annexation of the occupied territories. On the one hand, the captured territories were defined as strategically vital for the future defense of Israel (see chapter 7), while on the other, they were considered exchangeable for peace. The first stage of the Arab response after the war was formulated at the Khartoum Summit as the "Three No's"—no reconciliation (sulh), no recognition, and no negotiation with Israel.

Al-Fatah and other Palestinian political and guerrilla organizations tried to initiate popular resistance and guerrilla warfare within the occupied territories, but with limited success. Increasing numbers of Palestinian workers began to search for work inside Israel, and within about sixteen years, they became the major source of labor in areas such as construction, agriculture, sanitation, and other blue-collar jobs. Israeli products also inundated the Palestinian consumer market. Even the all-encompassing Arab economic boycott of Israeli products was bypassed by disguising Israeli products as Arab and exporting them to the Arab states by way of the West Bank and Gaza Strip. The economic dependence on Israel of the population of the occupied territories was established in the post-1967 period and has continued to deepen.

In the post-1967 period, two informal models were simultaneously employed by the Israelis. One was the so-called "[Yigal] Allon Plan," which envisioned reshaping Israel's boundaries by establishing frontier settlements on sparsely populated lands in the Jordan Valley. The other model reasoned that the Jewish presence must be strengthened in densely populated Palestinian areas in order to avoid any future possibility of giving up part of the Holy Land. This strategy implied that Jewish settlements could not be "uprooted," and that the land on which they were built would became part of the eternal inheritance of the Jewish collectivity. This latter assumption was shown to be completely baseless following the Camp David Peace Accords between Egypt and Israel, in which it was agreed that the exchange of territories for peace was a valid principle.

With the change of government in 1977, and the victory of the right-wing Likud party, the territories of the Sinai Peninsula were returned to Egypt. At the same time, however, colonization of the core territories of the biblical "Land of Israel"—the West Bank (renamed "Judea and Samaria")—was made a top priority on the national agenda. The major engine behind this colonization effort was the development of a settler sociopolitical religious movement called Gush Emunim (Bloc of the Faithful) and its settlement branch, Ammana. The rise of Gush Emunim was one ramification of the mass protest movement born from growing discontent in the aftermath of the 1973 war, a war in which Israel was strategically surprised by a coordinated attack of Syrian and Egyptian troops, which inflicted heavy causalities. The 1973 war called into question Israeli military superiority in the region and reemphasized the Israeli state's vulnerability.

Different Israeli political groups deduced different "lessons" from the 1973 war (see also chapter 3). From one angle, the logical conclusion of the war was the necessity of peace and readiness to pay territorial prices for such peace (this line of logic is best represented by the "Peace Now" movement). Holding three million Palestinians without any citizens' rights was considered morally evil and dangerous for the ethnic composition and security of the Jewish nation-state. The conclusions and interpretations of the situation from the other end of the political spectrum were that there is no chance of a Jewish polity being accepted in the region, and that only its military and political might, including control of as much territory as possible, can ensure its very existence.

By 2000, about 180,000 Jews, spread over 140 settlements, had colonized the West Bank and Gaza Strip, totaling about 12 percent of the total population of these areas. Sixty-five percent of these Jews lived in several large town settlements, and most residents were employed inside the Israeli border (or the 1949 ceasefire "Green Line"). All in all, this colonization drive did not achieve its basic aim of building such a massive Jewish presence in the occupied territories that any possibility of withdrawal would be impossible. This failure seems to stem from the fact that, unlike the early Zionist colonization efforts, this time around, the effort did not enjoy broad consensus among the Jewish citizens of Israel. There was, however, enough Jewish settlement to threaten control of limited land and water resources.

Making a rather rough division of the settler population, we can say that they are of two types. About half are ideologically or religiously committed to settle the "Land of Israel," producing a territorial and political fait accompli. The other half are Israeli Jews in search of cheaper housing and a higher quality of life (the settlements are heavily subsidized by the government). Although the settlement process was not carried out under the umbrella of a nationwide ideological consensus and was, in fact, the subject of grave controversy within the Jewish polity, causing a major societal and political cleavage between so-called hawks and doves, no settlements would have been established had the Israeli state not considered these territories a frontier zone. The former of the two groups believes that Israel must adopt an active, "strong" policy toward the Arabs in general and the Palestinians in particular. This includes the annexation de facto or even de jure of the lands of Greater Israel, as justified by security, nationalist, and religious concerns. A minority of the hawks has even advocated the partial or total expulsion of Arabs from the "Land of Israel." In the opposing camp are those Israelis with "dovish" orientations, who believe that a peaceful solution between Arabs and Jews is still possible in the region (see chapter 7). The preconditions for peace and reconciliation, they argue, are a much "softer" and less aggressive policy on the part of the Israeli state, as well as a readiness to exchange land and dismantle settlements in return for peace.

THE INTIFADA AND THE OSLO ACCORDS

Up to the present, the main controversy within the Jewish polity has centered on the question, "Has the state of Jewish colonization of the occupied territories reached the 'point of no return'?" Several years of mass immigration, at first from the Soviet Union and later from the former Soviet republics, have brought about one million immigrants, increasing the number of Jewish citizens in the state by about 20 percent (see chapter 5).

On December 9, 1987, a general popular uprising broke out in the Gaza Strip and spread to the West Bank. A unified leadership of the uprising formed inside the occupied territories, with its directives ratified by the "outside" leadership of the PLO. The Israelis were helpless and unable to repress the rebellion, which was carried out by young men and women throwing stones at Israeli troops. The Israelis reacted by using excessive force, breaking bones and giving beatings, shooting live ammunition and later rubber bullets, imposing curfews and other collective punishments, demolishing houses, and holding thousands in administrative detention and prison. As a symbolic act, the 19th session of the PNC declared an independent Palestinian state in November 1988.

The Palestinian popular uprising was complemented by escalation of guerrilla activities inside Israel, including the stabbing of civilians and the use of firearms to target private and public transportation. The cost/benefit equation of the "colonial situation" began to change, with the costs becoming obviously higher for the Israeli state. The ultranationalist Likud government did not provide any real answers to this new situation, with the exception of increasing its aggressive rhetoric, which simply widened the gap between the ideology of "Greater Israel" and the reality of a feeling of precarious personal security among the Israeli people.

Another major concern of the Israeli public and its leadership was that, despite its formidable military strength, the state's power was continually subject to attrition and slow deterioration as a direct result of its "policing" functions in the occupied territories. As the Palestinian popular uprising continued to exact a toll for direct Israeli control of the Palestinian population, the costs for the Israeli military system grew, and gains for the Israeli economy decreased. Many Israeli military units drastically cut their basic and advanced training; and, even worse, the mentality of the Israeli military as a whole changed from that of an elite corps able to conduct extensive, blitzkrieg-style, large-scale wars to that of an internal security force. An additional burden on the Israeli military was the protection of small, sparsely populated Jewish settlements dispersed among a dense Palestinian population. In short, the Israeli military learned the limitations of military power vis-à-vis an active civilian resistance consisting mainly of stone-throwing children and youth.

In the 1992 Israeli elections, the Labor party returned to power, promising to solve internal security problems by granting autonomy to the Palestinians, as agreed in the Camp David Accords. The ability of

Israeli political culture to adopt, with relatively little major domestic resistance, an accord with the Palestinians under the leadership of the PLO (with which contact had only shortly before been legally off limits to any Israeli) should be considered a major historical upheaval. This is even more dramatic when we consider that this agreement means, not only acceptance of the PLO and its demands for legitimacy, but a far-reaching change in the status quo on the ground. The first stage of this is acceptance of Palestinian autonomy in the Gaza and Jericho areas, and then probably in most of the West Bank. This includes a major relocation of Israeli troops as a kind of "disengagement" between the two collectivities.

How are the "Declaration of Principles" and the Cairo Agreement of May 5, 1994 (the basis for the "Gaza and Jericho First Plan"), and their de facto implementation, possible from the Israeli point of view? Will September 13, 1993, the date of the signing of the Declaration of Principles by the Israeli prime minister and the chairman of the Palestine Liberation Organization, be a significant turning point in the hundred years of Jewish-Arab conflict? Is this a movement toward genuine reconciliation or just another piece of paper? We shall evidently have to wait a few years more for the answers.

Despite its "revolutionary character," this new policy is well rooted in the power-oriented Israeli culture. From the beginning of Yitzhak Rabin's Labor party's return to power, a rigid policy toward the Palestinians was demonstrated through the mass deportation of Islamic activists, extension of curfews on the Palestinian population, and closure of the territories. Rabin's macho image had been previously well established when as minister of defense he formulated a "bone-breaking policy" in response to the Intifada. He is thus well identified with the power-oriented culture.[13] As an aside, the previous rightist and "patriotic" Likud administration, despite its rhetoric, is more strongly identified with the "weak" components of Israeli political culture, because most of its political moves have been "anxiety-arousing" tactics, in contrast with the "activist" and security-oriented components of Labor's message.

Thus, a power-oriented analysis of the situation leads to the conclusion that indirect control of the Palestinians is a better and cheaper strategy than direct control, especially of a completely ungovernable area

13. Some talked in this context about the "banalization of brutality" in Israeli culture. See Lissak, "Intifada and Israeli Society."

such as the Gaza Strip. The transfer of local rule to a Palestinian authority that would take over police and security services was the logical conclusion to be drawn by the power-oriented Israeli culture. In any case, Palestinian "autonomy," or, in the alternative scenario, a sovereign state divided territorially between the Gaza Strip and the West Bank and compressed between Jordan and Israel, would be more of a strategic asset than a threat.

The PLO and its leadership have already made a few essential moves in this direction. The first of these moves was the 12th PNC (July 1974) resolution "establishing a Palestinian national authority in any area liberated from Israel"—the so-called "mini-state option." The second move was made when, in 1988, in Geneva, Yasser Arafat denounced terrorism and declared, on behalf of the PLO, recognition of the rights of all parties concerned in the Middle East conflict to exist in peace and security, including the states of Palestine, Israel, and their neighbors. These were abstract declarations, however, without any concrete policy and institutional applications, and they aroused strident antagonism from other Palestinian factions. Even so, the entire process of accepting the Israeli offer and its implications was a revolutionary move for the PLO.

None of this is to say that the PLO's leadership, represented at the time by al-Fatah and encouraged by part of the local leadership in the occupied territories, was unaware of Israeli motives and the unfavorableness of the terms from the PLO's point of view, nor of the danger of becoming, not only a weaker partner to the Israelis, but their soldiers of misfortune as well. Their Palestinian and Arab rivals continue to remind them of these facts all the time. The misfortune is that both Yitzhak Rabin and Yasser Arafat were labeled traitors by parts of their own constituencies. Indeed, after the political mistake of supporting the Iraqi invasion of Kuwait, only a weakened al-Fatah leader, threatened by a growing Islamic movement within the occupied territories, could be coerced into accepting almost near-capitulation terms in order to survive. On the other hand, the deal proposed by the Israelis was better than any other previously proposed to the Palestinians by their enemies. Most important, however, the inner dynamics of the process will most probably lead to the formation of an independent Palestinian state.

From the opposite perspective, the Oslo Accords are perceived as a psychological, cultural, and political acceptance of the legitimate existence of a Jewish state in the region. This should be appreciated as the second biggest Zionist achievement, right after the establishment of the state of Israel in 1948 and the subsequent war victory that completed the first stage of Jewish state-building efforts.

Nevertheless, for the majority of Israeli Jews, regardless of the different evaluations of these agreements and the Israeli leadership's motives for agreeing to the establishment of the Palestinian National Authority, the Accords and their implementation were a political earthquake. The explicit recognition that Palestinians as a people have collective rights over what is known as "The Land of Israel" and the likely establishment of a sovereign Palestinian state were not by any stretch of the imagination commonly acceptable ideas, even though they have long been promoted by certain elite groups. For a while, it seemed that the majority of Israeli Jews hesitantly supported rapprochement with the Palestinians. In addition, the major source of parliamentary opposition, the secular right-wing Likud party, was unable to suggest a convincing alternative policy to withdrawal from major Palestinian urban centers and refugee camps, which since the 1987 Palestinian uprising had become a major burden on the Israeli armed forces, state, and society. The only strong and salient opposition during most of the period was provided by nationalist and Orthodox religious supporters of the settler population and by the settlers themselves. Major resistance and demonstrations against the "peace process" were organized by some extraparliamentary groups, while the majority of the population stood on the sidelines, expressing high ambivalence toward the government and its policy and adopting a position of "wait and see."

Thus, in a relatively short period of time, Rabin's government tried to impose major change within Israeli political culture. By passing responsibility for control of the majority of the Palestinian population in the Gaza Strip and the West Bank to the PNA, the government established a political fait accompli without touching any Jewish settlements in the occupied territories. Any attempt to dismantle settlements was considered likely to trigger large-scale popular resistance, if not civil war. Vast resources were invested in bypass roads in order to minimize friction between Palestinians and settlers, and PNA collaboration with Israeli security forces was supposed to prevent attacks against targets within Israel and against the Jewish settlers.

Fundamentalist religious groups argued that Rabin's policy was disastrous, and that his government could not legitimately give up parts of the Jewish "holy land" because it was a minority government, formed with the unprecedented support of two non-Zionist Arab parties (see

chapter 4). Secularist right-wing parties did nothing to distance themselves from these arguments, in the expectation that they would penetrate the electorate's consciousness and aid them politically.

From the beginning, Rabin's coalition expected the support of three
"Jewish" parties—Labor, Meretz, and the traditionalist Mizrahi Shas
party. However, shortly after establishment of the coalition, the Shas
party abandoned ship,[14] and Rabin's coalition remained a minority government, supported by Arab parties, whose seats added to those of Labor and Meretz amounted to 61 of the 120 parliamentary seats. For the
first time, an Israeli government depended on Arab parties for support,
something hitherto considered unthinkable in the ethnocentric discourse
of Israeli political culture. The government itself appeared uncomfort-
able with this situation.

On November 4, 1995, Rabin was assassinated by a young Jewish
religious nationalist, who took the rhetoric about the "non-Jewish"
government and its "traitorous policy" to its logical conclusion. In the
months before the murder, a vocal campaign led by religious groups
had included influential rabbis cursing the government and Rabin personally and discussing his culpability under halachic law[15] and the necessity of sentencing him to death. Rabin's assassination provoked
deep shock among the majority of the Israel public. People, mainly
secular youth, kindling candles and singing songs of mourning and
protest, suddenly filled squares and streets, especially in the metropolitan areas. The leitmotif was "How were we [the secularist peace seek-
ers] able to let them [the religious fundamentalists] kill Rabin?"
"Where were we during the right-wing demonstrations that depicted
Rabin as a traitor?!" For a moment, it appeared that a new kind of
civil and secular society was in the making, built around a new secular
saint or martyr, Rabin. The mass media amplified the feeling that the
murder had crystallized a new generation with a central collective experience and spiritual revelation, resembling that of the "JFK generation" in the United States.

---

14. The Shas party left Rabin's government partly because of the personal problems
of its charismatic young leader Arieh Deri, who was charged with corruption, and partly
for political reasons. The party's spiritual leader, Rabbi Ovadia Yosef, is regarded as a
moderate on issues regarding the Jewish-Arab conflict, but most of the party's supporters
are hard-liners.

15. Jewish law in Israel is applied to the sphere of private laws, such as marriage,
divorce, burial, and the determination of Jewish ethnic nationality, but not to the public,
political sphere (see chapter 6). This is one of the many compromises the Israeli state has
made between its basic civil and primordial orientations.

Indeed, the assassination caused the secular right-wing opposition considerable embarrassment and temporarily silenced even the most vociferous and aggressive religious opposition to the peace process.[16] For a short time, the murder had an intense political boomerang effect, with a prevailing expectation that "Rabin's legacy" had completely conquered public opinion, to the tune of a continued mandate for the Labor government. This evaluation, along with the desire to receive popular approval for his leadership, and to establish a stronger government coalition without depending on Arab parties, led Rabin's successor, Shimon Peres, to advance the election date by five months. Converting the moral indignation caused by the assassination into political gains proved to be an impossible dream. The assassination served to sharpen social identities and boundaries, but did not legitimize change. On the contrary, as one camp sharpened its boundaries and mobilized its supporters, the political dynamic led to a countermobilization of the rival camp. In fact, as the election campaign began, people slowly returned to their pre-assassination stances. If any change occurred in the 1996 election, it appeared within the two major political blocs, and not between them, as occurred in the 1999 elections.

From the perspective of the "civil" elite, the four years under Labor-Meretz rule were characterized by an accelerated process of "normalization," "secularization," and "civilianization" of Israeli politics and society. This "normalization" process included the attempt at historical conciliation with the Palestinians and the strengthening of Israel's political and economic position in the Middle East, as well as a series of internal reforms. The basic perception was that the quality of Israel's internal regime was strongly connected with "normalization" of its external status and vice versa. The Knesset continued to adopt a series of citizens' rights and "human dignity" laws, and the Supreme Court sped up what Justice Aharon Barak called the "constitutional revolution" by rendering several liberal and "enlightened" decisions.[17] From the perspective of the religious, traditional, or simply conservative segments of the Jewish population, these four years were perceived as the years of "de-Judification" or "Hellenization" of the state. The Israeli state and society's basic "Jewish" identity became, alongside the Palestinian prob-

---

16. Typically, on the right, the shock was expressed by wonder over "how a Jew could kill a Jewish prime minister" and less over the general implications of an assassination for the political system and culture.

17. The "constitutional revolution" in fact began at the end of the Likud government, despite the general public perception that associates it with Labor-Meretz rule.

lem, the hottest public issue, bringing the whole society to the brink of a culture war. The religious-nationalistic conservative streams felt threatened by "decadent Westernized and Americanized" culture, which they feared would take over "Jewish society" and transform Israel into "just another nation." They saw the 1996 election as the last chance "to save" the Jewish state from destruction and mobilized all their human and material resources to win it.

The basic problem of the Israeli control system, the existence of about five million Jews and close to four million Palestinians within the territory of "Greater Israel," explains its policy deadlock.[18] In the long run, if Israel wants to maintain its basic character as a "Jewish state," whatever that means, it will be forced to make painful territorial and political concessions. This will have a drastic impact not only on Israel's internal social fabric and culture but on its regional and international position. The results of the February 2001 election for the premiership can be interpreted as a strong backlash on the part of a considerable portion of the Jewish electorate against what were seen as far-reaching concessions to the Palestinians (but with which the latter themselves were nonetheless quite rightly not content). When asked to accept what were perceived as unacceptable losses, albeit mainly symbolic ones, both sides showed themselves to be not yet culturally ripe for reconciliation.

18. See Kimmerling, "Boundaries and Frontiers of the Israeli Control System."

CHAPTER 2

Building an
Immigrant Settler State

Analyzed in terms of the state/civil-society paradigm that seeks to "bring the state back into" sociological discourse, contrasting it to civil society,[1] the Israeli sociopolitical system presents something of a puzzle, because there is contradictory evidence about the strength of the Israeli state, its capacity to govern, and its ability to make critical decisions.

On the one hand, the Israeli state has been classified, by Joel Migdal, for example, as a "strong state" with a tremendous capacity to mobilize its citizens (e.g., for wars or shaping an emergency economy).[2] This capacity is characterized by considerable law-enforcement power, which penetrates into almost every social formation and grouping of Jewish citizens, as well as by the ability to maintain surveillance over the Israeli Arab population and over noncitizens.[3] To these characteristics, one

---

1. One major limitation of the state/civil-society paradigm is its inability to make a clear distinction between "the government" and "the state," especially with regard to specific policy implementation. Here an analytical distinction is proposed between "the government" and "the state," using the concepts of "identity" and "state's logic." See Migdal, *Strong Societies and Weak States;* Nordlinger, *Autonomy of the Democratic State;* Evans, Rueschemeyer, and Skocpol, "On the Road toward a More Adequate Understanding of the State"; Krasner, "Approaches to the State."

2. Migdal, "Crystallization of the State and the Struggle over Rulemaking." See also Barnett, *Confronting the Cost of War.*

3. This excludes several enclaves of ultra-Orthodoxy, which, mainly for ideological and theological reasons, have traditionally maintained partially separate, parallel institutions to those of the state. See Friedman, "The State of Israel as a Theological Dilemma." The Israeli state's relations with different kinds of (citizen and noncitizen) Palestinian populations will be discussed later.

must add the state's extraordinary role in the economic sphere: its ownership and control of enormous material and financial resources, and
also its ability to control and intervene, through various agencies, in
almost any economic activity. The state's ability to regulate economic
activity is evidenced, not only by its high capacity to raise taxes and
formulate monetary policy,[4] but also by its ownership of over 90 percent
of the land within its territory and enjoyment of an overwhelming influx
of resources from external sources (loans and grants from other states
and organizations such as the WZO, as well as private donations). Additionally, until the mid 1980s, the state not only owned its own economic (or business) sector, but also both closely controlled the public
sector and was highly involved in the private business sector.

On the other hand, and perhaps in light of these characteristics, some
have characterized the situation in Israel as "trouble in utopia."[5] This
view implies that the autonomy of the Israeli state tends to be low,
placing it at the mercy of rival groups.[6] As these authors put it, the
"ungovernable" tendencies of the system reflect an overburdened condition that stems from the state's inability to meet the contradictory
political demands of certain groups and spheres, which are rooted in
opposing fundamental ideological positions. These positions result from
the state's dual identity, or what Hegel calls a "historically produced
sphere of ethical life," grounded in the identities of two rival civil societies (*gesellschaftlich* and *bürgerlich*)—one based on primordial ties and
the other on civic orientations.[7] In analyzing the dynamic between these
rival ideological positions, like this book as a whole, this chapter takes
a somewhat different approach to the Israeli collectivity, diverging from
the conventional and orthodox views that have dominated the macro-
sociology, social history, political science, and historiography of Israel.[8]

4. This statement is conditional, because it refers mainly to the income taxes of wage-
earners, especially in the public and governmental sectors of the economy. "Real taxation"
of the self-employed is much less impressive. Undeclared incomes are estimated at from 5
to 15 percent of Israel's GNP, as compared to about 10 percent in western Europe. See
Ben-Yehuda, "Social Meanings of Alternative Systems"; Zilberfarb, "Estimate of the Black
Market in Israel and Abroad."
    5. Horowitz and Lissak, *Trouble in Utopia*, pp. 22–23.
    6. Dietrich Rueschemeyer made a similar observation in private conversation. The
same line of argument, presented in a more moralistic manner, appears in Harkabi, *Israel's
Fateful Decisions.*
    7. Hegel, *Grundlinien der Philosophie des Rechts*, p. 342.
    8. For examples of these approaches, see Eisenstadt, *Israeli Society* and *Transforma-
tion of Israeli Society;* Horowitz and Lissak, *Origins of the Israeli Polity;* Shapiro, *Democracy in Israel;* Galnoor, *Steering Politics.* For a detailed, but conservative description
of the Israeli political system, see Arian, *Politics in Israel* or Dowty, *Jewish State.* These

In order to develop this argument, it is necessary to introduce an additional dimension to the notion of the state that has been neglected by scholars of the state/civil-society paradigm. The founding father of this approach was Max Weber,[9] and the additional dimension is collective identity, the unique "fingerprint" that distinguishes each state-society complex and is created through interaction between the state and civil society. Collective identities tend to impose explicit and implicit rules on the game, which serve to establish the perceived degree of freedom permitted by the state to its subjects from its position as "power-container" and without regard to any specific value system or culture.[10] As powerful and strong as it may be, however, the state cannot detach itself from the identities and mythic self-perceptions of its society's various populations.[11] In the case at hand, "society" refers to the population who identifies with a somewhat abstract notion of "Israel" that cuts across institutions such as the state, family, civil institutions, and voluntary associations (in the pre-state period, the Yishuv, or Palestinian Jewish ethnic community, was perceived similarly; see chapter 3). In addition, we are dealing here with the notion of a nation-state (the term "nation" indicating a generalized kind of primordial or ethnic identity with some structural implications), wherein "Israel" is primarily and ultimately conceived of as a "Jewish nation-state" (see chapter 6). In order to understand the major trend of development in this state, its strengths and weaknesses, and its degree of autonomy, it is thus necessary to analyze the diverse meanings of the term "Jewish nation-state," together with the structural and cultural aspects of the state.

The term "state autonomy" refers to the ability of the state to prevent unsolicited interventions from, and the imposition of particularistic def-

---

volumes reflect various shades of a Judeocentric perception of Israeli society and its boundaries, as well as a strong implicit or explicit perception of continuity in the basic rules of the game. For a critique of such somewhat simplistic overviews of Israeli sociology, schools, and paradigms, see Ram, *Changing Agenda of Israeli Sociology;* and for an earlier analysis, see Kimmerling, "Sociology, Ideology and Nation-Building."

9. See Weber, *Theory of Social and Economic Organization.* More recent elaborations of this approach that should be mentioned include Evans, Rueschemeyer, and Skocpol, "On the Road toward a More Adequate Understanding of the State"; Migdal, *Strong Societies and Weak States;* Azarya and Chazan, "Disengagement from the State in Africa"; Nettl, "The State as a Conceptual Variable"; Nordlinger, *Autonomy of the Democratic State;* Alford, "Paradigms of Relations between State and Society"; and Krasner, "Approaches to the State." The European version is well represented by Birnbaum, *States and Collective Action.*

10. Giddens, *Nation-State and Violence.*

11. Sometimes such identities are encapsulated and condensed into one supposedly coherent term of "nationalism" (see chapter 6 below on the Zionist case).

initions of collective identity by, one or another segment of civil society. The intervention of a specific collective identity can determine the rules of the game or the practices of a certain distributive or coercive policy (both by making formal, constitutional impositions and by shaping informal political culture).[12] A spectacular demonstration of the social and political strength of particularistic identities powerful enough to destroy states and erect alternate strong ties and loyalties in their place can be seen in the dismantlement of powerful multinational states such as the Soviet Union and the Yugoslav Republic, in which particularistic groups associated themselves with ideologies that acted as alternatives to the officially defined identity of the state.

In contrast, the term "state strength" refers to the state's ability to enforce law and order, to mobilize the population for war, and to manage distributive and extractive fiscal policies, as well as to its ability to impose its own definition of collective identity on all segments of society.[13] The first dimension of the notion of the "state" adopts the traditional Weberian concept. This concept views the modern state as a corporate body that has compulsory jurisdiction and claims a monopoly on legitimate means of violence over a territory and its population, a monopoly that extends to all action that arises in the territories under this entity's control.[14]

The state must have an institutionalized organizational structure, minimally including military and police forces, some sort of tax-collection and resource-redistribution apparatus (the state bureaucracy), some rule-making institution (parliamentary or otherwise), a decision-making institution (rulers and their delegates), and a judicial body (courts that act on the basis of a written code). These traits, however, constitute only one dimension of any state.

The second dimension is what makes each state cognitively and *culturally* different from the next, that is, its collective identity, collective memory, and culture. This body of collective knowledge is the core that tends to persist in the event of changes of government or even of the

12. Mann, "Autonomous Power of State."
13. See Evans, Rueschemeyer, and Skocpol, "On the Road toward a More Adequate Understanding of the State," 347–66, and most of the authors mentioned in n. 9 above. I cannot, however, accept their one-dimensional structural views of the state. For a more critical approach, see Mitchell, "Limits of the State."
14. In the case of Israel, this control over territories and populations has extended beyond the limits of the state's sovereignty, into the West Bank and Gaza Strip since 1967 and into the so-called Security Zone in southern Lebanon after the invasion and withdrawal in 1982.

state's regime.[15] It is not a mere matter of convenience that each state
has its own name, banner, symbols, and anthem. The question of what
makes the French state "French" and the Swiss state "Swiss" is much
more essential. The collective identity determines, not only the geographical and societal boundaries of the collectivity,[16] its basic credo or
political culture, its specific "civic religion,"[17] and its civil society, but
also the implicit and explicit rules of the game.[18]

Finally, "state's logic" is understood to mean the basic codes, traditions, rules of the game, and practices that are unaffected by changes
of government, administration, or even entire regimes. This "logic" is
imposed by geographical constraints rooted in the human and material
resources possessed by the state, its identity, collective memory, traditions, historiography, and political culture. This logic is employed
mainly in the state's bureaucracy and in other state agencies, which represent particular intrastate agency identities and class interests. Thus,
the degree of change when a Tory government in England is replaced
by a Labour government, or when a Democratic administration in the
United States gives way to a Republican one, is basically limited and
restricted. Even after the Russian Empire became the Soviet Union and
then returned to being the Russian state, some basic practices and perceptions of *the* Russian state persisted through the "revolutions" and
were even protected and amplified by the new regimes. This is not to
say that the "state's logic" and the practices derived from that logic
cannot be objects of change. These changes, however, do not necessarily
overlap with changes in government or even regime. Some changes in
regime can even be connected to previous changes in the state's logic,
which are by and large influenced by the state's position as an actor in
the international arena.

15. If the change in regime is accompanied by changes in (1) the social and political
boundaries of the collectivity, which lead to (2) changes in the collective identity, we may
see a substantially different character in the newly emerged state. A transition from an
autocratic or totalitarian regime to a democratic system constitutes a change in regime
but not in identity. The "Hungarian" identity of postcommunist Hungary is not different
from its identity during the communist era. The two most striking examples are, of course,
the decomposition of the USSR and subsequent restructuring of "Russian identity" and
the national-ethnic identities of other states of the federation, as well as the decomposition,
"ethnic cleansing," and boundary redrawing taking place in former Yugoslavia. No doubt
we are witnessing a rebuilding of old-new primordial identities.
16. See chapters 3 and 6 below; Kimmerling, "Between the Primordial and the Civil
Definitions of the Collective Identity"; Kimmerling and Moore, "Collective Identity as
Agency, and Structuration of Society."
17. Bellah, *Beyond Belief.*
18. Keane, *Democracy and Civil Society;* Taylor, "Modes of Civil Society."

Nonetheless, a state is not a homogeneous and harmonious entity; it includes several branches and institutions, based on different values and power foci. The very doctrine of "checks and balances" among different state agencies presumes the conflicts of interest that are built into the state. These power relations are evident, not only between the executive, judicial, and legislative branches, but also within them, such as among the executive agencies of the military, the central bank, and the office of the prime minister or the president. When one part of the executive branch gains power or greater autonomy, the others may lose power or prestige, but the state as a whole does not become weaker or stronger.

THE COLONIAL STATE OF PALESTINE

It is generally assumed that what is officially titled the "State of Israel" directly originated in the Zionist movement.[19] In addition to the political mobilization of persecuted Jews and encouragement of their immigration to "Zion," however, the establishment of a Jewish state on the soil of the "ancestral homeland" was enabled by the support of the great powers. Although the Zionist idea and movement constituted a necessary condition for the creation of a Jewish polity in Palestine, the British mandatory or colonial regime established after World War II was an equally important factor.[20] While it was intended to maintain and guarantee British interests in the Middle East, the British administration was also intended to lay the foundations for the establishment of a "national home" for the Jewish people in Palestine.[21]

Mandatory Palestine was a typical colonial state. Its residents (a Palestinian Arab majority and a growing Jewish minority) did not have the right to determine policies and could only exert influence through

19. See chapter 1 above; Avineri, *Making of Modern Zionism;* Laqueur, *History of Zionism;* and Vital, *Origins of Zionism.* To the author's best knowledge, Israel is the only nation that officially includes the term "state" in its title.

20. The boundaries of colonial Palestine were originally intended to include large areas that are today part of the Hashemite kingdom of Jordan. In light of British commitments to Sharif Hussein of Arabia, the emirate of Transjordan was created for Abdullah ibn Hussein in 1922, and its territory was excluded from the jurisdiction of the British Palestinian state.

21. The concept of the "national home" was deliberately rendered obscure, in order not to commit highly to the final form and scope of the Jewish polity. For the Zionists, however, it was interpreted in practical terms to mean a future sovereign Jewish state. The lack of clarity was rooted in the British desire to overcome opposition both within Great Britain and among the Arabs of the Middle East, and especially in Palestine, and not to contradict Britain's so-called "dual obligation" (expressed in Sir Henry MacMahon's letters to the sharif of Mecca).

negotiation and bargaining. Bargaining included the use, or threat, of both controlled and uncontrolled violence against the colonial power, Great Britain, and its local agencies and representatives.[22] Like any other state, colonial Palestine maintained a regime of law and order through the mechanisms of a local police force and other security agencies. The colonial state was also responsible for:

- Establishment of a judicial system and passage of laws applying to the area within the colony's territorial boundaries
- Creation of a modern bureaucracy
- Issue of coins and stamps, development and implementation of monetary and fiscal policies, and systematic tax collection
- Funding typical state activities (road construction, telephone, telegraph, postal services, and radio broadcasting) through state revenues
- Provision of education and health services; facilitation of normal civilian life and minimal welfare; and
- Granting concessions, including rights for the establishment of an electric company, which brought about the rapid electrification of the country.

In addition to its support of both limited agrarian reform (mainly by encouraging the Palestinian Arab peasantry to redistribute their communal lands among households and register them as private lands) and a cooperative marketing system for agricultural products, the mandatory regime also provided partial protection to infant industries, loaned money for economic development, and extended credit for agricultural production. Passports and identity cards attesting to Palestinian citizenship were issued. Thus, in the brief span of thirty years, the regime created, not only a legal "Palestinian identity" and a limited notion of citizenship, but also a potential political identity for at least some of its Arab residents, who constituted a large majority of the population until the end of the colonial regime.

Mandatory Palestine was a minimalist state, which directly intervened in only a limited number of areas, preferring to extend wide-ranging autonomy to the two major national communities (Arab and

22. Mezer, *Divided Economy of Mandatory Palestine*; Miller, *Government and Society in Rural Palestine, 1948*; Reuveny, *The Administration of Palestine under the British Mandate, 1920–1948*; Kimmerling and Migdal, *Palestinians*; and Kimmerling, "Process of Formation of Palestinian Collective Identities."

Jewish) under its territorial jurisdiction. Prima facie, both communal entities can be defined, following Charles Taylor's definition, as civil societies in the maximalistic meaning of the term.[23] They were based on free association and were not under the tutelage of state power, yet by structuring themselves as complete systems, they were able to significantly determine or affect the course of state policy. If, however, we consider Hegel's conception of civil society as the societal space in between the family and the state, both communities in colonial Palestine were much closer to imagined familylike associations based on primordial ties than to the rationally based secondary groups that its theoreticians implicitly or explicitly presume to constitute civil society.[24]

Prior to and during the initial stage of the creation of mandatory Palestine, the British and Zionist movements operated in accordance with two latent but jointly held assumptions, on the basis of which Great Britain agreed to assist in the establishment of a so-called Jewish national home. The first assumption was that the creation of necessary political preconditions would bring about massive Jewish immigration, measured in the hundreds of thousands, if not millions. This immigration presumed a radical change in the demographic and sociopolitical character of the territory under the British mandate, rapidly making it an entity with a Jewish ethno-national majority population. The second assumption was that Palestine's Arab population would not express firm, organized resistance to the process of massive Jewish immigration, or, alternatively, that it would lack the political and organizational ability and skill required to mold such resistance into effective political action. Strong Palestinian Arab opposition to mass Jewish immigration and to intercommunal Arab-Jewish land transfers subsequently confronted the British colonial regime with unacceptably high economic and political costs.[25]

Thus, within a short period of time, the assumptions upon which the British pro-Zionist policy was based were proved wrong. First, it emerged that the Zionist movement's ability to recruit Jewish immigrants was limited, and that a fundamental and rapid demographic transformation of Palestine's Jewish population would not take place. Second, once they learned of the content of the Balfour Declaration,

23. See Taylor, "Modes of Civil Society," 95–118.
24. In fact, many of the civil societies in the contemporary Middle East are based on ethnicity or religion and deviate considerably from conventional forms of civil society. See Kimmerling, "Elites and Civil Societies in Middle East."
25. See Kimmerling, *Zionism and Territory.*

Palestinian Arabs began to organize themselves into a political protest, and even active resistance, movement in order to sabotage the British policy's declared aim of creating a "Jewish national home" and turning the country's Arab majority into a minority within a Jewish state.[26] This resistance movement shifted into high gear with the outbreak of the Arab revolt of 1936–39.[27] Palestinian Arab demands centered on the issue of the transfer of power, and ultimately sovereignty, to the national majority in Palestine. In order to attain this goal, Palestine's Arabs formulated interim demands, including the establishment of a legislative council, which would be elected democratically by the country's residents, that is, with an overwhelming Arab majority. They demanded, at the least, drastic restriction of Jewish immigration and legislation that would prevent the transfer of land-ownership from one community (the Arabs) to another (the Jewish).[28]

When the British realized that their two basic assumptions were not, in fact, valid, they adapted their policy to suit the reality they confronted. The principal objective of British policy in Palestine became ensuring political stability in the area with the aim of continued control at a lower cost. In the wake of the Arab revolt of 1936–39, and in view of the heavy economic and political burden of quelling it, the option of abandoning Palestine became an actual alternative. The outbreak of World War II, however, forced Britain to defer decisions about the future of the mandate and of Palestine. Eventually, British departure would lead to one of two probable scenarios: either transfer of sovereignty into the hands of the Arab national majority or territorial partition of Palestine. The Peel Commission first proposed the latter.[29] The Palestinian Arab community rejected partition as a viable option, while the Zionists tended (until the 1942 Biltmore Convention) to accept partition in principle but not the specific plan suggested by the Peel report.[30]

26. See chapter 1 above and Porath, *Emergence of the Palestinian National Movement, 1917–1929.*

27. Porath, *Palestinian National Movement: From Riots to Rebellion;* Kimmerling and Migdal, *Palestinians,* pp. 96–121.

28. Prima facie, the avoidance of transfer through the sale of lands from Arab ownership to Jewish title did not require the colonial state's legislative intervention. In a situation of internal cleavage, however, internal social control over this kind of "deviance" is limited (see Kimmerling, *Zionism and Territory*).

29. United Kingdom, Royal Commission on Palestine, Cmd. 5479.

30. The Jews hoped for an increased territorial share in Palestine. On the whole controversy within the Zionist movement around the partition plan, see Galnoor, *Partition of Palestine.*

THE JEWISH COMMUNITY IN PALESTINE
AS A "STATE IN THE MAKING"

Beginning in the mid 1920s, the Jewish immigrant settler community in Palestine became well aware of the possibility that within a relatively short period of time, in accordance with the worldwide decolonization process, sovereignty over the colonial state would pass into the hands of the territory's majority population (that is, its Palestinian Arab residents). In order to prevent such an eventuality, the Jewish community had to establish a parallel framework to that of the colonial state. In other words, there was a need for a Jewish "state in the making" that could provide the territory's Jewish residents with most of the essential services offered by any state. Defense, administrative machinery, education, welfare, health, and employment services were absolute necessities.[31] The state in the making could also mobilize the exclusive loyalty of the Jewish community's members without risking a (premature) head-on collision with the colonial state.

The colonial regime provided the Jewish immigrant settler society mainly with the security umbrella needed for the community's growth and development in the face of the Arab majority's opposition. Although the Jews were not always satisfied with the pace and extent to which British security was supplied, in the long run, they were the major beneficiaries of the regime. The accumulation of institutionalized power and the formation of an organized machinery of violence by the settler society, together with the ability to mobilize Jews in Palestine and in the Diaspora for political ends, constituted two necessary conditions for the existence of Palestine's Jewish community as a viable political entity regardless of its size. Furthermore, the so-called organized Yishuv provided an immediate alternative to the colonial state that was destined to disappear together with the British colonial regime. In creating an entity with such considerable political potential, the Jewish community was forced to concentrate most of its institutions and manpower into the autonomous "state in the making." Thus, the boundaries between "state" (i.e., the central political institutions) and "society" (nonpolitical but exclusive ethnic institutions) were completely blurred, as institutionalization of political organizations and leadership intensified internal social control and surveillance.

31. Horowitz and Lissak, *Origins of the Israeli Polity*. See also Shapiro, *Formative Years of the Israeli Labor Party*.

"Knesset Israel," the quasi-governmental institution of the immigrant settler community in Palestine, overlapped, to a great extent, not only with the leadership of the Zionist parties,[32] but also with the Executive Committee of the Jewish Agency, the local operational branch of the World Zionist Organization. Within this political complex, the Histadrut, or General Labor Federation of Jewish Workers in Palestine, was founded in 1920. This organization itself amounted to a quasi-statist mechanism. In addition to performing the usual functions of a trade union, the Histadrut owned manufacturing plants and construction firms (Solel Boneh and later the Koor consortium), marketing and purchasing cooperatives, a comprehensive health and hospitalization system, a bank, an employment bureau, a newspaper (*Davar*), a publishing company (Am Oved), and a competitive and mass-oriented sports organization (Ha'poel).[33] An entire subculture based on symbols—a (red) flag, anthems, ceremonies, parades, and festivals and holidays (May Day)—was also developed.[34] Owing to its vast economic and profit-oriented involvement and its status as a major employer in the system, the Histadrut was never regarded solely as a union movement that protected workers, but rather as an additional nation-building organ with its own economic and political interests vis-à-vis the other state- and society-building institutions, on the one hand, and the workers, on the other.

Not all the Jews in Palestine were part of this "state in the making." For example, in the eyes of the local Orthodox Jewish community (including branches of Agudat Israel, the largest religious party in the Jewish world at the time), the colonial state was the sole recognized political authority.[35] The state in the making also excluded members of the Communist party, and to a certain extent, parts of the long-established Sephardi Jewish community, who were culturally and politically linked with the previous Ottoman regime, as well as the small Yemenite Jewish community. An issue that produced much controversy in the Jewish community of Palestine was the communal position of the Revisionist

32. Primarily after 1933 with the dominant Mapai party and its leadership.
33. Ha-Poel could be used as a militia for internal and external purposes (similar to the German *Schutzbündnis* organizations).
34. Shalev, *Labour and the Political Economy of Israel*; Grinberg, *Split Corporatism in Israel*.
35. The Jewish commonwealth could be established only by the coming of the Messiah; Zionism was thus considered a false messianic movement, which, like previous messianic movements, would end as a great catastrophe for the Jewish people. See Friedman, *Society and Religion*.

Zionist movement, which opposed the socialist-led coalition in the World Zionist Organization, arguing for a more assertive Zionist policy and for a bigger share of power, positions, and material resources. Another highly crystallized and institutionalized portion of the Jewish community in Palestine, the municipalities, held a central position in the polity. Even so, they were not fully integrated into the state in the making, mainly because they enjoyed the advantage of independent financial resources. The municipal councils, primarily those with nonsocialist petit bourgeois majorities, such as the municipalities of Tel Aviv and Ramat Gan, were autonomous to some extent both from the British and from the central Jewish political centers. They played a mediating role between the colonial state and the Jewish ethnic community.[36] It should be emphasized that the very presence of these excluded groups indicates how clearly the boundaries of the state in the making were demarcated.

Although the organized Jewish community was not without its internal struggles and tensions, it had evolved unique mechanisms that could serve as safety valves to prevent the intensification of confrontations. One mechanism was a coalition of benefactors who raised external capital through "national funds" collected by various worldwide Zionist organizations and distributed by the local leadership. This was needed because the Zionist venture was a uniquely nonprofit and noneconomic settler movement,[37] which had chosen its target territory, not with a view to wealthy and abundant land, natural, and human resources, but instead at the behest of a nationalist utopia, driven by religious and primordial sentiments (see chapters 3 and 6).

THE STATE

With its declaration of independence in May 1948, in the course of what it refers to as "the War of Independence," on part of the territory originally included in the British colonial state, the State of Israel set two primary goals. The first was to establish clear-cut boundary lines between the state and society and to achieve a dominant symbolic status for the state, or what might be called a "high stateness." The second was to obtain an optimal level of dominant state institutions vis-à-vis other historical power foci in society. In the pre-state era, the boundaries between these foci and those of the state in the making were blurred or,

---

36. Ben-Porat, *The Bourgeoisie: The History of Israeli Bourgeoisie.*
37. See also Kimmerling, *Zionism and Economy.*

in some cases, nonexistent. The Israeli state carried out its boundary-establishing activities in a gradual and systematic manner in order to prevent the creation of instability and the weakening of its own position in relation to the pre-state power centers.[38] At the same time, it was in the state's best interests to maintain its alliance with groups that could ultimately assist it in penetrating new areas and peripheries and establishing a hegemonic order (see chapter 3).

The ability to extend state autonomy to and to control new peripheries was of crucial importance, because Israel was rapidly turning into a country of unselective mass immigration, and the political and cultural assumptions of the new immigrants were strikingly different from those of the pre-1948 Jewish community in Palestine.[39] Other groups were also incorporated into the state and society but excluded from power and peripheralized. These included about 150,000 Arabs who remained within the territory of the newly established state, and Jewish Orthodox, non-Zionist groups that did not recognize the legitimacy of the secular Jewish state.[40] At first glance, it would appear that the state was successful in its aim of controlling new peripheries and preserving the original distribution of power in society by creating a bureaucratized hegemony (see chapter 3). Both the popular image of that era in Israel's history and the findings of social science research studies indicate that the state appeared to be in control of the process, while simultaneously maintaining a high level of autonomy vis-à-vis other actual and potential foci of power.[41] Control was concentrated in the hands of the ruling Mapai party, which shared power in an uneasy partnership with the Histadrut, the "Workers' Society" (Hevrat Ha'Ovdim, or Meshek Ovdim, the political-economic-cultural complex of Histadrut-owned companies),[42] and the Jewish Agency.[43] The power of these four unequal partners appeared solid and impregnable, despite the perennial struggles

38. Such as the Jewish Agency (the Sochnut, the local branch of the World Zionist Organization), the "Labor Society," the municipalities, and the political parties (Mapai in particular).

39. See chapter 3 below and Zloczover and Eisenstadt, *Integration of Immigrants from Different Countries of Origin in Israel.*

40. Friedman, "The State of Israel as a Theological Dilemma." From the beginning, most of Orthodoxy and the religious parties tended to recognize the state at least de facto, and a United Religious Front participated in the first governmental coalition. Coercive secularization of new immigrants provoked a great deal of anxiety and anger, however, which led to a deeper split between Orthodoxy and the Zionist state.

41. Kimmerling, *Zionism and Economy,* pp. 97–122; Matras, *Social Change in Israel.*

42. Aharoni, *State-Owned Enterprises in Israel and Abroad.*

43. Medding, *Mapai in Israel.*

among them over the sharing of authority (but not over the rules of the game).

The leaders of the ruling coalition were members of an elite group with certain salient sociological characteristics: they were all of eastern European (primarily Polish or Russian) origin and had arrived in Palestine in the second or third wave of Zionist immigration (between 1904 and 1923). Together with their offspring and with a number of individuals who had been co-opted into the elite group, the leaders constituted an oligarchy, whose hegemony over Israeli society appeared indisputable and unassailable until the late 1970s.[44]

Among the first practical measures undertaken by the fledgling Jewish state was the rapid transfer of most key Jewish Agency personnel to leadership roles in the state apparatus, and the concurrent separation of the Jewish Agency from the state. In accordance with the Status of the Jewish Agency Act, the state assigned the Jewish Agency functions that were clearly defined and that were, in essence, marginal within the state.[45] In this manner, the state sought to secure its autonomy vis-à-vis both the World Zionist Organization and world Jewry. A more complex strategy was, however, required in order to wrest independence from the institutions and values of the Workers' Society, which represented the interests, not only of the Histadrut, but also of other organizations, such as the Mapai party, the remaining Histadrut-oriented political parties, and the pioneering Zionist rural settlement movements. When David Ben-Gurion established the dogma of state autonomy and supremacy,[46] accompanied by a large degree of militarism,[47] as both a rallying symbol and an immediate objective, his aim was the transfer of control of key institutions from special-interest groups to the state. It was still not clear, however, who would be ruling whom. Would the Mapai party, with its dominant position in the Histadrut, utilize the powerful new instrument of the state in order to stay in power? Or, conversely, would the Mapai party and the Workers' Society become informal, operational branches of the state?[48]

44. For a detailed discussion on the practical and theoretical meanings of hegemony, see chapter 3 below. See also Shapiro, *Democracy in Israel* and "End of the Dominant Party System."

45. Liebman, "In Search of a Status."

46. Coined as "statism," or *mamlachtiut* ("kingdomship") in Hebrew. See Kimmerling, "Israeli Civil Guard."

47. See Kimmerling, "Patterns of Militarism in Israel," and chapter 7 below.

48. Grinberg, *Split Corporatism in Israel.*

In line with the concept of "state sovereignty," which became synonymous with state autonomy, the pre-state paramilitary organizations, the Haganah, Palmach,[49] and the revisionists' Etzel and Lechi were disbanded. Ninety percent of the country's land, key industries, and even the school system were nationalized (or statized), as was control over the distribution of external resources (donations from world Jewry, reparations from Germany, and, at a later stage, foreign aid and grants from the United States). Nonetheless, the struggle for control of Israel's society and economy that ensued between the state and the dominant Mapai party did not come to a decisive conclusion during the 1950s. There were three reasons for the continuation of the tug-of-war. First, most of those who occupied key positions in the state apparatus also held key positions in the Mapai party. Second, strata totally dependent on the state had not yet been created. Third, the Histadrut and the traditional ruling party held sway over vital mechanisms of control and sociopolitical mobilization of the new peripheries, which the state could not readily dispense with in light of the waves of mass immigration.

The symbiosis created between the state and the Mapai party also provided a convenient medium for enabling the Arab minority that had remained within the boundaries of the new state to be absorbed into Israeli society and the new political and economic structure through formal citizenship (see chapter 5). This was only a partial absorption, however, and did not enable the Arabs to compete with "protected" Jewish new immigrants in the labor market or with subsidized Jewish agricultural products.[50] Furthermore, owing to the symbiosis, the activities of the minority group could be monitored, and they were thus almost completely deprived of access to land and excluded from labor and other markets.

Only through the four-way coalition of the state, the Jewish Agency, the Mapai party, and the Histadrut, and the cooperative frameworks established among these institutions, could a "drastic change" ("chaos" from the perspective of the Jewish veteran population) in the Israeli state be prevented. In addition, although emergence of the new state inevitably posed certain threats to the legitimacy of the pre-state distribution of power, both the four-way coalition and the cooperative frameworks

---

49. Palmach was a paramilitary unit within the Haganah affiliated with Mapam, the left wing of the Zionist Labor movement, which had close ties with the Soviet Union in the 1940s and 1950s.
50. Lustick, *Arabs in a Jewish State.*

ensured preservation of the previous system of distribution. These threats were rooted in major demographic and cultural changes, a total redrawing of ethnic and national boundaries, and a dramatic alteration in the structure of interests of the segments of the newly created state (see chapter 3).

In spite of these threats, a process of social mobility among the veteran Jewish population accelerated. The establishment of the state and the concomitant "absorption" of a mass immigration that doubled the country's population within only three years brought about an almost total transformation of the Israeli class structure. In addition to producing a significant increase in both the power and bureaucratic structures of the state, this influx of immigrants led to an impressive upsurge in the number of citizens directly dependent on the state and available for exploitation by the ruling party during elections. This era saw the creation of large state and public bureaucracies, which absorbed the overwhelming majority of veteran Jewish members of the collectivity. Thus, many of the collectivity's members became either officials with civilian or government security agencies, teachers, police officers, physicians, dentists, lawyers, accountants, academics, mass-media personnel (occupations then under the state's tutelage), or career officers and noncommissioned officers in the Israeli military.

While many of these individuals became part of the country's ruling class, there were also those who became active in the field of economic entrepreneurship, which was subsidized by the state, and they thus helped establish a new middle class.[51] This new middle class provided a counterbalance to the economic and political power bases of both the Workers' Society and the old bourgeoisie, which were already in place upon Israel's proclamation of independence. In contrast to the "established" bourgeoisie dating back to the pre-state period, the new entrepreneurial class, which lacked necessary financial resources, was completely dependent on the state and, like the Workers' Society, required access to public funds and concessions, whether direct or indirect.

The new immigrants, especially those from Middle Eastern countries and North Africa, were expected to become part of the working class in rural and urban areas and to be absorbed by the labor market in

51. Rosenfeld and Carmi, "Privatization of Public Means, the State-Made Middle Class, and the Realization of Family Values in Israel." After the 1952 elections, the bourgeois General Zionist Party became the second biggest party in the parliament and formed a coalition with Mapai. Since then, a slow privatization of public means has begun, which was accelerated after the 1977 electoral upheaval.

agriculture, industry, and services. Owing to their social and geographical isolation from the veteran community, the immigrants were provided with separate social services, which in turn increased their isolation and dependence.[52] Unlike other actors in the "game," the new immigrant class was powerless, even to the extent of being unable to convert its "adjustment" difficulties into a mythology replete with heroic symbols, as had happened during some of the previous waves of immigration (see chapter 3). Many of the early Zionist settlers had not only mythologized their struggle, but had gone one step further: they had managed to convert the Zionist pioneer myth into both status and power. In contrast to the waves of immigration prior to 1948, the waves of immigration in the post-1948 era were neither heroized nor mythologized.[53]

As part of the previously mentioned process of spatial isolation and social exclusion, social differentiation, gaps, diverse strata, and political subgroups began to form within the new immigrant population.[54] The division of the immigrant population into subgroups tended to take place along ethnic lines, with the eastern Europeans usually distinguishing themselves from the Asians and North Africans through the pace and nature of their social mobility.[55] The newly formed strata in the immigrant population were mobilized to carry out tasks assigned to them by the state; in this way, they counterbalanced the veteran, more established strata of the country's Jewish population, and made a significant contribution to the growth of the state's autonomy and power. Nonetheless, the symbiotic relationship between the Mapai party and the state was strengthened by the *ways* in which new immigrants were incorporated into Israeli society.

Obviously, the above processes were neither planned nor consciously willed into reality; rather, they were the outcome of the dynamics of control over various resources or routes of access to these resources, via language, culture, skills, personal connections, and so forth. In other words, these processes resulted primarily from the inner logic involved in building the Jewish nation-state and from the desire to enable the state to function autonomously without becoming an agent for the interests of other groups. At the ideological level, the

52. Lissak, *The Mass Immigration of the Fifties.*
53. Spilerman and Habib, "Development Towns in Israel."
54. Gonen, "Population Spread in the Course of Passing from Yishuv to State."
55. Swirski, *University, State, and Society in Israel.*

concept of Zionism was reduced to the task of building up a strong state, while other goals of Zionist ideology (i.e., welfare, equality, quality of life, etc.) became secondary in importance. It was felt that only the state could ensure both the security and continued existence of the country's Jewish community in protracted conflict with a hostile environment.

As additional groups came into being in Israel, and as more established groups gradually accumulated power, the link between the state and the Mapai party began to weaken. The state was not trying to free itself from the party's support; Mapai simply declined, finding it increasingly difficult to rally support among the new immigrants. In time, Mapai turned into a financial, political, and symbolic burden shouldered by the state. The state also succeeded in blaming the Mapai party for the material and symbolic hardships and insensitive "absorption" policies of the 1950s and 1960s.[56]

The fading symbiosis between the state and the Mapai party exploded into open conflict when Ben-Gurion and his young lions were kept at arm's length from central positions of power. The result was the so-called Lavon Affair (1960–61)[57] and diminution of the state's strength and autonomy in favor of those of the Mapai party. For a brief period, Mapai seemed to regain its dominant position. Israel was perceived as a "party-state" that maintained "formal democracy" with formal rights (such as the franchise), while ignoring important citizens' rights, especially those of minority and marginal groups.[58] Although they voted in free elections and enjoyed certain freedoms, Israelis could not, in fact, remove the ruling party from its position of power, because of the country's sociopolitical structure and the oligarchy's cultural hegemony. As far as symbiosis between the Mapai party (which was supported by and,

56. After the defeat in the 1996 election of the Labor party (Mapai's successor), its new leader, Ehud Barak, asked forgiveness of all the generations of immigrants from Arab lands for the party's insensitivity in handling their "absorption." As the 1999 elections approached, Barak made great efforts to blur the party's roots in Mapai, adding to the party new elements identified with Mizrahi and religious causes.

57. The Lavon Affair was an internal conflict within the ruling Mapai party, which finally led its main leader, David Ben-Gurion, to split from the party. The official controversy surrounded the role played by Defense Minister Pinchas Lavon in a security "mishap" in Egypt in 1954 and the way in which the investigation should have been handled. In fact, the struggle was between the party's old guard and its younger generation (headed by Shimon Peres and Moshe Dayan). Ben-Gurion tried to use the younger generation to regain his personal "statist" control over the party. After failing, he formed a new party (Rafi) and later withdrew from politics altogether. In the long run, the internal quarrel weakened the party but not the state.

58. Shapiro, Democracy in Israel.

in turn, provided support to the Workers' Society) and the state was concerned, the Mapai-Histadrut partnership appeared to have regained dominance; the country's political situation appeared increasingly similar to that of the pre-1948 period, when the state, or rather the state in the making, was run by the Mapai.[59] The cultural-political dominance of this period is presented and analyzed in the following chapter.

In 1977, the situation changed dramatically. The process that had begun shortly after the 1967 war culminated, and the new middle class, which had abandoned the patronage of Mapai,[60] now began to direct its support to the fledgling Democratic Movement for Change.[61] When Mapai's traditional arch-rival Herut[62] formed a coalition government in 1977, the link between the state and Mapai was severed, with the result that the party-state alliance system collapsed forever.

During its first decade in power, the Gahal (later Likud) bloc, consisting of Herut and its junior partners, failed to replace Mapai as an alternative system of linkage with the state and its elites. In contrast, the state managed to utilize some of the Likud's ability to reach previously alienated socioeconomic strata, increasing its base of support primarily among second- and third-generation Israelis of Mizrahi background.

Both the 1973 war and the 1982 war in Lebanon considerably damaged the image of the state and its military as efficient implementers of "rationally" formulated policies, and thus served to diminish the state's power and, to an extent, its very legitimacy vis-à-vis other groups. At the same time, however, this diminution of the state's power and legitimacy did not bring about concomitant growth of a new dominant political party or other alternative social agency. At first glance, no socioeconomic stratum rooted in the civil society arose to compete with the state's efficiency and strength in supplying desiderata to its citizens, and no alternative social order or changes in the fundamentals of Israel's foreign or domestic policy were brought about.

The subsequent economic boom and the territorial and demographic consequences following the 1967 war, as well as the messianic political mood in which the entire Jewish population was trapped, postponed

59. Shalev, *Labour and the Political Economy of Israel.* See also Levy, *Trial and Error.*
60. In its new guise as "The Alignment" (Ha'Maarach), which included Mapam, a party to the left of Mapai.
61. See Arian, *Politics in Israel.*
62. In a joint electoral list with the Liberal party and other small factions, later called Likud, and led by Menachem Begin.

any internal struggles. From the collective sense of being a small (if not tiny), besieged state, under continuous threat of destruction, there emerged the self-image of an almost omnipotent regional military and economic power.

The settlement frontier, which had been closed following the 1948 war, was reopened, as was the struggle over the state's borders, size, and character.[63] Although expansion of boundaries, territorial space, and preservation of what were perceived as military assets were ingredients of the state's logic, annexation of the "liberated territories" contradicted one of its central pillars: the need to preserve the state's clear-cut ethno-national majority and prevent its becoming a binational entity. To further complicate the issue, the land of these territories was perceived as religiously and civil-nationally "holy." Thus, the territorial consequences of the 1967 war introduced a dilemma and internal contradiction into the Israeli state's logic.

The state's political character has been significantly changed by several factors: the Palestinian uprising of 1987 and its spread into the "Jewish territories," the need to absorb some 800,000 new Jewish immigrants from the former Soviet Union, the economic and social hardships that threatened the delicate fabric of Jewish society, the changes in the world political system following the collapse of the Soviet superpower, the results of the Gulf War, and American pressure to link aid (in the form of loan guarantees) to the "peace process." These factors have led to changes of government in 1992, 1996, and again in 1999, causing perpetual "counterupheavals" of the Labor and the Likud, oscillating between two mutually contradictory state logics: desire for territorial control and expansion, on the one hand, versus an aspiration to ethnic homogeneity and neighborly and world legitimacy for an immigrant settler state, on the other.

Concomitantly, basic changes have occurred in the Israeli state's political-economic structure. By various means, the state has been concerned with and invested in the country's industrialization since its beginning. The state directly invested in or heavily subsidized not only state- or public-owned enterprises but also private entrepreneurs.[64] By and large, however, the Israeli economy combines state enterprises, especially military heavy industry since the 1960s (mainly of the

63. Kimmerling, *Zionism and Territory*, pp. 173–76.
64. Aharoni, *Political Economy of Israel*.

Histadrut),[65] with a smaller private sector. Following a series of mostly state-initiated crises (e.g., the 1960s and 1996–99 recessions,[66] the late 1970s hyperinflation, and the mid 1980s bank-shares collapse, in which the state was obliged to take over all major Israeli banking), the economy underwent a centralization process, accompanied by an increase in the power of the central bank and the role of its governor and the professional echelons of the Bank of Israel and Ministry of Finance. The state's interests and logic were often guarded against sectarian or welfare lobbies by professional economists within the civil service.

The public or Histadrut-based sector was dismantled. Part was privatized and part (the Koor industrial cooperative and Bank Hapoalim and its industrial and financial subsidiaries) passed at least temporarily to state control.[67] Gigantic and all-embracing business conglomerates, some of them familial groups and multinationals, began to dominate the economy.[68] Concentration of ownership became the major trend, and, in 1993, the total sales of the top 100 industrial firms already made

65. From 1967 to 1985, Israel's expenditure for military and diverse security-related enterprises was about 22 percent of the GNP. In 1990, it declined to 10 percent. Israel manufactured advanced self-developed tanks, a missile system, missile ships, and an advanced jet fighter (the refusal of the United States to continue partial funding of which halted its development).

66. Regarding the 1960s recessions, see Shalev, "Labor, State and Crisis" and *Labour and the Political Economy of Israel*.

67. On January 1, 1995, the National Health Insurance Law went into effect. This law provided every Israeli citizen and alien with a basic, state-insured basket of medical and hospitalization services and medications, and opened the health care market to free competition. Historically, Kupat Cholim, the Histadrut health care company, had had practically a monopoly on health care service, providing health care for about 80 percent of the insured population. Being insured by Kupat Cholim and membership in the Histadrut became almost synonymous in Israeli culture. Thus, most of the population had, in fact, been forced to pay either membership fees to the trade union or health insurance payments, one-third of which went to the Histadrut. Since the 1980s, the perpetually increasing cost of medical services has caused Kupat Cholim to accumulate heavy debts and deficits, which the state has been forced to cover from time to time. This has also been the situation with pension funds and other social services of the Histadrut (e.g., senior citizen homes and day care centers). As the state took over these responsibilities and privatized these services, the Workers' Society was dismantled and the powerful Histadrut became a federation chiefly of several small, but powerful pure trade unions. See Ramon, "New Histadrut on Strong Pillars"; Grinberg, "Political Economy of the Dismantlement of the Old Histadrut."

68. The most important conglomerates were the Koor industrial group, the Hapoalim and Leumi financial groups (the latter of which had previously been a banking group owned by the World Zionist Organization), the IDB Corporation business group (affiliated with the Discount Bank and owned by the Reccanati family), and the Clal and Eisenberg (family-owned) cross-sectoral business groups. These last two groups combined industries, financial institutions, transportation, energy, and infrastructure firms. In 1995, the Eisenberg group also incorporated the previously state-owned Israel Chemicals Ltd. (ICL).

up 30 percent of the GNP, and 130 industrial firms, less than 1 percent of the total number of firms, already employed 31 percent of the total industrial labor force. Out of 54,000 corporations, the top 1 percent generated 67 percent of corporate tax payments.[69]

Apart from the central bank, two additional statist institutions gained much power, mainly at the expense of other political institutions, such as the political parties and the parliament: the High Court of Justice and the office of the prime minister. Since the late 1980s and early 1990s, the High Court, led by Chief Justice Aharon Barak, has opened its gates to citizens' suits of general interest and has decided that any issue is adjudicable. The High Court has also proclaimed itself a "constitutional court," able to examine any law passed by the parliament according to the vague criteria of "enlightenment" and the "spirit of democracy."[70] During the past decade, the High Court, which in fact has invited citizens to petition most political acts, has become a major and powerful political actor in the Israeli political arena, filling the vacuum left by other institutions. In fact, the court has become the main, and almost last guardian of veteran Ashkenazi, secular, liberal, semi-universalistic Western bourgeois values.[71] This has also aroused a great deal of antagonism toward its decisions, mainly on the part of religious elements, who perceive the court as "non-Jewish" and imposing "liberal tyranny."

According to the new election law that came into effect in 1996, the prime minister is now directly elected by the people and not appointed intermediately by political parties. A quasi-presidential regime has thus emerged, which overempowers the office of prime minister without offering proper political checks and balances. The power-deflated parties and the weakness of other ministerial posts have introduced great

69. Maman, "The Social Organization of the Israel Economy." In addition, inequality in Israel rose continuously. After taxes, by January 1998, the poorest 30 percent of Israelis received only 7 percent of all income, while the richest 30 percent received 62 percent. Meanwhile the state has greatly reduced taxes on business and does not tax major sources of capital gains at all. As for the role of transfer payments (social security payments), no clear trends can be observed since the mid 1980s. Social security payments reduce the commonly used Gini measure of inequality by a steady proportion of around one-fifth. They typically reduce the proportion of families living under the so-called poverty line by much more than this—around 60 percent (although this figure fluctuates a bit from time to time).

70. It should be noted that the High Court adopted this American model without the existence of a coherent Israeli constitution and in contradiction to Israel's initial political culture. This and additional political, economic, and social phenomena are considered by some analysts as a dangerous "Americanization" of the Israeli culture.

71. These values are analogous to those of "WASPs" in the United States.

instability into the Israeli political system, as demonstrated by the unusually brief tenures of Benjamin Netanyahu (1996–99) and Ehud Barak (1999–2001).

FROM THE STATE OF ISRAEL
TO THE ISRAELI STATE—AND BACK?

The incremental process of transition from a unitary nation-state to a de facto binational state began in the period immediately preceding the 1967 war. During that period, when changes in the sociopolitical structure of Israel's Jewish society became apparent, the country's first "national unity government" was established and the Herut party, whose ideals and institutions had traditionally been stigmatized, received legitimization. Its members, who had always been considered outsiders, were now allowed to become part of the legitimate power system. Israel's spectacular victory in the 1967 war reinforced the image of the state as an effective actor. It was the state, and not the Mapai party, that had reaped victory, created a sense of security, brought about "a return to the Land of Israel's historic borders," and bolstered the nation's pride.[72]

A new factor that was beginning to gain prominence in Israel's political stratification was the rapid buildup of strength tied mainly to the state rather than to the Mapai party. This was evidenced by the country's military-industrial complex, consisting of the armed forces and elite senior officers, officials in the foreign and defense ministries, the country's military industries and big businesses (private and public, such as the Histadrut enterprises), and cultural elite groups, including members of the mass media.[73] Despite their Mapai roots, all of these were essentially state-oriented. Some of these components were operational arms of the state or parts of the state's growing bureaucracy, which derived their funding primarily from direct or indirect state subsidies, concessions, or special benefits. Common to all individual and group members of the complex was their ultimate loyalty to the state, rather than to any specific interest group, including the Mapai party.

While it appears that the locus of power shifted gradually, such that it was almost indiscernible, in actuality the shift was built into the situation and into some elements of the initial political culture. Since June

72. See chapter 3 below and Kimmerling, "Change and Continuity in Zionist Territorial Orientations and Politics."

73. Mintz, "The Military Industrial Complex"; Peri and Neubach, *Israeli Military-Industrial Complex.*

1967, the entire area of colonial Palestine, with considerable additions, if we take into account the Syrian (Golan) Heights, has been annexed de facto by Israel.[74] This annexation did not come about because any authority made a positive decision to effect it, but rather because no alternative decision was taken and because no individual group had the strength to make any alternative decision. De facto, since 1967, Israel has thus been transformed into a binational Jewish-Arab state.

In this state, all political power—political rights, citizenship, human rights, access to resources, and the right to define the collective identity—has been concentrated on one side. The other, consisting of the state's veteran (pre-1948) Arab population, is accorded rights and access to material resources, but is absolutely never granted a share of the symbolic resources of domination.[75]

The *identity of the state* has been constructed as "Jewish" by means of various symbols and codes[76] such as the flag, the national anthem,[77] the official history,[78] and the official days of celebration and commemoration.[79] The right to belong to the Israeli state has been extended to Jews all over the world, who are by definition included in the Israeli collectivity (see chapter 6). Human rights for the Palestinian citizens of the state and inhabitants of the newly created control system are, however, conditional on terms of "good behavior" and loyalty to the state and are conferred in a selective manner.

At first glance, it might seem that if it were not for external constraints, the state might have annexed the conquered territories de jure. Such annexation could have been effected immediately after the 1967 war, as well as subsequently on various other occasions. With the rise to power of the rightist Likud party in 1977, for instance, many people expected or were apprehensive of a formal declaration of annexation, which would have been consistent with the party's platform. But it is not an accident that this annexation did not come about, even under the circumstances attendant on the formation of an extreme nationalist government.

The state was neither able and willing to make a declaration of annex-

74. Only East Jerusalem and the Syrian (Golan) Heights were annexed de jure.
75. See Stanley Greenberg, "The Indifferent Hegemony: Israel and Palestinians" (unpublished MS, 1985). For a parallel between South Africa and Israel of that time, see Greenberg, *Legitimating the Illegitimate.*
76. Dominguez, *People as Subject, People as Object.*
77. Handelman and Shamgar-Handelman, "Shaping Time."
78. See Kimmerling, "Academic History Caught in the Cross Fire."
79. Liebman and Don-Yehiya, *Civil Religion in Israel.*

ation nor able to enact a general law covering the territories conquered in 1967, since such a move would have opened a Pandora's box and given rise to a demand for civic and political rights on the part of the Palestinian population of the territories and to a more subtle and sophisticated struggle for the entire land. The management by legal means of a conflict over political and civic rights "from within" in a state that defines itself as democratic is much more complex and uncertain than the continuation of a power struggle conducted by means of violence, in which the Jewish state enjoys a decisive advantage. It is no wonder, then, that a number of Palestinian intellectuals privately considered the idea of proposing to Israel a formal and complete annexation of the occupied territories,[80] given the absence of any tangible possibility of expelling masses of Palestinians from Israel's spheres of control. A de facto political annexation, accompanied by an autonomous settler movement, such as has been going on since 1967, represents, from the point of view of state-building, the optimal solution. It must be stressed that without the Israeli state's tacit or explicit acceptance, not to mention the heavy subsidization and its military protection, not one of the 140 settlements established within the occupied territories (populated today by about 160,000 settlers) could or would exist. The status quo amounts to a more efficient and enabling form of annexation than any legalized or declared sort of annexation.

Although Israel's policies oscillated between the elections of 1992, 1996, 1999, and 2001, from the state-building perspective, the results of new policies have been predictably familiar. Efforts were made to differentiate between occupied territories and "administered" peoples[81] by including in the "autonomy" offered to Palestinians only the densely populated areas of the West Bank and Gaza, and excluding from "autonomy" East Jerusalem and the Jordan Valley, which was designated a "vital security zone" (see chapter 7). The end result of these policies will be the creation of two overpopulated Palestinian enclaves, separated

---

80. See Shehadeh, *Third Way;* Peleg and Selikter, eds., *Emergence of Bi-National Israel,* p. 204.

81. The idea of granting supposed "autonomy" to peoples, but not over lands, is in line with Moshe Dayan's attempt in the late 1960s to make a "functional division of rule" between *lands* ruled by the Israelis and *peoples* ruled by the Jordanians. In the long run, the solution probably envisioned a confederation or federation of the Palestinian enclaves with Jordan. But it was not likely that the Bedouin-dominated Hashemite kingdom would be willing to change its very identity by inclusion of the highly politicized Palestinians. This would have meant a very quick "Palestinianization" of Jordan, and not a "Jordanization" of the Palestinians. Here again we have a question of state identity. See Sivan, "Intifada and Decolonization."

territorially both from each other and from any other Arab-controlled space. These will form an autonomous but divided Palestinian entity or state—in other words, a reincarnation of the 1967–92 state of affairs, in which the Israelis continue to control the entire area of colonial Palestine, refraining from settlement-building in the most populated areas, but not in other territorial spaces. The dynamics of peace talks, the need to support the mainstream Palestinian leadership (versus the emerging Islamic fundamentalist movements), and the changing world order should, however, force Israel to adopt a much more flexible policy that will take into account the Palestinians' needs and national pride.

The territories in the domain of Israeli control since 1967 do not amount to a conventional colony within Israel, as has been claimed by several scholars and thinkers. A pure colony is a form of political and socioterritorial arrangement that, notwithstanding foreign control, is located *outside* the boundaries of the colonial state itself, and to which that state relates essentially instrumentally. The West Bank and Gaza Strip represent an integral part of the building and expansion efforts of the territorial self-image of at least one of the versions of collective identity of this immigrant settler state.[82] In some cases, when a colony begins to represent a heavy burden for the colonial power, the forces controlling the state begin to make cost-benefit calculations, and if these parties reach the conclusion that the game isn't worth the candle, they abandon the colony as fast as possible.[83] But these parties will never concede control over an area perceived as integral to the state itself, even if continuation of the control represents a sacrifice and a cost exceeding any benefit that comes from possession: in this case, the price of maintaining the territory does not matter.[84]

---

82. Paradoxically, Algeria, which would appear to be a perfect example of a pure settler-state-building effort, proves this thesis. Algeria was indeed defined as an indivisible part of the French fatherland, despite the fact that, apart from the settlers (the so-called *pieds noirs*) and elements of the right wing and the armed forces, most of the French did not perceive the territory located on the other side of the sea to be an inseparable part of the French state. Proof of this was the relative ease with which General Charles de Gaulle, upon his rise to power, was able to destroy this nonobligating consensus and construct a different sociopolitical reality. In the case of France, outside of an extremist minority, there was neither religious intervention nor a wide perception that the "loss" of Algeria might present a danger to France's very existence or a destruction of the cosmic order. A loss of control over the territories of the West Bank, the Gaza Strip, and even the Syrian (Golan) Heights is, however, perceived this way by most Jewish Israelis.

83. Lustick, *Unsettled States / Disputed Lands*.

84. One of the conspicuous implications or costs of the transformation of the Israeli state into a binational system of control was the reversal of the roles played by the Israeli armed forces, which changed from that of a military whose basic character was designed

THE CIVIL VERSUS THE PRIMORDIAL IDENTITY OF THE STATE

Prior to 1967, the Zionist movement managed to build a Jewish political entity on the territorial margin of the "Promised Land" of "Zion": namely, on the coastal plain, which, according to biblical mythology, belonged primarily to the land of the biblical Philistines (see chapter 1). Because of the structure of the local Palestinian society, Jewish immigrants were unable to occupy the central uplands (with the exception of the Jerusalem region) that once constituted the legendary biblical kingdoms of Judea and Israel.[85] The establishment of the State of Israel alongside the sanctified territory of the "Promised Land,"[86] but not in this core territory, helped the Zionist sociopolitical system create a secular society and protect the state's autonomy in the face of pressure from religious and nationalist groups (see chapters 3 and 4). With the conquest of the West Bank and its redefinition as "Judea and Samaria," the situation changed dramatically. The encounter between the sacred and the mundane provided several advantages for groups capable of exchanging "holiness" for participation in the system, and these advantages continued to increase given the primordial components of the state's identity.

Before the 1967 war, elitist religious groups had been relegated to the periphery of the system, despite the fact that their roots were identical to those of the country's state-oriented middle class. Once the West Bank came under Israeli control, these groups began to move toward the symbolic center of the system and, at the same time, to gather political strength, converting their "closeness to holiness" into political power (see chapter 3). This also led to an increase in the prestige and power of the Likud party,[87] which knew how to establish attractive alliances with traditional and religious groups and make the best use of overt and covert protest based on Jewish ethnic codes. All the groups allied with Herut had one grievance in common: they had been marginalized by the establishment, which they perceived as class-oriented, socialistic, and secular. Beginning in 1977, the Herut-led coalition produced both

to preserve the existence of a state under attack from without to that of an internally oriented police force, or militia, to protect the interests and dominance of one community against its rival.

85. See Kimmerling, *Zionism and Territory*, p. 26.

86. Better known in the Christian world as the "Holy Land."

87. The successor of right-wing Revisionist Zionism and later of the Herut party.

groups of settlers determined to expand the state's territorial control into the occupied territories and pressure groups demanding that the state change its basis from a class and socialistic orientation to a more religious one. It should be noted that the coalition resulted from the convergence of several struggles—class/ethnic, political, and religious—and was not the outcome simply of a struggle among political cultures.

The presumed cultural-religious encoding of the State of Israel as "The Land of Israel"[88] was not only a transformation of the nation-state into a binational state, including within its boundaries about three million noncitizen Palestinians, but also a clear sign that power relations *within* the Israeli Jewish community had changed. It must be emphasized that the several elite groups who pushed for redefinition of the collectivity's boundaries and its basic identity immediately after the 1967 war, and who founded the "Land of Israel Movement," originated in the mainstream secular activist segments of Laborite and socialist Zionism.[89] Only after the weakening of the elites of the ancien régime as a result of the 1973 war was the political and the symbolic struggle over implementation of the "Land of Israel" ideology passed to the national religious and secular nationalistic elite groups. These groups then transformed this struggle into an internal struggle over rule of the collectivity as a whole (see chapters 3 and 6).

As the identity and structural dimensions of the state's inner logic necessitated *permanent* definition of the binational situation as a *temporary* situation, the state had to establish new types of coalitions with new strata. In order to continue defining itself as a Jewish nation-state, Israel had to maintain its control of these territories without annexing them. At the same time, the state carried out several important activities within the captured territories: control of land transactions, monitoring the manner in which water resources were utilized, and the introduction of settlers from "preferred" population groups from within the dominant society. The Palestinian residents of the occupied territories constituted both a labor market and a consumer market for Israel, establishing a dual market system along the lines of national origins.[90] In

---

88. Peleg and Seliktar, eds., *Emergence of Bi-National Israel,* call this "new" entity "The Second Republic." I prefer, however, to label it the "Israeli state," in contrast to the State of Israel established within the territorial and population framework arising from the 1948 war. The Israeli state controls nonannexed territories and populations without citizenship rights far beyond its legitimate authority.

89. Sprinzak, *Ascendance of Israel's Radical Right,* pp. 38–43.

90. Shalev, "Labor, State and Crisis," pp. 362–86.

military, political, and economic terms, it became clear that the perceived profits to the state (and to most socioeconomic groups within the state, except the settlers) from control of the territories exceeded the costs, at least until the end of 1987.

THE STATE UNDER CROSS-PRESSURES

Because of the binational situation that has been created, two political orientations have crystallized in the dominant Jewish society, which challenge the continuation of the status quo in the occupied territories (see also chapter 7). Each of these orientations has its own set of motives and institutions for demanding an end to the binational situation. One orientation wishes to annex the territories and has as its ultimate goal (sometimes overtly and sometimes covertly) the creation of conditions suitable for the transfer of all (or most) of the local Palestinian Arab population from their lands and for the resettlement of Jews in their place. This orientation is viable only as long as the perceived costs of maintaining control of the territories remain within tolerable limits.[91] Following the Palestinian rebellion, the whole cost-benefit balance of holding and settling the so-called "territories" was reversed in great measure toward increased "state costs."[92]

Even if the Israeli case does not fit the colonial paradigm, some of these processes are familiar from the experience of other settler colonial regimes,[93] in which a situation is ultimately produced in which the settlers (who are subsidized and supported by the state and who in exchange serve as its local agents) force the state to act against its own best interests. Thus, the state is forced, either formally or informally, to annex the colony as a part of continuous state-building efforts, or to continue to hold on to it even when the costs of possession exceed the advantages, and even when such action threatens the very existence of the mother country. Even when the costs are high, the continuation of control is generally justified by a mixed bag of pragmatic and security-

91. This orientation favors a voluntary reduction in state control of resources, such as lands, natural resources, water sources, and consumption markets created by domination of another people, cheap labor, and the like.

92. The costs to the state were in many areas. The major terms mentioned by intellectuals and media were transformation of the military from armed forces designed for large-scale fighting to a police force with its own mentality; the brutalization of Israeli society; and damage to Israel's image abroad. All in all, the feeling was that continued holding of the conquered territories weakens the Israeli state.

93. Such as France in Algeria and England in Ireland.

related rationales and ideological and/or religious concepts that touch on the very nature of the mother country's collective identity.

Another aspect of the Jewish state's inner logic is represented by the second orientation. The basic assumptions of this orientation are a worldview that is more or less antithetical to the orientations of its opponent. These assumptions include the following:

1. The idea that the attainment of a peaceful resolution to the Jewish-Arab (and especially Palestinian) conflict is possible, although it will not be easily accomplished; such a solution depends, among other things, on the political behavior of Israel.

2. The belief that the Arab-Jewish and Palestinian-Jewish conflicts are not different in nature from any other negotiable dispute, and that they have little in common with the persecution of Jews in the past.

3. Perception of peace as one of the most desirable collective goals, because its achievement is a necessary (although not sufficient) condition for the attainment of other aims, such as a more egalitarian society, economic growth, immigrant absorption, welfare, technological, scientific, cultural, and artistic progress, and so on.

4. The understanding that both civil society and the state have civic bases, and that membership will be based sooner or later on *citizenship*, which is not necessarily related to nonuniversalistic attributes, such as religious, ethnic, or racial affiliations.

5. The notion of citizenship as conditional and depending on the fulfillment of mutual obligations. The state must provide its citizens with internal security, law and order, protection from external threats, well-being, and all generally accepted civil and human rights. The obligations of the citizens are mainly to obey the state's laws, to perform military duties (if needed), and to pay reasonable taxes.

6. The belief that the existence of the state and membership in the collectivity are not ultimate values; they are functions of the quality of life that the state offers its citizens.

7. The supposition that the Israeli state is part of Western civilization. As an accepted member in this "club," it assures a wide measure of social pluralism, which is not necessarily to say a multicultural system.

This orientation basically perceives the world system, especially the Western world and North America, as a friendly culture of reference. Yet, as most sectors of Israel's political economy seem to belong to the developing countries category, this orientation favors the intervention of forces from the outside world so as to assure the economic, political, and cultural "improvement" of Israeli society. The world system is perceived by this orientation as a potential ally in its struggle to attain influence in Israeli society.

Each of these orientations adopts its own methods for recruiting state support for "the cause" and believes that the rationale for support lies in the state's own value system. In doing so, each orientation provides an authentic but partial gloss of Israel's collective identity as a Jewish nation-state, and ignores the fact that a significant portion of the state's identity, symbols, and decisions regarding areas targeted for Zionist settlement can be traced to Jewish religion (see chapter 6). What is common to both orientations is the belief in Israel's exclusive Jewish ethnic identity; in other words, both orientations are determined that Israel will not become a multinational state in formal terms, although it is a multinational state in point of fact. All of the other reasons cited for returning to the status quo ante of the nation-state, preservation of democratic values, public morality, and so on, are motivated not by exclusively political considerations, but rather by concern for the nature and procedures of the regime (see chapter 6). Only when they are directly related to the possible weakening or demise of the state can the reasons given by an orientation for its position be considered to be of a purely political nature, such as the "separation" (from Palestinians) slogan adopted by Rabin's government and later again by Ehud Barak.

At the same time, it cannot be argued that a state's policies will always be determined on the basis of its unique political logic. If changes are evident in the state's cost-benefit balance or in the group interests[94] on which the state logic is based, state policies will be altered accordingly. The alteration might even be based on the values represented by one of the opposing security orientations (see chapter 7) or state-building subcultures based on an alternative definition of identity. Indeed, this was seen, at least on a rhetorical level, in changes of the "priorities of the

94. For example, on the one hand, big business groups have an interest in making concessions and achieving peace (regional peace and stability are perceived as "good for the economy"); on the other hand, the lower-middle-class Mizrahi Jews perceive relinquishing control over the Palestinians as downward group mobility.

state" following the return of the Labor party to power in 1992 and in 1999. Policy alteration does not always occur, however, even when the circumstances justify a change, nor is there any guarantee that the state will always adopt a pragmatic policy enabling it to adapt to new circumstances. Like any organization, the state can be the cause of its own weakening (in terms of overall position or resource mobilization) or even the cause of its own destruction.[95] Special attention needs to be paid to the fact that there are two diametrically opposed ways of reasoning in Israel, each of which is derived from an alternative definition of collective identity. Although each of these lines of reasoning represents only one aspect of the state's logic, it is very convenient for the state to have the two existing side by side, because, from the perspective of statist logic, they complement each other. When it appears that deadlock has arisen, and that decisions cannot even be made about internal conflict resolution, the state is in a position of strength, because its political logic apparently embodies both opposing lines of reasoning, perception, and construction of sociopolitical and military realities.

As demonstrated in this volume, Israel is presently facing a situation of somewhat diminishing "stateness." The reason for this diminishing effect is the fact that the state has extended its control over a population that is relatively large in proportion to the size of the Israeli population, and that completely rejects the idea of being a part of that state. Furthermore, the Palestinian population presently under its control does not accept the legitimacy of Israeli authority, producing a vacuum of legitimacy in the territorial dimension of the state. Moreover, between 1967 and 1992, the autonomy of the state has continuously diminished in the face of ideological groups that stress its "primordial Jewish" identity. In addition to producing a profound ideological crisis among the Israeli public, this situation seems to call into question the authority and efficiency of the Israeli regime in general. The crisis, however, stems primarily from the fact that Israel is a strong state capable of maintaining the status quo, rather than from any apparent weakness on Israel's part in the areas of decision-making, decision implementation, and conflict resolution. The state institutionalizes conflicts, not because it cannot solve them, but rather because it finds these conflicts conveniently suited to its own purposes. When a state institutionalizes conflicts that are not

95. We have the example of the Maronite polity in Lebanon, which was unable to resist the temptation of territorial expansion into areas populated by Moslems, as well as the more recent examples of the Balkans and the former Soviet Union.

beyond its capacity for resolution, its power is augmented, and the other competing agencies on the sociopolitical map are neutralized. The 1992 and 1999 elections, in contrast to the 1996 and 2001 elections, which emphasized primordial identity, provided an opportunity for the "state-related" societal groups to again increase the autonomy of the state vis-à-vis groups associated with primordial parts of its identity.[96] This led to a slowdown in the state's expansion into the Palestinian spaces (by freezing the settlement process), and to a reversal of the process of integration of the occupied territories into Israel. The most important factor for diminishing the amount of stateness, however, has been collapse of hegemony over the state's Jewish and Arab *citizens* in terms of complete acceptance of the state, as well as its legitimate authority and rules of the game. From this angle, the state's symbolic power (its stateness) has been in continuous decline, although its instrumental power and organizational capacity as the central allocation and redistribution mechanism still remain very high. This situation is a direct result of the shattering of the monocultural system of the community and its replacement by a plurality of cultures, further described and analyzed below.

96. See Kimmerling, "Elections as a Battleground over Collective Identity."

CHAPTER 3

The Invention and
Decline of Israeliness

There was, unfortunately, no commonly agreed upon replacement for the national identity that had been invented for the new Israeli state when the built-in structural and ideological contradictions of that identity led to its decline and decomposition. For the purposes of this chapter, the process is divided into four periods: (1) The creation of a local Jewish ethno-communal identity in colonial Palestine,[1] (2) the attempt to create a hegemonic national identity, dominated by a bureaucratized monocultural system, (3) the challenging of this hegemony by one of its own inner components, the national religious subculture, and (4) the final disruption and decomposition of the hegemonic culture and the fragmentation of the collectivity into a plurality of competing cultures, engaged in a wide variety of changing relations. The present stage is characterized by a plurality of cultures and subsocieties within the state, in the absence of a multicultural social order.

---

1. I refer to the so-called British Mandate period in Palestine, from 1917 to 1948, as the British colonial period. Palestine was for all practical purposes a British colony and was run accordingly. Use of the term "mandate" for the period came to blur its colonial character and roots. The British partially changed their policy on Jewish settlement when it became clear that the Zionist movement would be unable to change the demographic composition of the country as soon as had been expected. See Kimmerling and Migdal, *Palestinians.* On the economic aspects of this order, see Metzer, *Divided Economy of Mandatory Palestine.* For a wider international overview of the initial and the diplomatic developments that led to the British rule, see Karsh and Karsh, *Empires of Sand.*

THE YISHUV AS POLITICAL-CULTURAL IDENTITY

Beginning in 1882, Jewish immigrant settlers began establishing small Jewish settlements, or colonies, in Ottoman Palestine. These settlements would never have been able to develop into a strong, viable, and autonomous ethno-community, however, without the political alliance, after World War I, between the British colonial power and the World Zionist Organization, which both opened up and secured the country to Jewish immigration and land purchases.[2] With the several consequent waves of Jewish immigration, the Jews succeeded in developing a small but well-organized polity, which separated itself as far as possible from the British colonial state. The Jewish immigrant settlers constructed their political, economic, and cultural institutions within a social and mental "bubble." In actuality, they were dependent on local Arabs even in such crucial spheres as the real estate market, for labor, and for most agricultural products and livestock. Security was supplied by the British rulers. The Jewish immigrant settlers acted as though the Arabs and the British were "irrelevant," however, and designed their institutional infrastructure and collective identity to be self-sufficient and autonomous.[3]

Yishuvism, the collective identity of the Yishuv, or Palestinian Jewish ethnic community, was created gradually and incrementally. Within its imagined boundary, it included all the Jewish residents of the country who accepted the basic premises of the local version of Zionism, as well as some peripheral inclusions, such as of the "old Yishuv."[4] Yishuv society was stratified. Symbolically, the communal agricultural settlements

2. The unexpected strength of Arab resistance led to restrictions on Jewish immigration and land purchases based on the "economic absorption capacity" of the country, measured mainly by unemployment. By and large, however, except for the 1945–47 period, the Zionist movement was unable to recruit many more immigrants than allowed by the British quotas or to buy extensive tracts of land. See Kimmerling, *Zionism and Territory* and *Zionism and Economy*.

3. In a great measure this was possible because considerable material resources were transferred unilaterally from abroad by different agencies. See Metzer, *Divided Economy of Mandatory Palestine*. For the political organization of the Jewish community of Palestine, see Horowitz and Lissak, *Origins of the Israeli Polity*. For an example of the cultural organization, see Cordova, "Institutionalization of a [Jewish] Cultural Center in Palestine."

4. The "old Yishuv" consisted of the ultra-orthodox Ashkenazic community that predated the immigration that began in 1882. It was concentrated mainly in Jerusalem, Tiberias, Safed, and, until the 1929 massacre, Hebron. The Sephardic community, which had been part and parcel of the local Ottoman elite, was partially absorbed into the Yishuv community. Small Yemenite groups, conceived of as "natural Jewish labor" that could compete with Arab labor, were also located on the periphery. See Shafir, *Land, Labor, and the Origins of the Israeli-Palestinian Conflict*.

(and their so-called *chalutzim*, or pioneers) and agricultural workers[5] occupied the top ranks in the prestige hierarchy, but political power was held by city-dwelling party bureaucrats and leaders.[6] Those who arrived in the second and third waves of immigration from Russia and Poland were considered the "cream" of the community. The secular and religious middle classes of new cities such as Tel Aviv, Ramat Gan, and Haifa played a key role in the economic and commercial development of the Yishuv, and contributed to its cultural development, but were excluded from symbolic and political power.[7] Notwithstanding vociferous ideological controversies and quarrels over the distribution of resources, Yishuv society and culture were highly homogeneous. Despite talk of building a "new [and muscular] Jew," the Yishuv saw itself as a small, weak minority, held down by the local British administration and the "hypocritical" English government in London and under permanent siege by the Arabs.[8] Additionally, the pioneers of the Yishuv were engaged in an endless struggle with nature—including swamps and malaria—in the unfriendly land they had chosen to colonize, which became the subject of an epic of heroism and sacrifice. These perceptions and this social construction of reality contributed to the cohesion of the Yishuv and to the creation of a collective identity that became a part of individual identity. A "man of the Yishuv" (*adam min ha'yishuv*)[9] meant a responsible, civilized person, ready to be recruited to some extent in order to fulfill the goals of the collective.[10] In exchange, a "man of the Yishuv" was entitled to material and social benefits such as health care, education, and employment, mainly provided by the influx of "national funds" from abroad, as well as to a feeling that he was part of the community.

The basic premises of the Yishuv identity and the presumed communal rules of the game were:[11]

5. But not the private landowners of the colonies (*moshavoth*), who were regarded as bourgeois.
6. See Shapiro, *Formative Years of the Israeli Labor Party.*
7. Exceptions included leaders such as Meir Disengoff of Tel Aviv and Abraham Krienitzy of Ramat Gan.
8. At this point, the Arabs were not yet thinking in regional terms; almost no independent Arab states existed at the time.
9. Although there existed no feminine parallel, the notion included women as well.
10. Mythologically, this mobilization was considered unconditional and total. In reality, however, only the pioneers were totally and unconditionally "at the disposal of the idea."
11. Most of Israeli sociography overemphasizes the weight of "Labor Society" in the Yishuv. See, for example, Horowitz and Lissak, *Origins of the Israeli Polity;* Eisenstadt, *Israeli Society.*

1. All or part of the land included in the British Palestinian state
    was the basis for an autonomous, exclusive, and separate "Jewish
    commonwealth."[12] All Jews in "exile" who accepted Zionist
    premises should be entitled to immigrate to the country. Until
    the community strengthened and consolidated demographi-
    cally,[13] economically, and politically, only the most "suitable el-
    ements" should, however, be encouraged to immigrate. That
    meant that in the Zionist preparatory camps (haksharot) abroad,
    only young, skilled men and women were accepted, and they
    were then distributed proportionally among the different ideo-
    logical camps already existing in the country. The British admin-
    istration issued "certificates" (immigration permits) only to "cap-
    ital owners."[14]

2. Inasmuch as there was no good reason for individual Jews to
    immigrate to Palestine, the Yishuv community constructed itself
    as a direct continuation of ancient biblical Jewish society, whose
    inheritors the immigrant settlers were supposed to be (see chap-
    ter 1).[15]

3. Zionism selectively used traditional Jewish religious motifs and
    symbols to attract Jews and to give the settlement internal and

12. The ambiguity of the term "Jewish commonwealth" was not accidental. Nor was
it used merely to avoid arousing harsh Arab reactions. As a result of the powerful impact
of European state-oriented nationalism on Diaspora Zionism, an independent and sovereign "Jewish state" was envisioned by most Zionist leaders, including Herzl, as part of
the "normalization" of the Jewish people. Various versions of socialism were, however,
the most powerful component in Palestinian Zionism, and for these internationalist and
communitarian ideologies, the role of the state was ambiguous and regarded with suspi-
cion. Practical Zionists gave priority to building a Jewish society, and Vladimir Jabotinsky,
for example, saw the establishment of a national state as a means to this. The same
hesitancy toward a statist approach was prevalent in the Zionists' liberal orientation and
in cultural nationalism (as with Achad Ha'am's favoring of a Jewish "spiritual center" and
cultural autonomy). Only following the awareness of the scope of the Holocaust and the
Biltmore Conference (Biltmore Hotel, New York, May 1942) did Palestinian Zionism
adopt an explicitly statist approach. Prior to this, in 1937, the Peel Commission had
already suggested partition of the country into Jewish and Arab states. Practically speaking, however, the establishment of a Jewish state at this time would have meant limiting
the "Jewish space" to which Zionism aspired.
13. The demographic aspiration of the Yishuv was to comprise at least 50 percent of
the total population of the country.
14. The tacit agreement between the Yishuv leadership was that the British administration would set the annual quotas for Jewish immigration and the Yishuv would decide
what kind of people should be entitled to immigrate.
15. Katz, Jewish Nationalism, p. 57. Palestine was one of the most miserable target
territories for colonization. The land was poor, scarce, and costly. It lacks any precious
natural resources. The political conditions were unfriendly. See Kimmerling, Zionism and
Economy, pp. 7–9.

external legitimacy. The basic text was the Bible (the Old Testament), with the addition of some other "external texts," such as Josephus,[16] the *Book of the Maccabees,* and the literature created by the European Jewish enlightenment of the eighteenth and nineteenth centuries.[17]

4. The adoption of Hebrew (with the local Sephardic accent), instead of Yiddish, with its rich secular culture, was perhaps the most profoundly revolutionary step taken by the Yishuv community.[18] Hebrew symbolized both discontinuity from exile-developed culture and the supposed reconstruction of biblical Israel, as well as unintentionally infusing religious terminology and cultural operational codes into the Yishuv's collective identity.

5. As a part of this attempt to secularize religious symbols, texts, and collective memory, a hybrid Jewish calendar was constructed, incorporating some Jewish holidays, such as Passover (reinterpreted as "Liberation Day"), Succoth (the celebration of land, harvest, and nature), Tu B'Shevat (the Zionist Arbor Day), Purim as a popular carnival day (especially in Tel Aviv), Lag B'Omer (a celebration of the revolt led by Bar Kochba against the Romans), and so on. In addition, two new, completely secular holidays were adopted: the Eleventh of Adar, commemorating Joseph Trumpeldor, the first Yishuv hero, who fell while defending the small northern settlement of Tel-Hai against King Faisal's troops, and May Day, celebrating the international solidarity of proletarians.[19]

ISRAELI NATIONALISM

During the first decade of the formation of the Israeli state, a formidable and exceptional effort was made to construct a new collective identity,

16. In Josephus, they found the story of Masada, which they reinterpreted as a saga of Jewish heroism (as opposed to suicidal zealotry). Masada became a secular holy place and a target of pilgrimage. See Ben-Yehuda, *Masada Myth,* and Zerubavel, *Recovered Roots.*

17. See chapter 4 and Feiner, *Haskalah and History.*

18. Only later was the choice of Hebrew also explained in terms of the need to find a common language with Mizrahi Jews. See Harshav, *Language in Time of Revolution,* and Shavit, *History of the Jewish Community in Eretz-Israel Since 1882.*

19. May Day was a secular labor celebration but became a holiday for the entire Yishuv. Arabs were excluded from the proclaimed international solidarity of workers.

which was also explicitly intended to be a new Israeli nationalism. In some respects, this new Israeliness should be regarded as a continuation of the pre-state communal identity and of the Jewish ethnic nationalism developed within the Yishuv. Of course, this new nationalism also included and exploited some major elements of Diaspora Zionism. By and large, however, Israeli nationalism was a project of building an imagined community based on new principles and was designed to achieve additional and very different purposes than the original collective identity of the Yishuv. This project was based on the assumption that it would be anchored in a culture that would simultaneously be created and diffused as part and parcel of this nationalism.

The creation of this new identity became a necessity for the preservation of the stability and continuity of the initial social order of the immigrant settler Jewish community of colonial Palestine, and for the balance of political, economic, and cultural power already existing within the community since 1933 (when the Mapai party took control of the Jewish Agency for Palestine, the local branch of the World Zionist Organization). This necessity arose following rapid, large-scale, varied demographic and cultural changes as a result of immigration and the 1948 war.

Within three years, the Jewish population of approximately 650,000 had doubled, while of the approximately 900,000 Arabs who had inhabited the territory that came under control of the Israeli state, fewer than 150,000 remained (see chapter 5).[20] The veteran population regarded the new Jewish immigrants from Europe both compassionately and also suspiciously as Holocaust survivors. They were viewed as "wrecked people" (avak adam) with a "Diaspora mentality" and were suspected of channeling their suffering into anger against the veteran Israelis, without being aware of the heroic efforts of the veteran ascetic pioneers of the Yishuv. They eventually took over power within the state, endangering its initial characteristics and culture by outnumbering the veterans.

The other part of the mass immigration, those who immigrated from Arab lands, reached a critical mass of about half a million immigrants during the first decade of the state, upsetting the system even more. These Jews from Arab and Muslim lands (or "Arab Jews," as defined by Albert Memmi)[21] initially remained largely outside the Zionist na-

20. Morris, *Birth of the Palestinian Refugee Problem, 1947–1949.*
21. Memmi, *Who Is an Arab Jew?*

tion-building project. Yemenites who had been persuaded by Shmuel
Yavnieli to immigrate to Palestine in 1914 were considered "natural
workers," able to compete with Arab labor because of their physical
fitness and adaptation to the climate, and their frugality made it possible
to pay them low wages.[22] But whereas the Yemenites were a small, segregated group that never challenged or endangered the social and ideological foundations of the system, from the perspective of the European
veterans, the mass immigration of non-European Jews threatened to
"Levantinize" the Yishuv, downgrading it to the "low quality" of the
surrounding Arab states and societies. In stereotypical terms, these immigrants were perceived as aggressive, alcoholic, cunning, immoral,
lazy, noisy, and unhygienic. From this point of view, their "cultural
cleansing" in the Yishuv melting pot was perceived as a necessary condition for the very survival of the collectivity.[23] At the same time, they
also were depicted as possessing some degree of authenticity, of "biblical
Jewishness," and of sexuality and mystery, especially the women. Thus,
for example, a good deal of Israeli sociological research in the 1950s
was preoccupied with the subject of prostitution among North African
immigrants, but never with Polish or Romanian Jewish prostitution.[24]
The *Ostjuden,* themselves "orientalized" by their Westernized, emanci-
pated German and French coreligionists in Europe, treated Jews from
Arab countries (or Edot Ha'mizrach) as culturally backward orientals,
lacking the skills and knowledge to meet the challenges of the modern,
secular world in general and the unique egalitarian nationalist order of
the Yishuv in particular.[25] The Arab lands from which these Jews came
had never experienced the Enlightenment, and they knew nothing of
Zionism's battles with competing Jewish social and ideological currents.
In fact, they were perceived as representing an alternative type of Jewishness, very similar but not identical to the kind that Zionism had met
with and struggled against in "exile."[26] The most practical and immediate anxiety aroused by the social category constructed as Edot

22. See Kimmerling, *Zionism and Territory;* Shafir, *Land, Labor, and the Origins of
the Israeli-Palestinian Conflict;* Nini, *Kinneret's Yemenites.* The Kinneret Affair was an
example of the inability of the Ashkenazic elite to handle other Jewish cultures and eth-
nicities.

23. Rejwan, "Two Israels."

24. See Kimmerling, "Sociology, Ideology and Nation-Building."

25. German and Austrian Jews called Jews from eastern Europe *Ostjuden* ("eastern"
or "oriental Jews"). See Aschheim, *Brothers and Strangers;* Cuddihy, *Ordeal of Civility;*
Rejwan, "Two Israels."

26. See Deshen, "Judaism of Middle-Eastern Immigrants," and Hirschberg, "Oriental
Jewish Communities."

Ha'mizrach was that they would "re-religionize" and "Levantin-ize" the collectivity, changing the internal political balance of power. There was also a fear that they would lower the general quality of society, making it more economically, technologically, and militarily vulnerable.

The political, social, and economic status of the remaining Arab population also demanded definition. As has been noted, the Yishuv was ethnically relatively homogeneous, and after the establishment of the new state of Israel, the Arabs who remained were considered a hostile minority, a kind of Trojan horse, a potential danger to the fundamental security of the nation.[27] Nonetheless, the remaining Arabs were granted Israeli citizenship and declared to possess equal citizen rights. As is well known, however, they were denied any influence in the polity and were heavily oppressed by the machinery of the Israeli military government (see chapter 5). Most Arab lands were expropriated, and Arabs were kept out of the labor market, so as to protect Jewish immigrants from the competition of their cheaper labor. At the same time, as part of their Israeli citizenship and formal equal civil rights, a special curriculum was set up for Arab schools with the explicit intention of denationalizing and "de-Palestinianizing" them by creating a new "Israeli Arab" identity for them.[28]

THE CULTURAL AND POLITICAL ANXIETY OF THE YISHUV VETERANS

In addition to the anxiety over loss of control and surveillance over all these new populations, the veteran establishment was also frightened by the prospect of being removed from its position of political, ideological, and cultural dominance. The new immigrants from Europe were suspected of sympathizing with communism, and the Jews from Arab lands of sympathizing with the right-wing Revisionists, the historical rivals of the dominant "Labor Society" establishment and political culture. In order to meet these threats, the state was organized as a highly centralized and all-encompassing institution. As noted earlier, a new state civil religion, with its own cults, ceremonies, calendar, holidays, and com-

27. See Landau, *Arabs in Israel;* Jiryis, *Arabs in Israel;* Kimmerling and Migdal, *Palestinians,* ch. 7; Zuriek, *Palestinians in Israel.*
28. See Mar'i, *Arab Education in Israel;* Al-Haj, *Education, Empowerment, and Control.*

memorations was constructed, first around the military,[29] and later around the Holocaust.[30]

The state bureaucracy and its agencies were greatly expanded, and the dominant Mapai party, the Histadrut political-economic labor union complex, and branches of the World Zionist Organization were incorporated into a strong state-building project. As the supremacy of the state and its bureaucracy vis-à-vis these agencies was not always so clear-cut, this incorporation was not reached without struggles (see chapter 2). But beyond the internal struggles, all these agencies and their power elites shared a common concern about the collectivity's identity and the way to preserve their own dominant positions.[31]

The most important project for preserving veteran predominance, however, was less an institutional one and more a cultural and cognitive project. The purpose was, as mentioned above, to create a new collective identity or nationalism—Israeli nationalism—shaped by a model that would firmly fix the original Yishuv culture as the only legitimate model within the collectivity and as a source of cultural capital.[32] Central to this new identity was the idea of the state, or in J. P. Nettl's term, "stateness," and the melting pot doctrine, which presumed that the primary goal of state agencies such as the school system, youth movements, and, particularly, the military was to create a uniform new Israeli person and personality.[33] The melting pot, a giant mincing machine, was supposed to incorporate most of the newly immigrated Jews, but not the Arabs, who were to be excluded from the new Israeliness until the new immigrants could be resocialized, a process that might take a generation.[34]

29. See Azaryahu, *State Cults.*

30. See Segev, *Seventh Million.*

31. Take, for example, the so-called Lavon Affair, which was considered a historical turning point and a major crisis in Israeli political culture, leading many intellectuals to rebel for the first time against David Ben-Gurion's authoritarian rule. A crisis erupted following the discovery that an Israeli espionage and sabotage group in Egypt had been ordered to strike American targets there to inflame tension between the U.S. government and the Nasser regime. To exculpate himself, Prime Minister Ben-Gurion blamed the failed operation on the minister of defense, Pinhas Lavon. A careful examination shows, however, that not a single basic premise of the regime was questioned as a result. See Keren, *Ben-Gurion and the Intellectuals.*

32. For a presentation of this model, see Almog, *The Sabra.*

33. See Nettl, "The State as a Conceptual Variable"; Kahane and Rapoport, *Origins of Postmodern Youth;* Roumani, *From Immigrants to Citizens;* Lissak, "The Israel Defense Forces as an Agent of Socialization and Education"; Levy, *Trial and Error.*

34. See, for example, Bar-Yosef, "De-Socialization and Re-Socialization." The key term was "modernization." Secularization, Westernization, and general acceptance of the

Special consideration and top priority in this transformative project were granted to the Edot Ha'mizrach, mainly because their critical mass and cultural distance from the main Jewish population put the whole system under stress.

The melting pot doctrine was implemented through a contradictory societal mechanism of geographical segregation and separation. Many new immigrants, mainly those from Arab countries, were settled in peripheral areas and coercively "peasantized" or proletarianized (see chapter 5).[35]

In the past, the "agriculturization" of the Jews had been a central part of the larger Zionist project of increasing Jewish productivity and was considered by the so-called "pioneers" to play a major role in "healing" the people. The communal agricultural communities, such as the small *kvuzah* and larger *kibbutz,* were the flagships and emblems of the local nation-building project. But most of the new immigrants being compressed into small, newly formed agricultural frontier settlements, some of them on the sites of appropriated "abandoned" Arab villages, had nothing to do with the heroism, glory, and asceticism of the founding fathers' pioneering spirit. Later, the "development towns" appeared in the same peripheral areas, usually built around heavily subsidized industrial plants in need of low-skilled labor to perform demanding work.[36] More fortunate new immigrants found housing on the peripheries and in the slums of the big metropolitan areas, if they were able to leave the transitional camps (*maabarot*).[37] The transitional camps were transformed later into small concrete blocks of public housing, or *shikunim*. These small, two- or three-room apartments were sometimes sold (with mortgages), but more often were rented out cheaply, and were far too small for the large families of the immigrants from Arab countries. The rented apartments also did not allow any opportunity for the accumulation of property and titles and their inheritance from generation to generation.[38]

---

model of the Israeli man/woman as a package deal were supposed to fall under this umbrella. Some folkloristic expressions of the original culture were tolerated.

35. See Willner, *Nation Building and Community in Israel;* Weintraub, Lissak, and Azmon, *Moshava, Kibbutz and Moshav;* Swirski, *Israel: The Oriental Majority.*

36. Spilerman and Habib, "Development Towns in Israel."

37. Bernstein, "Immigrant Transit Camps."

38. The first major attempt to allow the inhabitants of these apartments to buy them at a reasonable price was made in 1997–98 following lobbying by a coalition of small militant and elitist Mizrahi social movements and nonprofit organizations, such as Neighborhood Voice, Project Genesis, and Democratic Rainbow.

Thus, aside from the harsh economic and material conditions they faced in their new country, and despite the aggressive policy of "Israelification,"[39] most of the new immigrants, in particular those from Arab lands, were prevented from feeling part and parcel of their new society. Their culture was considered as far inferior and belonging to the spatial and social peripheries of society; the preferred culture was almost inaccessible to them and their spatial and social mobility were blocked.

Some of them expected that coming to the Jewish holy land would be a religious revelation, or even a messianic experience, owing to the historical linkage between Jewish ethnicity and Jewish religion (see chapter 6). The "official" Jewish state they met was almost completely alien to their perception of any kind of "Judaism." Small national religious and ultra-Orthodox groups did exist in the country, but they practiced the Ashkenazic versions of the religion, which did not appeal to the oriental Jewish immigrants. Despite this lack of appeal, as the result of an initiative of young *haredi* (non-Zionist ultra-Orthodox) rabbis to save their "souls" from secularization and "Zionization," some talented children of the Edot Ha'mizrach were educated in the independent ultra-Orthodox or *haredi* school system, beginning in the mid 1950s. Following political arrangements between the ruling party and its national religious political allies, the Mizrahi and Ha'poel Ha'mizrahi parties, a few of these children were directed by an elaborate quota system into the state national religious school system.[40] This relatively marginal phenomenon had far-reaching consequences later on.

BUILDING HEGEMONY

It is commonly accepted that hegemonies are based on groups of social elites, or the common interests of political, economic, and intellectual elites. The political elites are the producers and implementers of societal decisions. The economic elites are in charge of the production of the material goods and resources of the collectivity and, together with the political elites, of their distribution among the different segments and classes. The intellectual elites are the producers of ideologies, including

39. Very much resembling the pre–melting pot "Americanization" policy aimed at non-WASP American immigrants. See Davie, *World Immigration.*

40. From the constitution of the state until the present day, the curricula of these state schools have been under the sole jurisdiction of the Department of Religious Education of the Ministry of Education and under the permanent and exclusive control of the National Religious Party.

nationalisms and religions, and other values of the collectivity. They create the meanings, the world order and the boundaries of the imagined community, which is one central dimension of nationalism.[41] They are the major producers of cultures, subcultures, and countercultures, as well as the public domains and spheres that are necessary conditions for the existence of an active civil society. The intellectual elites include philosophers, writers, poets, artists, academics, and "spiritual leaders," whether secular or religious. Most professional researchers of intellectuals argue that a person cannot be considered an "intellectual" if he or she is not involved in public discourse and a participant in the creation of the moral boundaries and rules of the collectivity.[42]

Since Antonio Gramsci's reformulation of the dynamics of hegemony- and counterhegemony-building, the role of intellectuals in these processes has been assumed to be fixed. The problem of a hegemony-building project in a basically anti-intellectual "revolutionary" immigrant settler society, however, has never been completely solved. For example, as Anita Shapira has demonstrated, the Hebrew University and its "professorate" were from the beginning marginal and marginalized by the dominant political elites of the Labor establishment.[43]

Even if there is not yet sufficient research on this critical theoretical and empirical subject, the impression is that the major intellectual elites, who were correctly suspected of not being completely committed to the power-oriented "socialist" version of the nation- and state-building project, were supplanted by secondary elites,[44] consisting mainly of veteran secondary and elementary schoolteachers, journalists and peripheral writers, poets, and self-educated politicians. Apart from their main vocation, the secondary elites had also in the past been responsible for the revival and spread of the Hebrew language as a vernacular, and for producing Hebrew textbooks in various fields.

Seemingly, their major enterprise was the inclusion of Bible instruction in the secular Hebrew school curriculum and the invention of a new

41. Anderson, *Imagined Communities.*
42. See, for example, Adamson, *Hegemony and Revolution;* Bocock, *Hegemony;* Mouffe, "Hegemony and Ideology in Gramsci"; Radhakrishnan, "Toward an Effective Intellectual."
43. Shapira, "The Labor Movement and the Hebrew University."
44. For example, some prominent figures at the Hebrew University ("the Mount [Scopus] men") were identified with the small stigmatized Brit Shalom (and later Ichud) association, which promulgated the idea of a binational Palestinian collectivity. Berl Katznelson and other members of the socialist elite ("the [Jezreel] Valley men") strongly objected to such "defeatism" and constructed an exclusionary Jewish ethno-nationalism. Hattis, *The Bi-National Idea in Palestine during Mandatory Times.*

type of knowledge, "Motherland studies" (*moledet*), which combines biblical mythology, geography, archeology, topography, and hiking. The secondary elite was also involved in a vast enterprise of selective translation of classic world literature into Hebrew, as the continuation of the Jewish enlightenment and Yishuv culture. Even though most of them did not belong to the Labor establishment, their national vision coincided almost completely with the nation-building vision of the national socialist political elites.

Yishuv society and its political culture had been strongly collectivist, but had emphasized at least a semblance of voluntary participation in the collectivity. Now the state's coercive doctrine, *mamlachtiut* (statism, or *raison d'état* ideology), was located at the center of personal and collective existence and essence, as a part of hegemony building. No longer were amateurish grass-roots initiatives tolerated or encouraged, and the previous "pioneering spirit" (*chaluziut*) was bureaucratized. The state developed its own cults and civil religion. At the center of this civil religion was the military—the most obvious state institution and value (see also chapter 7).

Not only was the military assigned the tasks of waging war and protecting the "national security," but also it was to be the major mechanism for creating the new Israeli man and woman, at least in the younger generations. This was a creature similar but not identical to the mythical sabra (*tzabar*). She or he was supposed to be healthy, muscular, a warrior, industrious, hard-working, rational, modern, Western or "Westernized," secular, a vernacular, accentless Hebrew speaker, educated (but not intellectual), and obedient to authorities (that is, to the state and its representatives). This aspired-to "type" was to be produced in the image of the first-generation natives, the offspring of Ashkenazic immigrants. Some small variants of this ideal type were allowed, but the margins of tolerance were relatively limited. Other "types" of Jews were excluded or marginalized by this model.

At this stage, it is important to add a theoretical conceptualization of the hegemonic approach in order to understand better how notions of agency and bureaucratization actually operate. In order to build a hegemonic situation, it is not enough to have a band of idea, value, and identity producers. It is also not enough to possess a strong elite system with common interests and background. A strong, deep, wide, and routine agency system, supported by the state's bureaucracy, is also a necessary condition. These agents actively or passively: (1) are used as models for imitation in all spheres of life; (2) adopt and carry out the hegemonic values, exemplified by their own way of life; (3) teach and socialize (or "de-socialize" and "re-socialize") the "others," showing them the right way of life; and (4) are used as agents for social control and surveillance of deviants.

From this perspective, most of the secular (and in some measure also the religious) veteran population were consciously or unconsciously recruited as agents of the prevailing Zionist Ashkenazi hegemony. Even without any explicit directives from the top, both sides regarded most encounters between veterans and new immigrants as "corrective experiences."

SECULARIZED RELIGION

Ideologically, the system continued to be built on selective adoptions of Jewish religious, sometimes messianic symbols and motifs. Nonetheless, because the modern Jewish colonization never succeeded in penetrating the heartland of the country, the hilly regions of the ancient kingdom of Judea, or the core territories of the so-called "Second Temple Commonwealth," "New Zion" was located on the periphery of the old one. The Zionist colonization enterprise was built mainly along the coastal plain and in the great valleys, while most of the "holy sites" remained outside the Israeli state's boundaries until after the 1967 war. Even small West Jerusalem was a pallid replacement for the "real holy city." The Wailing Wall and the Temple Mount were not only outside the geographical and political boundaries of the collectivity, but also outside its mental or cognitive boundaries. The geographical and political departure from "holiness" made possible the secularization of the land and symbols, and the creation of a basically hegemonic secular society. This was despite the firm religious foundations of Zionism, embodied in its very choice of Palestine as the target land of immigration and colonization. The target land had not been designated because of its abundance of natural resources, good climate, or convenient geopolitical accessibility, but rather because of its appeal to a portion of the Jewish people and its "holiness" and sentimental value.

Use made of the Bible is a good example of this process of secularization of central motifs of the Jewish religion and bestowing secularized national meaning on them. The Old Testament is no doubt a religious text and a moralistic book par excellence. The aims of its writers, codifiers, and producers were to teach which practices were permissible and desirable "in the eyes of God" and which were not. Gershom Scholem remarked in 1926 that "God is talking [anyway] from the scripture and the secularized Hebrew language, even if they [the secular Zionists] are not aware of it."[45] From the beginning, the Jewish settler society of Palestine adopted the Bible as a constitutive text, and considered it a national history and title to the land currently settled by the native Arabs, who manifested both active and passive resistance to Jewish colonization. The Book of Joshua, the narrative of the ruthless conquest of the Land of Canaan by the ancient Jewish tribes, was especially appealing, because of the direct linkage it provided between the mythical time and the *here and now*.[46] After the establishment of the state, the scholarly and the popular teaching of the Bible and its cult were constructed as the most central part of the Israeli state civil religion, as has been well demonstrated by C. S. Liebman and Eliezer Don-Yehiya.[47] Prime Minister David Ben-Gurion organized well-publicized Bible study classes in his home for officially invited intellectual and political celebrities, adding to his aura as a "philosopher king." Hundreds of imitative Bible seminars (*hugey Tanach*) were established countrywide.

The Bible was interpreted as both a kind of ethnocentric nationalist-militaristic basic law and a universal humanist and socialist message, leaning on the visions and prophecies of texts such as the books of Isaiah and Jeremiah. The wider public was involved by means of a newly invented cultural institution—Bible-knowledge competitions, which were broadcast by the monopoly state radio service and intensively covered by the newspapers. A new popular hero emerged, the "Bible champion."[48] The clear message was that the present Israeli state is the direct heir of the biblical Israelites and the mythological kingdoms of David and Solomon, but the theocratic character of the latter was largely blurred. Despite all these efforts, it was not easy to establish secular Zionist hegemony and impose the state on the civil society previously rooted in the Yishuv. The first great achievement of the state, the abolition and dismantling of all the pre-state underground and paramilitary

45. Ravitzky, *Messianism, Zionism and Jewish Religious Radicalism*, p. 27.
46. Tamarin, *Israeli Dilemma*.
47. Liebman and Don-Yehiya, *Civil Religion in Israel*.
48. The first winner of the Israeli "National Bible Quiz," on August 4, 1958, was Amos Hacham. He also won the "World Bible Contest" held on August 19 of the same year in Jerusalem. Hacham was educated in the traditional way to memorize the entire text by heart.

groups affiliated with political parties and factions (such as the Palmach, Haganah, Etzel, and Lechi) and their melding into one unified military force, was not easily duplicated.

EDUCATION AND THE FIRST MIZRAHI REBELLION

The first *Kulturkampf* broke out in 1949. One of the first Israeli laws mandated free and compulsory education for all children between 5 and 14 years old, and committed the state to funding elementary education. During the Yishuv period, education was a purely political enterprise, and most of the schools were affiliated or identified with political or ideological currents. Three major educational streams existed, subsidized by the Yishuv's "national authorities." The General Stream, which identified with the General Zionists, the Farmers' Association, and secular Revisionist elements, was the largest Jewish school system in colonial Palestine and included more than the half of the pupils. This was the educational system of the urban and rural bourgeoisie, but because of its superior quality, the offspring of many members of other parties attended it. About 28 percent of the pupils attended the "Workers' Stream" schools founded by the Histadrut and supported by the dominant (Mapai and Mapam) parties. About 20 percent studied in the "National Religious" stream schools of the Mizrahi and Ha'poel Ha'mizrahi parties. A small minority of Jewish children attended British or private schools, mainly non-Zionist Orthodox traditional schools—*yeshivas* and *cheders* (kindergartens).

Continuing this pattern, the new education law obliged the state to fund the party school system for the veteran population. The vast majority of new immigrant children, however, were concentrated in immigrant camps and in *moshavei olim* (smallholder settlements) that were entirely under direct state control. In these camps, the so-called uniform education approach was developed. This was the first attempt at state, secularist resocialization and an aggressive application of the melting pot doctrine, mainly to the children of Edot Ha'mizrach and Yemenis. Thus, prayer was not permitted, nor was the wearing of skullcaps and prayer shawls; the sidelocks of Yemenite children were cut. These practices met bitter resistance from Yemeni and North African Jews, and riots broke out. The memory of these acts became part of the collective memory and identity of these immigrants, as well as of all the Jewish religious communities in Israel, as a warning about the state's attitude to religion and religiously observant people. The United Religious Front, which had formed the first coalition government with the Mapai party, resigned from it in protest. The government fell, and a new election was announced.

In the meantime, in January 1949, the government appointed a commission of inquiry headed by Gad Frumkin, a Sephardi colonial era High Court judge. The Frumkin Committee unanimously rejected the melting pot doctrine and accepted the principle that all parents have the right to educate their children according to their personal beliefs and values.[49] The major consequence of the Frumkin Committee's recommendations was the creation of the "Religious Workers' Stream" by the Histadrut, headed by Dr. Yeshayahu Leibovich, in order "to absorb" the immigrant children from Arab lands. The immigrants regarded this new framework as merely a subtler path toward their secularization and integration as second-class citizens into a secular Ashkenazic pseudo-Jewish state.

A wild competition of "soul hunting" (including "kidnapping") evolved, and by 1953 the "Workers' Stream" had become the biggest system, succeeding in absorbing most of the new immigrant children. Following this success, the Mapai party was not happy to relinquish education to the state,[50] and a bitter controversy ensued until the parliament enacted the Statist Education Law (Hoq Hinuch Mamlachti) in 1953, which partially regulated the politically and culturally segmented education system. The "General" and the "Workers'" systems were merged and became the Mamlachti (Statist) nonpolitical network. Despite the rhetoric of saving the schools from politicization and avoiding any further culture wars, two different religious sectarian school systems remained intact.

When Israel was established, the "independent" *haredi* school system requested the state's financial support, but under the condition that it remain completely autonomous. This was, in effect, de facto recognition of the state by the major Orthodox anti-Zionist party, Agudat Israel. The party even participated in the first governmental coalition under the umbrella of the United Religious Front, but left during the uniform education crisis. Agudat Israel agreed to the funding of the *haredi* schools by the Zionist state mainly for financial reasons. All those aware of the theological problems that the Holocaust and the secular Jewish state posed to *haredi* Jewry, as well described by Menachem Friedman,

---

49. For the whole affair, see Zameret, *Melting Pot;* Lissak, *Mass Immigration of the Fifties.*

50. Zameret, *Across a Narrow Bridge.*

cannot ignore this turnover.[51] This was the first essential step toward the slow inclusion of most of the *haredim* as yet another segment of the cultural and political mosaic of the Israeli state. The state's agreement to fund a completely independent but small religious school system was at the time a successful tactic for excluding the *haredim* from the collectivity, while concurrently maintaining their dependence on the state machinery. The same logic was applied to exemption from compulsory military service for Yeshiva students—one of the most blatant expressions of the new Israeliness and its sociocultural boundaries.

It is harder to explain the readiness of the state, following its own logic, to permit the existence of a separate national religious school system. Supposedly, this system was a part of the Ministry of Education and came under its full control. However, it has, in fact, remained under exclusive control of the National Religious Party. The state thus offered the population three educational options: the secular national, Ashkenazi national religious, and Ashkenazi ultra-Orthodox school systems. The traditionalist Edot Ha'mizrach, the most denigrated culture (apart from the Arabs, who lacked an autonomous educational system), had no independent schooling opportunities within this framework.

The religious-cultural rebellion of the Mizrahim (see chapter 5) was long delayed after the violent protests based on their socioeconomic grievances. In 1959, riots broke out in the poor neighborhood of Wadi Salib in Haifa, following a local incident. Violent clashes between newly arrived ghetto dwellers from North Africa (especially Morocco) and the police spread all over the country. The riots were spontaneous, lacked leadership, organizational framework, spokespeople, and articulated demands. Nonetheless, they entered the Israeli and Mizrahi collective memories as a kind of warning of the potential danger of eruption of violent ethnic conflict between Jews, or so-called ethnic cleavage (later called "the ethnic devil").[52] The 1950s ethnic protests lacked any legitimacy in terms of the rhetoric of "common Jewish solidarity," were easily extinguished, and did not challenge the hegemonic regime. A com-

---

51. Friedman, "The State of Israel as a Theological Dilemma"; id. "Haredim and the Holocaust."

52. In Israeli Zionist discourse, "ethnicity" (*adatiyut*) is related to the differences between Jewish immigrants from Arab lands and Jews who emigrated mainly from eastern European countries, the Ashkenazim (considered "Westerners"). This plurality of origins and cultures is considered by political culture and social scientists as "cleavage," or something that can endanger society and the state.

mittee of inquiry, nominated following the riots (including two prominent sociologists) concluded that the loss of patriarchal authority in the
Mizrahi family and partial modernization of the new immigrants were
the main causes of the riots and denied that there was any factual basis
to the rioters' allegations of discrimination.[53]

In 1971, the Jerusalem slum neighborhood of Katamon became the
center of a militant protest movement called the Black Panthers.[54] This
time the protest was better organized, articulated, and directed, but its
achievements were still very limited, and some of its leaders were co-
opted by the establishment.[55] In the 1980s, the protest was renewed by
the less militant Ohalim ("Tents") movement, which channeled its efforts into improving housing and the rehabilitation of slum neighborhoods.[56]

Until the appearance of the Shas movement (see chapter 5), however,
Mizrahi protests were unable to challenge the hegemonic order, mainly
because any such challenge needed to come from the center and not
from the periphery, and to be connected with the central symbols of the
hegemony itself. Thus, the first real challenge appeared from another
direction, the national religious sector. Only after this sector made the
first cleft in the hegemony could the Mizrahim enlarge it.

THE NATIONAL RELIGIOUS REVOLUTION

In the eyes of the ultra-Orthodox, Israel's national religious population
were considered worse than secularists, bearers of an unacceptable version of religion, a false messianism, or Shabbateanism.[57] Most of their

53. See Bar-Yosef, "The Moroccans."
54. They intentionally adopted the militant American black movement's title in order
to shock the public and to draw a parallel between the oppression of the American blacks
and the "blacks" of Israel (i.e., the immigrants from Arab lands and especially those of
North African origin).
55. Bernstein, "Black Panthers"; Swirski, *Israel: The Oriental Majority.*
56. Hasson, *Urban Movements in Jerusalem.* In 1977, when Menachem Begin and the
Likud party came to power, an elaborate plan for underprivileged neighborhoods, mainly
funded by North American Jewish communities, was successfully accomplished. This plan,
however, was directed at improving the physical conditions and not the social, so its
success was of limited scope and impact. In the 1990s, a new Mizrahi movement, "The
Democratic Rainbow," and other organizations oriented their efforts toward the privatization of public housing, in order to make capitalization on their properties and familial
inheritance and accumulation possible for the lower classes.
57. Many religious and traditional Jews still believe in a miraculous messianic return
to the Holy Land and redemption at the apocalyptic end of days. More recently, a similar

rabbinical authorities were considered inferior to the great *haredi* rabbis. They were considered as having crossed halfway over to secularism and annihilation (*shmad*). In the eyes of secular society, even though the national religious were of the same middle-class, veteran Ashkenazi origin as the dominant segments of society, their youth were considered outsiders to the dominant sabra ethos and folklore. When drafted to the military, they were usually assigned to military rabbinate units rather than to the prestigious elite fighting units.

As mentioned, however, the very existence of religious Zionism and religious Zionists was extremely important for the legitimacy of the secular Zionist movement, both in the context of the Arab-Jewish land dispute and in light of the opposition of *haredi* Jewry. For these reasons, national religiosity was part and parcel of the secular social-nationalist hegemonic culture, despite its socially and symbolically peripheralized location within this culture and collective identity. The establishment was even ready to pay a heavy price in order to include the national religious in the collectivity.

Authority over personal status issues, such as marriage, divorce, and burial, was transferred from the civil to the rabbinical courts, and the halachic laws of Shabbat and Kashrut (the kosher dietary code) were applied in most of the public sphere (see chapter 6). Moreover, the very definition of the boundaries of Jewish nationality was altered to conform to halachic definitions. Curiously enough, despite the enormous effort invested in the creation of a new Israeli identity and nationalism, this identity was legally reduced to citizenship rather than nationality. Nationality officially remained registered (in ID cards, for example) in ethno-religious terms (e.g., Jewish, Muslim, Christian, Druse). This demonstrated that despite the secular inclinations and self-identity of the founding fathers, the collective identity was constructed of three intermingled components: secular nationalism, primordial ethnicity, and religion. These components complemented one another, but also perpetually conflicted.

The most important nationalist theologian, Rabbi Isaac Hacohen Kook, solved the national religious ambivalence toward secular Zionism

---

phenomenon broke out among the followers of the late Menachem Schneerson, a Brooklyn Hassidic rabbi. The supposed redemption is linked with a miraculous incorporation of Greater Israel (i.e., the territories occupied in the 1967 war) into the Israeli state and the transformation of Jewish Israeli society into a holy-moral community.

(see chapters 1 and 4). Traditional Jewish theology suggested moral terms for messianic redemption: all Jewish people must become either fully observant or completely nonobservant. Upon fulfillment of this condition, the messiah will appear, the Jews will miraculously return to Zion, and the Temple will be rebuilt. Kook inverted the sequence of causality. The return to Zion became the first stage in God's grand design, and the secular Jews became God's messengers, even if unaware of their mission.

According to Kook, redemption has already begun in the here and now. It is a process of reuniting the holy trinity—the Land of Israel, the People of Israel, and the Torah of Israel. As the first two overlap, the fulfillment of the third is inevitable. The first two parts of the predicted process are fully compatible with the hegemonic culture, and the third is simply a matter of time and conditions.

Without waiting for full redemption, young religious nationalists at the Kfar Haroe yeshiva and the Mercaz Ha'rav Yeshiv accurately interpreted the militaristic Israeli cultural map and volunteered for elite military units. Combining their religious studies with military training, they placed themselves shoulder to shoulder with kibbutz youth—the core component of the Israeli ethos.

The big social and cultural transformation in Israeli society occurred as a result of the 1967 war, although only after the 1973 war were its far-reaching consequences clearly shown. The Israeli state took on the status of a regional power, the boundaries of its control were largely expanded, a large Arab population fell within these boundaries, and extensive frontier territories were reopened for settlement. Above all, new access to the heart of the ancient Jewish Holy Land was gained. As Moshe Dayan, the purely secular defense minister, expressed it, "We have returned to Shilo and Anatot in order never to leave." Deep religious if not messianic sentiments overwhelmed most Israelis, who perceived the results of the war as a "miracle" and evidence of the direct intervention of the Almighty in history. This euphoric power trip was accompanied by enormous embarrassment. It was unclear to what extent, if at all, the superpowers would allow the Israeli state to hold on to the newly acquired territories, and in what form.

The first official attitude was agreement to withdraw from all the conquered territory, except Jerusalem, in exchange for peace or some equivalent arrangement. "Peace" and "territory" are not, however, commensurable. "Peace" is an abstraction (and something Israel has not yet experienced), whereas "territory" is a measurable, concrete geopolitical asset (like land, water, and other natural resources).[58] The territories in question are also considered to provide security, as well as religious and national "holiness." What really made the situation extremely complicated, however, was the presence of a dense Arab population in some of the most central areas. The Syrian (Golan) Heights were, for the most part, ethnically "clean," but the West Bank and Gaza were "tainted" by more than a million Palestinians. The two basic long-term options were mass expulsion or annexation and conferral of Israeli citizenship, as was suggested by a group of activist mainstream intellectuals from the Labor camp. Both options were unrealistic, the first because of its moral and international implications and the second because it would transform the Jewish nation-state into a de facto binational entity, something few Israelis wanted. The old secular hegemonic ideologies were no longer able to supply answers in this rapidly changing world, and in the absence of political and moral guidelines, the "permanent-temporary" occupation of the territories led inevitably to lawlessness and alienation.

CONCLUSIONS: BREAKING THE HEGEMONY

The Gush Emunim subculture and ideology, as successful as it was, only partially overturned the original secular Zionist hegemony. It simply shifted the weight of already existing, or dormant, ideological and social components of secular Zionist socialist and *mamlachti* culture. Nonetheless, the religious settler society movement's penetration into the center of the sociopolitical sphere created the social and political conditions necessary for even more far-reaching changes. This was accomplished mainly by overemphasizing the religious and primordial elements in the definition of nationalism. The state lost part of its autonomy and became merely a means of resource distribution and redistribution, rather than the central and monopolistic symbol of the collectivity. Israeli society was split into several segmented cultures, of which the secular Ashkenazi middle class was only one.[59]

A new political alliance was established between secular chauvinism and religious ethnocentrism. In this alliance, the civil ideology of the secular Zionist segments was almost completely subordinated to Gush

58. See Kimmerling, "Peace for Territories."
59. For an analysis of two competing cultures within this new societal configuration, see chapters 4 and 5 in this volume; see also Kimmerling, "New Israelis."

Emunim's religious interpretation of "Judaism" at the expense of Israeliness. The traditional Edot Ha'mizrach, now redefined as Mizrahim (see chapter 5), were newly empowered under the common "Judaic" denominator.

As the definition of collective identity became less civic and secular and more "Judaic" and religious, many segments of the ultra-Orthodox non-Zionist (*haredi*) communities also found the collectivity and its *public domain* more friendly and open to their active participation. The new definition of Israeli nationalism in more religious terms also contributed to their move from the margins of the collectivity toward its center. Contrary to the convention that the ultra-Orthodox became more nationalist, it seems that collectivity identity and public discourse became more religious, enabling the ultra-Orthodox to become more active and be more welcomed as participants.

The turn from a more civic and citizenship-based identity toward a Jewish ethnocentric primordialism also repelled Israeli Arab citizens, who for a long time had been among the more enthusiastic partisans of common "Israeliness." Consequently, they have tended to withdraw from the public domain and claim cultural autonomy, consistent with recent trends within the Israeli state. It should be mentioned here that the slow "infiltration" of the Arabs into Israeliness was an additional factor prompting ethnocentrically oriented Jews to drop this identity.

By moving toward the center, however, one group does not erase other cultural groups. On the contrary, it strengthens their boundaries and internal institutional structure, because of the increasing friction with these other competing cultures, such as in the case of the *haredim*. Cultural diversity and the appearance of additional autonomous political-cultural groups seems to be the most recent outcome of the breakdown of the secular Zionist Ashkenazi hegemony and the decline or transformation of "Israeliness" as a reference group and a form of local nationalism. The holders of the "original Israeliness" today are faced with a difficult dilemma. They must choose between two alternative strategies of survival. One strategy is to continue their struggle to ensure some degree of privileged position within the state by arguing for the relevance of an all-encompassing "Israeliness" and their continued role as its authentic representatives. The alternative strategy is to redefine themselves as just another cultural group, identified mainly with the secular middle and upper classes. In either case, for better or for worse, they have reached the end of hegemony and enabled many other voices, ideologies, and cultures to come to the fore.

CHAPTER 4

The End of Hegemony and the Onset of Cultural Plurality

Israel's hegemonic secular Zionist metaculture has declined, and a different social order has risen in its place. The appearance and persistence of a new system of competing cultures and countercultures and an escalating cultural war between them and the still dominant culture has accompanied the decline of the hegemonic order. These countercultures are not based on innovative or new ideas, orientations, rules of the game, rituals, or practices; in fact, most of them were present even within the original Zionist hegemony, as described in the previous chapters. Lately, however, they have been becoming increasingly coherent, owing to a process of divergence within Zionist culture, in which more clearly defined clusters of beliefs, ways of life, ideologies, rituals, and practices are regrouping into finely delineated countercultures. Several others are newcomers to the Israeli state, or have moved from the far periphery toward a more central and salient location. At the present time, cultural wars between the segments oscillate and vary between periods of dormancy and sudden eruptions of open conflict, sometimes approaching civil war.[1]

---

1. Hegemonic culture is not only dominant but is also "self-evident," and it has the power to exclude any other culture from the collectivity's boundaries or define it as deviant (see Lukes, *Power*). In contrast, a dominant culture is the culture of the most powerful elite groups in a society, but does not possess a monopoly, owing to the legitimate existence of cultural pluralism.

THE DECOMPOSITION OF HEGEMONY

Alongside the already existing cleavage between Jews and Palestinians, the conquest of the territories called "Judea and Samaria" and the Gaza Strip in the 1967 war gradually introduced another major sociopolitical fault line into the system.[2] "Holy sites" out of the Israeli state's control since the 1948 war were once again in Jewish hands, raising strong religious (often messianic) sentiments among most of the Israeli secular and religious Jewish population. This overwhelming victory, after a long and traumatic period of waiting, was frequently presented in terms of divine intervention in Jewish history, the antithesis of the Holocaust and continuation of the "miraculous" victory in the 1948 war and the establishment of a Jewish sovereign state.

These intertwining processes of occupation and mounting religiosity led to the first stage of partial and incremental breakup of the hegemonic culture and crystallization of new countercultures. Three competing Jewish countercultures appeared on the scene to challenge the original Zionist ideology. One envisioned Israel as a Jewish state ruled by the Orthodox Jewish religious code, the Halacha and dogma such as Rabbi Joseph Karo's *Shulchan Aruch* (Code of Laws) and "The Thirteen Principles" of Maimonides.[3] The second counterculture aspired to turn Israel into a liberal, secular, and civic state for all its present Jewish and Arab citizens. Both countercultures were rooted in the original Zionist hegemonic culture. Each emphasized particular aspects of the original culture and took them to their logical conclusions.[4] The third counterculture, known as traditionalist culture, had less sharply defined boundaries, with a corresponding lack of clearly articulated beliefs and practices. Its eclecticism, in fact, in some ways resembled that of the original hegemonic culture.

Israeli traditionalism is based on an incoherent set of values, norms, beliefs, and practices, mainly borrowed from codified "high" Jewish religion, but mixed with many folkloric and "popular" religious elements (e.g., cults and holidays dedicated to local ethnic "saints"). One

2. See Horowitz and Lissak, *Trouble in Utopia;* Arian, Talmud, and Herman, *National Security and Public Opinion in Israel.*
3. Ravitzky, *Messianism, Zionism, and Jewish Religious Radicalism.*
4. For discussion of anxiety over the "de-Zionization" of Israeli society, see Silberstein, *Postzionism Debates,* which refers to the present era as "post-Zionist," a category equated to some extent with "postmodernism."

way to view traditionalism is to describe it as a less rigorous way to observe the precepts of religion, or a middle position in the secularization process, presuming the existence of a continuum between "complete religiosity" and "pure secularism." An alternative conceptualization of traditionalism is to regard it as a substantially distinct culture vis-à-vis both religious and secular cultures.

A fourth, non-Jewish counterculture, Arab culture, emerged as an insulated culture, and was, and still is, considered completely differentiated from "Hebrew" or "Jewish" culture. Almost all "cultural studies" in Israel simply ignored its existence and impact on general Israeli culture.[5] Following later immigration waves to Israel, one from Russia (or the former Soviet Union) and the other from Ethiopia, two additional countercultural "bubbles" appeared. Each wave contributed to the shaping and reshaping of the Israeli state by infusing new and alien ethnic, cultural, and economic factors into the system.

The social and conceptual boundaries of each of these countercultures are often blurred. Thus, for example, there are people who define themselves as "secular but maintain some traditions," or "traditional but obey religious precepts."[6] Table 2 shows the distribution of religious identities in a national sample of the Jewish population of Israel.

Each of these countercultures, however, possesses rules of behavior, supported by different lifestyles, that obligate certain groups of people in the state. Each also has institutional and political infrastructures that sustain the behaviors related to their distinct belief systems, develop them, and from time to time redefine some of their manifestations, content, and social boundaries. At least two of these cultures are geographically separated or segregated from and have no common "table manners" or marriage market with greater Israeli society.[7] Among the cultures, there are sometimes visible and observable divisions marked by garments and other external labels (e.g., skullcaps, haircuts, accents, and even language). Additionally, such differences can sometimes also

---

5. Even today the veteran Association of Hebrew Writers, which is supposed to be a trade union organization, does not accept Israeli Arab writers. In 1995, several Jewish writers and poets established a new association, with equal membership extended to all Israeli non-Hebrew writers and poets.

6. From this it appears that only about 35 percent of the population is "purely secular." A survey conducted in the early 1960s found that 30 percent of the Jewish population was religious, 24 percent irreligious, and the rest "in-between" (Antonovsky, "Sociopolitical Attitudes in Israel"). Here again religiosity is considered on a one-dimensional scale. A decade later, Katz and Gurevitch, *Secularization of Leisure,* enlarged the "in between" category and found 20 percent religious and only 16 percent secular.

7. Friedman, *Orthodox Society.*

TABLE 2

THE DISTRIBUTION OF RELIGIOUS
IDENTITIES AMONG THE JEWISH
POPULATION OF ISRAEL

Religious Identity	Percentage
Orthodox (*haredi*)	3.9
Religious (*dati*)	11.0
Traditional (*mesorati*)	26.8
Secular but maintain some traditions (*chiloni hamekayem masoret*)	23.4
Secular (*chiloni*)	30.3
Anti-religious	4.4

SOURCE: Moore and Kimmerling, "Individual Strategies for Adopting Collective Identities."

be observed within each of the cultures, which are themselves highly fragmented and include many competing and adversarial groups.

Of course, the existence of such complexly interrelated countercultures is by no means unique to Israeli society, and most of their characteristics and content are universal in nature. As usual, the many sui generis ingredients of the Israeli case, like those of any other, are rooted in the unique mixture of its components, historical development, and background.

THE SECULAR CULTURE

Secularism as an ideal type is only partially the inverse of religion. Rather, it can appear sometimes as "secular religion," or in its more politicized form as "civil religion."[8] Another phenomenon is "irreligion,"[9] which conceptually is completely indifferent to religious categories and ideologies, while secularism is a more or less coherent "atheist" ideology. Secularism is an ideology, or a system of beliefs, that sees individuals and collectivities as responsible for their own fate and destiny without the intervention of any transcendental power. The cornerstone of secularism is a belief in human reason, the naturalization of the supernatural, and rationality, which is institutionalized by science and various positivistic philosophical streams.[10] Some versions of secular

8. Bellah, "Civil Religion in America"; id., *Beyond Belief*.
9. Campbell, *Toward a Sociology of Irreligion*.
10. Pratt, *Religion and Secularization*; Panikkar, *Worship and Secular Man*.

belief also include the idea of legitimate pluralism and cultural heterogeneity, making room for "irrational belief" (i.e., religion) and for aesthetic and emotional products, such as the arts (whereas in religion the
arts are recruited for the reinforcement of the faith). The constructive
and destructive powers in secularism, "good" and "evil," are rooted in
human traits and humankind's ability for rational decision-making. Human reason, its "linear progress," and its supposed perfectibility cohabit
with human drives to self-destruction, such as the Freudian "id." Emotional and noncalculated behavior are not the subject of any divine or
satanic supervision or grand design, but are outcomes of the natural
social "milieu." Reward and punishment systems are not rooted in any
divine or supernatural accounting, but are located within an individual's
internalized values and self-esteem, the reaction of other individuals (social control), and a legal-juridical-sociopolitical system embodied by the
state. The secular world order, however, is full of ambiguities and ambivalence,[11] and religion itself does not essentially contradict urbaniza-
tion, modernity, rationality, and science. The initial agreement among
social scientists and philosophers over the disappearance of religion in
the modern world has been completely refuted.[12] Secularism and religion
have developed simultaneously and do not necessarily stand in a zero-
sum relationship.[13]

Historically, secularism has been seen as connected with the upper
classes of society, and religiosity, partly under the influence of Marx
(religion as the "opium of the people"), with the lower classes. Frederick
the Great has been cited as observing that religion is a necessity to dis-
cipline the masses and agnosticism is the privilege of the elite. Historical
empirical evidence does not validate this generalization and shows that
irreligion has existed under many historical and societal circumstances
among peripheral, but not necessarily deviant, classes and that religion
is not a universal phenomenon.[14]

The major attribute of secularism is the inclusionary characteristics
of the boundaries of its public realm. Thus, diverse religions or religious
motifs can be included in its belief system, as can other legitimate man-
made ideologies. Secularism itself can include one or more religions,
acting as autonomous cultural spheres within the secular realm, as well

11. Martin, *The Religious and the Secular*.
12. Stark and Bainbridge, *Future of Religion*.
13. Brown, "A Revisionist Approach to Religious Changes."
14. Campbell, *Toward a Sociology of Irreligion*.

as religious symbols and cultural products (e.g., religious liturgy) that are secularized and universalized. Religion is open to the same change, criticism, skepticism, and investigation as any other human phenomenon, with its totalistic and exclusionary forms regarded suspiciously at best and as dangerous at worst. In sum, God is not dead—as Nietzsche declared—but is rather a creature, man-made for human convenience, and subject to manipulation, shaping, and reshaping.

As previously stated, the Jewish immigrant settler movement in Palestine, especially after the second wave of immigration (1905–1914) created a society that was self-defined as almost purely secular. Even as many symbols and practices from Judaism-as-religion were absorbed into this culture, they were secularized and reinterpreted. Perhaps the most striking example of such adaptation and commodification was the place of the Bible (that is, the Old Testament) in the newly formed culture. The Bible was selectively constructed and reinvented as an ancient national history of the Jewish people, and the basic certificate granting the Jewish nation title to the Holy Land.[15]

Before the Holocaust, the Bible served as the central core narrative and the most powerful constitutive myth of the new collectivity, a bridge between the glorious past, the problematic present, and the desired future.[16] It was included in school curricula and used as a model in daily life for many practical purposes (such as finding names for newborns, attaching old names to "rebuilt" localities and social institutions, and as a source for examples of ideal behavior). Whether read selectively, accompanied by a modern "scientific" critical approach, or presented as "cultural heritage" or "literature," the Bible still remained a religious moralistic text. The multiple meanings of the Bible, as both a religious holy text and a national history, indeed played a key role in the constitution of the core narrative of this culture, but secular use of the Bible was constantly open to criticism, not only as the proportion of religious people among the general population increased and in response to the needs of the Zionist hegemony, but also owing to the inherent characteristics of the Bible as a religious and moralistic narrative. The major

15. This must be seen in the context of the counterclaim of the local Arab population to the possession of the exclusive right over the land and their perception of Jewish settlement as a colonial enterprise and the Jewish immigrants as aliens (see Kimmerling, *Zionism and Territory;* Kimmerling and Migdal, *Palestinians*). Hebrew, the language of the Bible, was also secularized about a hundred years before by the Jewish enlightenment (see Schweid, *Idea of Judaism as a Culture;* Shavit, *History of the Jewish Community in Eretz-Israel since 1882*).

16. Zerubavel, *Recovered Roots;* Zuckerman, *Shoah in the Sealed Room.*

and most active "hero" of the Bible as a narrative is God, and without a deep "censorship," no matter how it is interpreted, its omnipresence and moral message remains.[17] This double message of the Bible became one of the major ingredients in the hegemonic Zionist culture.

Nonetheless, despite the Hebrew culture's inability to completely detach itself from religious elements, a strong, self-defined local secular culture was created by the Jewish immigrants in Palestine, modeled on the great contemporary Western cultural centers. Together with the adoption of Hebrew as a vernacular and powerful unifying factor, a variegated "high culture" was created. Generations, groups, and schools of writers, poets, composers, painters, sculptors, architects, scientists, and journalists—some immigrants and some native-born—constructed a vital cultural field. Although the non-Latin origin of the Hebrew language is considered an obstacle to its accessibility, spread, and potential for market expansion, the "peculiarity" of Hebrew culture encouraged many translations. Moreover, the emergence of new modern Jewish cultural centers, especially in North America,[18] enlarged the market for Hebrew cultural items, almost globalizing it. Most of the great classics of Western literature were quickly made available in Hebrew.

Central culture-producing institutions, such as theaters, libraries, philharmonic and other orchestras, ballet companies, choirs, museums and galleries, universities, colleges, publishing houses, movie companies, mass media, and so on, were created as a part of the nation-building process. An extensive Hebrew educational system was developed, with the aim of creating a new "Hebrew person," and at least two great metropolitan cities—Tel Aviv and Haifa—developed as self-proclaimed secularist entities, complete with different secular cults and rituals. The elite daily newspaper *Ha'aretz* evolved as the traditional bastion of Israeli secularism, replete with a home-grown rhetoric and slang, and established a public realm of its own, with a *communitas* of writers and readers who share a common belief in secularism and civil society. Virtually no culture-generating institution found in any great center in the

17. See discussion at the Cherik Institute of Hebrew University on April 18, 1996, on the "Bible and the Israel Identity," with participation of Yair Zakowitz, Amnon Ben-Tor, Asher Shkedi, Gidon Aran, Shaul Katz, Michael Heyd, and others. For a vivid example of a recent attempt at revitalization of the Bible in a "secular" and nationalistic spirit, see Reisel and Reisel, *Secular Attachment to Judaism*. Many of the new generation of archeologists in Israel argue that their findings do not support the biblical story of the roots of the Jewish nation (see also chapter 1). Old guard Zionists vehemently reject these arguments.

18. See Kimmerling, "Boundaries and Frontiers of the Israeli Control System."

world is absent from the secular cultural map of the Jewish collectivity. Both in terms of quantity and quality, the scope of secular Jewish "culture production" relative to the size of the collectivity seems higher than that of any comparable collectivity.

Secularism as a loosely defined ideology and way of life, however, is still regarded as the prerogative of elite groups and is a class phenomenon. It is linked with the highly educated, affluent Ashkenazi middle and upper middle classes. Politically, it is mainly identified with the Civil Rights Movement, although the Orthodox and rivals of the Labor party tend to suspect the latter, and especially its kibbutz constituency, of being secular or "non-Jewish."[19]

The great influx of more than a half-million immigrants from the former territories of the Soviet Union threatens not only to change the fragile balance of power that exists in Israel between ethnic groups (so-called Mizrahi vs. Ashkenazi) and relations between Jewish and diverse Palestinian groups, but also between secular and religious Jews. In the long run, this immigration will probably alter the basic profile of Israel's political and social spheres, just as the 1948–54 mass immigration changed the social and political situation that had characterized the pre-state Jewish community in Palestine.[20] This immigration wave, which is basically the most secular ever to reach the country and is characterized by a middle-class social profile, will soon obtain considerable political power, not only as a reservoir of voters, but also in terms of the highly skilled, politically oriented persons who will represent the immigrants. A considerable portion, or even a critical mass, among these immigrants are "non-Jews" according to Halacha. Thus far, they have tended to conduct their social and cultural life within a "Russian bubble," but as soon as they integrate into greater Israeli society, the system will no longer be able to sustain the current religion-based marriage system.[21]

A distinction needs to be made between the state-produced quasi-secularist civil religion that places the state, its institutions (the military, bureaucracy, courts, and parliament) and culture at the center, and the

19. At a prominent public meeting, the well-known Lithuanian Rabbi Shach prohibited the Orthodox parties from forming a coalition with the Labor party, calling its members "rabbit [i.e., non-kosher animal] eaters."
20. Kimmerling, *Zionism and Economy.*
21. There are at present several hundred persons in Israel seen as "unqualified for marriage" or for burial according to religious rules owing to doubts about their "Jewishness." These are regarded as "marginal cases" and mainly ignored by the political system. Russian immigration dramatically increased the numbers of these "untouchables." This increase must lead to a legitimation of civil marriages, thus far unrecognized in Israel.

secular culture of civil society. Civil society secularism is based on a greater emphasis on individualistic values and individual self-realization. The appearance of such an individualistic and postindustrial secular culture was made possible only following the decomposition of Zionist hegemony, but was also the catalyst of this process. The increasing weight of individualism has been accompanied by feelings of anxiety and has been perceived as a disintegration of Israeli society and culture, a retreat from "genuine Jewish and Israeli values," and a general sign of moral weakness.[22]

The religious and old guard Zionist ideologues are not alone in viewing the new secular individualism as "decadence" or destructive hedonism. Several core members of the secular elite itself seem to feel threatened. For example, in an article entitled "There Is No Secular Culture in This Country," the prominent Israeli poet Dahlia Ravikovitz, a pillar of Israeli secular culture, wrote:

> I must say that I have not as yet found anything that we can call a developed secular culture in this country. I have only seen some pathetic attempts to create one overnight, on the part of the same people who laugh at the idea of the world created in six days. . . . I have not found in the Israeli secular culture any text or guide on how to gladden a bride and her groom, nor one that will console mourners. . . . Actually our secularist culture is a culture of nothingness. . . . I do not observe the commandments, and I am not religious, but the fact is that I haven't a secular alternative.

Ravikovitz's reflections echo the constant claim of Jewish Orthodoxy that secular segments of Jewish society lack any authentic culture except for a decadent hedonism, and that the secular are not "real Jews" but rather a "mixed mob" (*erev rav*).

The veteran secular population has slowly started to become aware of its narrow class character and of its loss of cultural and political hegemony. As long as they retain a residue of their former power within the state, secular Israelis are trying to shape class consciousness, to redraw boundaries, and to redesign the rules of the game from within. This population segment is currently in the organizational stage of wag-

22. The statist secular civil religion cannot be regarded as secular because of the definition of Israel as a "Jewish (nation) state" and the difficulties in defining "Judaism" in secular terms. Deshen, "Judaism of Middle-Eastern Immigrants," defines "secular nationalism" as one of four "patterns of Israeli Judaism," which excludes "secular nonnationalists from the boundaries of Judaism." Deshen also refers to the religiosity of the oriental Jews as a distinct "pattern" of Judaism, which I call "traditionalism." See also Shokeid, "Precepts vs. Tradition."

ing a more open and conspicuous cultural and class war. This reorganization is being carried out through a search among other population segments and competing cultures for allies with whom to form ad hoc political and social coalitions.

THE CONVERGENCE BETWEEN RELIGIOUS COUNTERCULTURES

Religion, as an ideal type, is an ideology or an aggregate of perceptions that presumes the existence of mostly omnipotent transcendental forces that dominate (and even create) the natural and social worlds.[23] The system has a binary character, using a sharp division between "good" and "evil" forces, which compete over human deeds and souls. The doings and undoings of human (and sometimes nonhuman) creatures are accountable and controlled by this-worldly and otherworldly rewards. A clear-cut code of behavior (or precepts)—derived from a holy source, usually as scripture—is imposed on a collectivity of believers. The degree to which these precepts are strictly observed is a reflection of the quality of belief in the "truth" of the religion. While religions use many ordinary terms and words drawn from secular experience, the ordinary sense of them has been expanded and translated to the sacred sphere.[24] The individual is usually not entitled to add or detract from the precepts or to interpret or reinterpret the scriptures, the values, or the precepts. For this purpose, there are professional authorities, such as high priests, rabbis, *qadis,* and *imams* (or, in the case of revolutionary reinterpretation, prophets), usually organized in a bureaucratic "church" or a communitarian or charismatic hierarchy.

Religion tends to be conservative and past-oriented (although it can sometimes support social or national revolutionary movements). Beliefs and behaviors of real, imagined, or invented ancestors are usually considered not only as perfect, but also as the ultimate, holy, and unchangeable model. World religions, with some exceptions, are also "totalistic," providing obligatory models of conduct in many or all realms of individual and collective behavior. Religion as such is exclusionary, inasmuch as it draws sharp boundaries between its members and those

---

23. Luckmann, "The New and the Old in Religion"; Wilson, *Religion in a Secular Society;* Turner, *Religion and Social Theory;* Beckford, *Religion and Advanced Industrial Society.*
24. Martin, *Breaking of the Image.*

outside its holy *communitas*.[25] Rights of participation in the public realm are granted only to true believers; this realm is most often a male society. Actual religion varies in great measure from this ideal-type presentation, and deep differences exist among particular religions, as well as within them.

Historically, Jews who defined themselves as religious were deeply divided in the stances they adopted toward modernity, Jewish enlightenment and secularism, Zionism, and, later, the very existence of a secular "Jewish state."[26] From the beginning, a small religious stream was established within the Zionist movement,[27] and even before the appearance of Zionism, there were rabbis who called for a mass "return to Zion." The real theological revolution, however, occurred in the late 1920s and was led by Rabbi Abraham Isaac Kook,[28] who reversed the whole Jewish-rabbinical paradigm and causal relationship concerning "redemption." Traditionally, the fulfillment by all Jews of all the "613 commandments" listed in the holy scriptures was the condition for the coming of the Messiah, the return of all Jews to Zion, and full redemption. Rabbi Kook reversed this, declaring that when as many Jews as possible fulfill the single commandment to "settle the holy land," the Messiah will appear to redeem "his people" politically and theologically, and will make them follow all his commandments and precepts. A cosmic redemption of the "whole world" will then follow. This new religious perception granted religious meaning and legitimacy to secular nationalism and the so-called socialist pioneer Jews by making them "tools" of a divine project of religious redemption. The Kookian theological revolution laid the foundation for the participation of its followers in the secular Israeli state and society in the here and now, and for a collaboration between this segment of religious Jews and the secular Zionists. It must be stressed, however, that the Kookian approach never abolished the ultimate goal of transforming the Jewish polity into a theocratic state ruled exclusively by halachic law.

It was thus not by chance that the first counterculture to assert itself successfully was the militant national religious culture of Gush Emunim, which created the territorial infrastructure for a new society of national

25. Luckmann, *Invisible Religion,* p. 3.
26. Ravitzky, *Messianism, Zionism, and Jewish Religious Radicalism;* Friedman, "The State of Israel as a Theological Dilemma."
27. Luz, *Parallels Meet.*
28. Kook, *Lights of Penitence;* Avineri, *Making of Modern Zionism;* and id., "The Zionist and the Jewish Religious Tradition."

religious settlers in "Judea and Samaria" during the 1970s and 1980s. Territorial settlement was not only part of a national political mission of conquest, occupation, and confiscation of "homeland" territories, and the expansion of the boundaries of the Israeli state, but also laid the infrastructure for the establishment of a moral community to be run according to the laws of Halacha and the judgments of rabbis. It seemed that Gush Emunim stood to conquer not only the uplands (both geographically and symbolically) but the hearts of the rest of the Jewish population of the country. Its adherents represented themselves as a replacement for the secular sabra kibbutznik fighter-settlers and, more important, sought to take the latter's place as the Zionist avant-garde in Israel. From "Judea and Samaria," the message was to spread over the entire country.

The national religious revolutionaries, driven by an aspiration for personal fulfillment, *bedarchey noam* ("a pleasant manner"), and burning faith in their path, and seeing themselves as representatives of the collective interest and the "true and pure Jew," aimed to establish a modern national halachic state in place of the polity corrupted in the previous stage of the "return to Zion." The success of this revolution of faith seemed assured, given the absence of any truly attractive competing ideology that could provide an answer to the political and social situation created in the aftermath of the 1967 and 1973 wars. In this regard, the settlements and the settlers in the occupied territories were just the tip of the iceberg. Religious Jews and groups who had not "settled" and were not allied with—or were even opposed to—Gush Emunim united behind what they viewed as the sublime aspiration to transform Israel into as "Jewish" a state as possible. Although Gush Emunim's brand of Jewishness was dominated by religious elements, its pioneering spirit and renewed militaristic, settlement security activism charmed even secular elite groups, especially communists and socialists, among whom great ideological crises had brought about deep internal rifts. In addition, by opening the frontier and acquiring control over all the land that had been the original objective of Zionist colonization, Gush Emunim reawakened dormant aspirations of the immigrant settler political culture that had lost their validity since 1948. Selective feelings for Halacha thus enabled some secular elites to ally themselves with Gush Emunim, whose deeds they also covertly admired.

The appearance of the national religious activism that first challenged the secular socialist political hegemony was preceded by a slow decrease in the power, prestige, and efficiency of state institutions (the military, for example) and, particularly in the aftermath of the 1973 war, a decrease in the centrality of the idea of the state ("statism"). The power of Gush Emunim was embodied in a promise to restore the power of the state, which its adherents sanctified, and to which they assigned themselves as agents, based on their interpretation of its interests. The preliminary success of the religious revolution, however, had two unintentional results, which essentially put an end to the Gush Emunim revolution, or at least moderated it. First, as the initial founders of Gush Emunim matured and became more "established," their revolution was "routinized"; they raised a new, essentially individualist generation that turned its back on the revolution. Second, the Palestinian revolt dispelled any delusions of distinguishing between control of the territories and control of their population. These two results also demonstrated that utopia has its own boundaries and limitations, and that the religious and nationalist fundamentals of Gush Emunim's version of messianism are at least as contradictory as they are complementary.

The Orthodox soon discovered that there is no need to be a Zionist, to don a knitted *kippa,* or to settle in Yesha (although it is permissible)[29] in order to be a Jewish nationalist. It is enough to be attached to various state symbols and actively participate in internal state power games, not only in order to augment one's share in the allotment of collective resources, but also in order to determine the character of the state.

As was evident from the very beginning of the Zionist venture, separation of nation and religion in the sociopolitical and cultural arenas proved difficult. One salient consequence of this overlapping was the subordination of personal status laws and the boundaries and criteria for belonging to the collectivity to the rule of Halacha. Upon its establishment, the state co-opted some rabbis and *dayanim* (rabbinical court judges) as clerks in the statist institution of the Chief Rabbinate. Over time, however, the actual and symbolic institutionalization of religion in the Israeli state changed the status of the Chief Rabbinate. This was not, as political scientists are occasionally accustomed to explain, an accidental phenomenon brought about merely as a result of the dominant party's preference in the 1950s and 1960s for forming coalitions with religious partners, who refrained from intervening in the management of foreign and internal policy, and preferred to safeguard their

29. Yesha is the Hebrew acronym for "Judea, Samaria, and Gaza." It also means "salvation."

sectarian interests, such as religious education, keeping the Sabbath, and Kashrut.

The processes of religionization were mainly the result of interaction between two factors: (1) demographic changes caused by unselective mass immigration that flooded the state with varied populations, mainly but not exclusively from Asia and Africa, who had only partially or not at all undergone secularization, and (2) the essential difficulty in separating religion and nationality in the Zionist version of Jewish nationalism. The secular coating of Zionist nationalism was very thin and fragile from the start. Certainly, the target land of the Zionist colonization and the majority of the slogans and the symbols through which the Jews were mobilized to emigrate to "Zion" were selectively appropriated from within the reservoir of the Jewish religion, and not necessarily from socialist and universal doctrines. Even the Hebrew language, the glorious creation of the renewed secular culture, was borrowed from the realm of religious holiness, with all its inherent layers of meaning.

Orthodox (haredi) religious subcultures had persisted as segregated and insulated societies for a long time,[30] despite post-Holocaust immigration to the state of Israel and demographic increase as whole branches of European Orthodoxy were reestablished in the Holy Land. Their anti-Zionist stance actually strengthened; their historiography designated secular Zionism as fully responsible for the Holocaust; and they thus came to perceive themselves as the only true remnants of the Jewish people. This anti-Zionist brand of Orthodoxy was a binary movement, separately based in the United States and in Israel. In this system, the American center was dominant, having the greatest and most charismatic rabbinical authorities, some of whom even refused to visit Israel.[31] Within Israel, most of the greatest rabbinical authorities were Orthodox, organizing themselves into the "Council of the Great Torah Sages." The Israeli Chief Rabbinate was considered as a subordinate, statist organ, staffed by second-rank rabbis. Even Kashrut certification by the Chief Rabbinate was considered suspicious, and a totally separate supervision mechanism was constructed and put into operation by the Orthodox. In terms of the food industry, a very strong and self-conscious consumer market developed, which has taken on political implications. Orthodoxy

30. Friedman, *Society and Religion.*
31. See Kimmerling, "Between 'Alexandria-on-Hudson' and Zion."

also established a parallel court system as a means of internal social control and maintenance of law and order, as well as to avoid the possibility of its adherents' participation in the secular statist judicial system.

An additional institutional dimension of this Orthodox society is its educational system, with curricula from kindergarten to the High Torah Colleges (Yeshivot and Kollelim) that are completely independent of state intervention. According to Menachem Friedman, Orthodoxy has, in fact, developed into "a society of learners," in which a considerable number of the males are involved in a lifelong learning process, supported materially by aid from abroad, by females working in peripheral markets, and, much later, by state subsidies.[32] The exemption of Yeshiva students from military service both provided a strong incentive for the younger generation to join and remain within the "learning society" and emphasized the boundaries between greater Jewish society and its Orthodox segments. It has also emphasized the strong gender divisions and stratified nature of the Orthodox social system.

From the point of view of the Orthodox, their communities are outsiders to the hegemonic culture, but hegemonic Zionist secular culture did not entirely agree. The self-imposed definition of "outsider" eroded over time: the political and military successes of the "Zionists" (mostly following the 1967 war) did not go unnoticed by Orthodoxy, and some began to wonder whether God had not blessed the Zionists after all.[33] With the 1967 conquest of the core Holy Land, the territory at the center of Jewish religious myths, a fusing process was triggered between the Orthodox and Zionist religious populations. This was reinforced by the increasing participation of Orthodoxy in the Israeli political game via political parties such as the veteran anti-Zionist Agudat Israel. At first, political participation was aimed at safeguarding the particularistic interests of the segregated Orthodox society within the state, but later it also aimed at influencing the wider society.

Two consequent processes occurred. First, religious Zionist Ashkenazi middle-class youth increasingly entered both the rank and file and elite units of the Israeli military, especially after arrangements were made allowing them to spend part of their service learning in Yeshivot.[34] This granted the religious youth considerable prestige in Israeli society, as

32. Friedman, *Orthodox Society*.
33. Friedman, "The State of Israel as a Theological Dilemma."
34. Bar-Lev, "Graduates of the High-School Yeshivoth in Eretz-Israel," pp. 175–87.

well as self-confidence, and pushed them from a peripheral to a central societal position.[35] The second process was the establishment of a religious settler society of the same social background in "Judea and Samaria," which fused the old Zionist hegemonic combination of nationalism and militarism with messianic elements.[36] This settler society differed from its parent model, however, in its emphasis on the halachic element and its attempt to establish a revolutionary holy community based as much as possible on the Orthodox religious codex.

Thus, the settlers of "Judea and Samaria" pushed Rabbi Abraham Isaac Kook's teachings to their logical extreme. The reunion of the "People of Israel" with the whole "Land of Israel" meant the termination of the first part of the redemption process. All that remained was to create a society based on halachic law: "Israel's Torah," in their terminology. Their religious practices drew them closer to Orthodoxy. The legitimacy of the state and sanctity of its organs were called into question, and its universal and modern character, which granted citizenship and democratic rights to Arabs and Jews alike, came to be perceived as non-Jewish. More and more, the values of "Judaism" were perceived as contradicting the values of "democracy." The state's authority was contrasted with halachic authority, and religious injunctions were perceived as unquestionably superior to civil law.[37]

The gentile world, Arab and non-Arab, was perceived as hostile, and its self-evident and permanent goal of annihilating the Jewish people as demonstrated by the Holocaust. Thus, an increasing similarity in ideology and practice between the religious settler society of the West Bank and Jewish Orthodoxy was observed. The settlers' partial adoption of Orthodox lifestyle did not go unnoticed and was welcomed by the latter group. On the other hand, some Orthodox have gone so far as to join the settlement effort, building exclusively Orthodox settlements (such as the cities of Beitar and Emanuel) in the occupied territories. Moreover, the Israeli-Palestinian Oslo Accords, which threatened to lead to a loss of Jewish control over substantial parts of "Eretz Israel," and put a stop to the development of a large territorial Jewish entity ruled according

35. See Kimmerling, "Determination of the Boundaries and the Frameworks of Conscription."
36. Aran, "The Beginning of the Road from Religious Zionism to Zionist Religion"; Lustick, *For the Land and the Lord.*
37. Thus, like Sophocles' Antigone, Yigal Amir, the murderer of Prime Minister Yitzhak Rabin, contrasted the law of the state with the law of the conscience, i.e., halachic law as interpreted by himself and his milieu, and claimed this as justification for what he had done.

halachic precepts, created a new kind of Jewish non-Zionist nationalism. Orthodox rabbis have both individually and jointly issued halachic and non-halachic decisions to the effect that giving up any part of the Holy Land to gentiles is forbidden by religious law. This relatively new involvement in political decisions has been reinforced by charismatic American Jewish religious authorities, notably the highly respected Hassidic Chabad Lubavicher Rabbi Menachem Mendel Schneerson, the seventh and last rabbi of the pedigree, who on his deathbed was declared to be the Messiah (and, by a fringe Chabad group, even God himself).

The impending crisis of "giving up land" and the death of the Chabad leader, who unprecedentedly did not leave behind a "successor," have created an atmosphere of doomsday and redemption. Despite the great variety of Jewish Orthodox religious groups, we are observing a rapid convergence among them, which allows us to refer to them as, on the one hand, a unified and distinct subculture, and, on the other hand, a product of the breakup of secular Zionist hegemony. The moral entrepreneurs of this newly formed counterculture have mainly been political. The innovative side of this culture represented by Rabbi Kook and continued by the original settlers of Gush Emunim has fallen back into the culturally frozen embrace of Orthodoxy.

CONCLUSIONS

The hegemonic secular nationalist Zionist culture was strong and flexible enough to include under its umbrella other varieties of Jewishness, reinterpreted as "Israeliness," as long as no major legitimacy problems arose. The nature of secularism permitted the inclusion within it of different, not necessarily secular, symbols, practices, and population segments as long as they did not implicitly or explicitly question the complete ideological, political, ethnic, and economic supremacy of the veteran ruling classes. "Liberation" of the "whole country" and actual contact with the heartland of secular Zionist mythology, as well as contact with the Arab population, short-circuited the system and caused social chain reactions. For the first time, a sovereign Jewish regime controlled the entire reunified territory of British colonial Palestine. Existential questions of collective identity that had been considered closed following the 1948 war, and the cleansing of most Arabs from Israeli territory, were reopened. The real ideological and social consequences of the new situation were delayed, like a series of aftershocks, although they had been inevitable from the beginning of the Zionist project.

Secular Zionism, whose universalistic and humanistic components were always weak, lacked the ideological tools to meet the challenge, thus paving the way for its religious wing to fill the political and ideological vacuum. Following the partial institutionalization of religion and primordialization of the public sphere, the "center" and participation in the "game" were made accessible to even those religious segments of the polity previously considered outside the boundaries of "accepted" Jewish nationalism. Religion, however, is never isolated from other ideological, social, and socioeconomic factors, such as ethnicity and class. Once the system was opened up, other segments of the Israeli state were able to find paths into the political game and contribute to the pluralization of the polity.

CHAPTER 5

The Newcomers

The partial success of Gush Emunim in redefining Zionism in more explicitly religious and ethnocentric terms, and its even more successful reshaping of the national agenda and allocation of material and human resources, shattered both the hegemony of secular Zionism and Ashkenazi ethnic dominance. New cultural, ethnic, and national groups, previously completely excluded from the boundaries of the collectivity or located on its margins, began to play increasingly central roles in the state at the expense of veteran cultural and political groups. The most important and influential newly empowered political-cultural movement was Mizrahi traditionalist revivalism.

THE TRADITIONALIST COUNTERCULTURE

Traditionalism can be regarded in two different ways. One is in terms of the degree of the distance from religious beliefs and obedience to the fulfillment of religious commandments—in other words, the degree to which behavior has been secularized. Religiosity is judged by the terms set by the most rigorous practice of a particular religion's precepts. In this case, the traditionalist regards himself or herself as a "partial" or even "deviant" person when compared to the "true believers" in his or her reference group. Guilt feelings or shame do not necessarily accompany these perceptions, because most societal spaces in life in Western society are morally stratified and encourage compromise. The second, and not necessarily contradictory, manifestation of traditionalism is as a separate belief system, which includes elements of formal religion alongside popular and folkloristic beliefs and practices. Such elements of popular religion, which are considered "proper" simply because they are rooted in a newly invented past, include cults of saints and holy persons, holy sites, superstitions, conservative mores, wearing of "modest" clothing, voting for "traditional parties," and so on. Generally, this imaginary or constructed past is considered "glorious" and better than the present. The desired future must always be shaped according to the ideals of the past. Traditionalism selectively adopts aspects of modern culture, its values, mores, and especially its technical and scientific commodities and comforts.

The initial assumption of the Enlightenment and modern social sciences is that humankind is constantly "progressing" from an era of "darkness," irrationality, and "primitive" religion toward a more modern, rational, and secular era. Here "modern" and "rational" are equated with "secular." This assumption has proved itself wrong. Various forms of religion have flourished together with "modernism" and have proved themselves part and parcel of the secular world.

The boundaries of Israeli Jewish traditionalism are highly fragmented and blurred and are based in ethnicity and, partially, in class. Self-defined traditionalism is anchored in the first, second, and third generations of immigrants from the developing societies of the Middle East and North Africa, the so-called Mizrahi, or oriental Jews.[1] Upon their arrival, the dominant Zionists promoted a long period of absorption and "modernization" as part of their "melting pot" ideology. These efforts met with only partial success, and most of the immigrants ended up in the lower strata of the class system. Nevertheless, many of these immigrants, especially from the second and third generations, have almost completely acculturated and have adopted the Ashkenazi perceptions of self and collective identity. Education, socialization, military service, and social, spatial, and economic mobility, accompanied by high rates of intermarriage, have also incorporated many Mizrahi immigrants into the Israeli social system and middle class.[2] The Mizrahi population

1. See Smooha, *Israel: Pluralism and Conflict;* Swirski, *Israel: The Oriental Majority.*
2. There are considerable differences among the Mizrahi Jews themselves in their reactions to the Israeli melting-pot policies. While the majority of those of Middle Eastern origin, especially those from Iraq, have demonstrated high mobility and "adaptation" capabilities, the North African immigrants have found themselves in a more marginal social position.

has developed its own version of Israeli culture, mixing the cultures of
its countries of origin with local varieties to create Mizrahi music, food,
local and national festivities, and saints (some of them reinvented and
replaced from their countries of origin,[3] and even a version of the Hebrew language spoken with certain types of accents. A vast industry
generating a parallel culture of music and songs, movies, and garments
has been established, which the mainly Ashkenazi elite regard as, at best,
"folklore," and, at worst, "low" or even "deviant" culture.[4] The turn
of some Mizrahi religious elite groups toward Ashkenazi Orthodoxy
was yet another path of paternalistic reculturation that ended up contributing to the building of a competing counterculture vis-à-vis the secular and religious Israeli Ashkenazi Jews, and was preserved within families and passed on and developed from generation to generation.
Generations of highly talented Mizrahi youngsters were accepted and
welcomed into the Orthodox "learning society" and aimed at complete
assimilation. But their acceptance was never total, and they remained
peripheral within the internal hierarchy of this culture. Their access to
prestigious positions and marriage into elite Ashkenazi families was
forestalled.

As a consequence, the Mizrahi students split from Ashkenazi Orthodoxy and formed their own version of Orthodoxy, around the charismatic figure of the so-called Sephardic Chief Rabbi Ovadia Yossef. The
Shas ("Sephardim Obey the Torah") party was created in 1984, and has
since struggled to liberate itself from the ambiguous patronage of the
(97-year-old) Ashkenazi Rabbi Shach and his successor, Shlomo Yosef
Eliashiv, who are considered by many in this culture to be the greatest
Orthodox rabbinical authorities in Israel.[5] Rabbi Shach has been accused by Shas of condoning innuendoes and incriminations about the
halachic and political competence of Shas's and Israel's Mizrahi religious
leadership.

Shas's forceful appearance on the Israeli scene was facilitated by its
leaders' considerable political and electoral potential and skill in converting access to material resources into successful institutions, including

3. Ben-Ari and Bilu, "Saints' Sanctuaries in Israeli Development Towns."
4. For many years, this music was not broadcast on radio stations or was relegated to
particular venues and sites of oriental music as "wedding music" or "bus station cassette
music." Slowly and selectively, however, it was included in "high culture," and some
oriental musicians and bands have achieved considerable respectability in the Israeli cultural field.
5. See Willis, "Sepharadic Torah Guardian"; id. "Shas."

an efficient political party, a separate school system, from kindergartens to teachers' seminaries, and separate neighborhoods for their constituents. Shas combines an ethnically based Orthodox elite with a large and inclusive periphery of people who obey religious precepts with great variation and flexibility. The Shas periphery (not all of them necessarily vote for Shas, but they nevertheless consider Rabbi Yossef a spiritual leader) mainly tend to define themselves as "traditional" (and not "religious"). This definition is central to their collective and self-identification. The social boundaries of this counterculture, like those of the secular culture, are not sharply defined, and there is no one way to "practice" traditionalism. Less than strict obedience is not considered a sin, and individuals and families have a large degree of freedom to interpret the binding "practices" mixed in with popular and traditional customs. The rise of the Shas counterculture liberated many second- and third-generation Mizrahi both from their political and cultural subordination to Ashkenazi non-Zionist Orthodoxy and from Zionist hegemonic culture, thus contributing to the breakup of that hegemony. The movement of Shas, the Mizrahi traditionalists, and the growing group of "born-again" Jews (baalei tshuva) toward the center of the Israeli sociopolitical map should perhaps be considered an even bigger social challenge than the "Emuni revolution," for three main reasons: (a) Shas's enormous demographic and constitutional potential, touching the material, class, and religious frustrations and collective memory of about half the Jewish population of Israel;[6] (b) its image of real concern for its adherents' social and material conditions; and (c) the fact that it tends to blur conventional boundaries between secularism and religiosity, although its leadership is committed to Orthodox religious practices and excellence in lifelong religious studies and scholastics.[7]

ARAB CITIZENS IN ISRAEL

Arab citizens of Israel were for a long time completely excluded from the hegemonic Zionist culture, just as they were confined to a separate bubble culturally, politically, and economically. The 150,000 or so Arabs remaining within Israel after the collapse of Palestinian Arab society

6. This was demonstrated in the 1999 elections, when Shas jumped from ten to seventeen seats in parliament, becoming the third-largest political party in Israel.
7. Except when some of their young and bright students are sent to permanent or temporary activities in political spheres, as emissaries of the movement.

during the 1948 war were a partial and fragmented society, lacking almost any elite groups, a middle class, or political and spiritual leadership.[8] They found themselves abruptly transformed from a powerful and self-confident national majority into a small, helpless minority in what was defined as a "Jewish nation-state."[9] The only social institution remaining after the 1948 catastrophe (*al-nakba*) was the nuclear and extended family, which was utilized as a means of control and surveillance by the state and its military government, imposed on the Israeli Arabs until 1968. To this, a state-controlled elementary and high-school system was added. Israel's school curriculum for its Arab citizens was designed to create a new ethnic identity, that of the "de-Palestinized" Israeli Arab. The history of Israeli Arabs was presented as consonant with the history of the state of Israel. They were taught the Koran (and the New Testament for Christian Arabs) as well as the Hebrew Bible and Hebrew literature.[10] Israeli Arabs became a bilingual and bicultural people, educated to obey "Israeli democracy," but, at the same time, they were systematically deprived of their land and access to welfare, jobs, housing, and other subsidized social goods. They were both excluded (except for small groups of Druse, Circassians, and Bedouin volunteers) from compulsory military service and denied full citizenship rights on the grounds that they had not fully fulfilled their citizenship obligations.[11]

For decades, any national or ethnically based Arab political organization or protest movement was choked off. Only the Israeli Communist party channeled Israeli Arab protests and fought for their rights within

---

8. See Kimmerling and Migdal, *Palestinians*.

9. On the situation of the Arabs in Israel, see Jiryis, *Arabs in Israel*; Kretzmer, *Legal Status of the Arabs in Israel*; Lustick, *Arabs in a Jewish State*; Grossman, *Present Absentees*; Benziman and Mansour, *Subtenants*; Peled, "Ethnic Democracy"; Smooha, "Minority Status in an Ethnic Democracy"; Rabinowitz, *Overlooking Nazareth*.

10. Mar'i, *Arab Education in Israel*; Al-Haj, *Education, Empowerment, and Control*.

11. Horowitz and Kimmerling, "Some Social Implications of Military Service and Reserves System in Israel." This ambivalent position has been expressed by several Arab writers, such as in the late Emil Habiby's *The Miraculous Story of the Disappearance of Said Abi Nakhs al-Mutashil* (1974), translated to Hebrew by Anton Shammas with the title *The Optimist,* and by Shammas himself in *Arabesques.* Shammas, an ex-Israeli poet, writer, and journalist, provoked embittered debate and indignation when he published "A New Year for the Jews," an article in which he accused Israel of excluding the Israeli Palestinians from participation in the common political cultural and collective identity. The prominent Hebrew writer A. B. Yehoshua was among the many respondents: "I am suggesting to Shammas that if you want to exercise your full identity, if you want to live in a state that has a Palestinian character with a genuine Palestinian culture, arise, take your possessions, and move yourself one hundred yards eastward, into the Palestinian state that will be established alongside Israel" (quoted in London, "Quilt of the Left"). See also Shammas, "Kitsch-22."

the Jewish state.[12] The Communist party also served as an intellectual hothouse for a new Arab cultural elite, who created an original local counterculture, almost completely isolated from cultural developments in other Arab countries. The party's newspapers, periodicals, and Arabic publishing house hosted and participated in the creation of opportunities for Israeli Arab poets, writers, thinkers, and journalists.[13] Later, especially after the inclusion of the Palestinians of the West Bank and Gaza Strip under a unified Israeli control system,[14] this cultural capital became part of the general cultural and political heritage of the Palestinian people.

Over time, the Arabs of Israel have accumulated not only cultural capital, but also considerable material wealth and political power. From about 7 percent of the total population in 1949, they have grown to approximately 20 percent of the population and 17 percent of the electorate in 1999. A Follow-Up Committee based on a joint committee of Arab municipality heads and mayors serves as the semi-official leadership of the Israeli Palestinian community and includes many of its prominent public figures and intellectuals. Following the 1992 general election, Israeli Arab parties came to be seen as part of the left-wing "bloc" that elected Rabin's Labor party and prevented the right wing from forming a unity government. In 1992, the late Emil Habibi, an Arab, won the prestigious Israel Prize for literature, and in 1996, the soccer team of the small Arab city of Taybeh won the second league cup and passed to the top national league.

In the wake of the Oslo Accords and the "peace process," which together are likely to lead to the establishment of a Palestinian state in the West Bank and Gaza, a rapprochement between Jews and Palestinians was perceived as possible from the perspective of both people. For the Israeli Arabs, who since 1967 have come to feel part of the Palestinian people, but at the same time are active participants in the Israeli state, involvement in Israeli politics, society, and culture on the basis of equal citizenship rights now seems desirable.[15] From the Jewish side,

---

12. Reches, *The Arab Israeli Minority between Communism and Nationalism, 1965–*

13. An example is the poetry of Mahmud Darwish, an Israeli Arab in exile, who is considered the "national poet" of the Palestinians and was the author of 1988 Declaration of Independence. Darwish, like Habibi, published most of his literary works in *Al-Jadida* and *Al-Itihad*, the periodicals of the Israeli Communist party.

14. See Kimmerling "Boundaries and Frontiers of the Israeli Control System."

15. Recently, a group of Palestinian intellectuals has voiced a demand for "cultural autonomy" within the framework of the Israeli state. This demand seems to raise a di-

participation of Arabs as active actors in Israeli politics has interested many segments of the secular, and especially left and libertarian, wings of Jewish society. The social construction of Arab citizens as a Trojan horse and self-evident "enemy" is now being strongly challenged. This is a part and additional cause of the decomposition of Zionist hegemony. The possibility of political alliances among central segments of the Jewish and Arab societies within Israel should lead to new social and cultural coalitions previously unthinkable and only recently possible owing to cracks produced in the hegemonic culture.

RUSSIAN-SPEAKING IMMIGRANTS

Nothing more clearly underscores the fact that Israel remains an active immigrant settler society than the waves of immigration first from the USSR and later from the Commonwealth of Independent States (CIS). The first wave arrived mainly in the 1970s, and the second in the beginning of the 1990s. This immigration, which now constitutes 17 percent of Israeli citizens, is also a dramatic example of the degree to which processes and changes in the world order can cause changes in the internal structure of a society and how difficult it is to plan and predict complex societal processes. In the first wave of immigration, approximately 200,000 immigrants arrived in Israel. In the second wave (between 1989 and 1998), about 720,000 Jews from the CIS came to Israel, while some 366,000 went to other countries. This immigration almost completely liquidated a large Jewish population. Together, the two waves constitute the largest ethnic group to have immigrated to the Israeli state.

This group, however, also appears to be the most heterogeneous ethnic unit in Israel from many perspectives; it might be appropriate to relate to it mainly as a cultural-linguistic group, rather than a group of differentiated "ethnic origin." Included under the Russian "linguistic umbrella" are immigrants from Asia (Uzbekistan and various states in

---

lemma for the Arabs of Israel, as it appears to contradict the claim for completely equal citizens' rights and full participation in terms of access to the public domain. It is not clear what the consequences of this demand for "cultural autonomy" are, besides the right to establish separate Arab universities and the ability to determine the curricula for all the Arab schools in Israel, as is currently the case for the separate Orthodox Jewish school system (see Bishara, "On the Palestinian Minority in Israel"). The claim to cultural autonomy raised fierce resistance in most parts of the Jewish political system, owing to the fear that this separatism will easily turn into territorial nationalism.

the Caucasus) and from Europe (the Ukraine, Belarus, and the Baltic states). These variations cover a large range of cultural, class, educational, and professional strata, in terms both of their place of origin and their status within the new society. There were also differences between the immigrants of the 1970s and those of the 1990s. Not only were the latter's main reasons for emigrating different, but they had lived through the early stages of an open, individualistic capitalist society, however unstable, and their perspective as a generation differed.[16] Moreover, there was a vast difference between the "absorbing" Israeli society of the 1960s and 1970s and that of the 1990s.

In spite of all the differences between them, these numerous immigrants perceived themselves as belonging to one distinguishable category—the "Russians." Israeli society also classified and perceived them mainly in terms of this "Russianness." As such, they shaped themselves into a subsociety, contributing to the centrifugal trend of adding elements and "islands" to Israeli civil society and giving the Israeli state a more culturally pluralistic character.

There was also a very meaningful economic aspect to the addition of this large number of Russian speakers and to the creation of a critical mass of consumers of Russian culture. A large market for cultural products and language and special food items was created, making these products "economically viable." Various initiatives, such as Russian schools and newspapers, were encouraged, and the ability to establish an autarky in many realms of Israeli society created ethnic and cultural boundaries around the "Russian" identity. The opening of global boundaries, including the cultural and physical boundaries of the CIS, the creation of Russian (and not just Russian Jewish) communities in North America and western Europe, and mobility and the reciprocal ability to travel between these communities,[17] added a new and very wide circle to international "Russianism." This spread of Russianism demonstrates the uniqueness of "Russian" ethnicity and also contributed to the crystallization of a separate "Russian" identity in Israel.

In addition, the "Russian" immigrants of the 1990s, particularly those that arrived at a relatively young age (up to 40–45), demonstrated a very substantial personal and collective ability to adapt as compared

---

16. See Gurr, "Between Immigration and Remaining"; Weisel, Leshem, and Adler, "Emigration Trends from Russia and Ukraine"; and Margolis and Singer, *What You See from There You Can't See from Here.*
    17. Including the existence of global Russian satellite and cable television broadcasts.

to ethnic groups and the Russian immigrant wave of the 1970s that preceded them to Israel. This adaptation was salient mainly in the areas of acquisition of employment (not always in their original fields and utilizing their true talents) and the purchase of apartments and household products according to the accepted standards of the Israeli middle class. A poll taken in April–May 1996 found that close to 95 percent of the immigrants were included in the labor force as employees, among them 75 percent full-time and 76 percent in steady work. Only 37 percent of these, however, were employed in the field in which they had worked in their country of origin. Another area of instrumental adaptation was quick acquisition of the Hebrew language for the purposes of both "dealing with Israeli bureaucracy" and effective competition in the labor market.[18] As mentioned, Hebrew language acquisition, particularly for immigrants of the large 1990s wave, was not necessarily accompanied by the adoption of the entire "package deal" of Hebrew and Israeli culture. It certainly was not accompanied by emotional internalization and identification with Israeli culture, but rather by rejection of that culture. Forty-five percent of Russian adults who had arrived in Israel since 1989 reported in 1995 that they spoke at least "pretty good" Hebrew. As with all the indexes of instrumental adaptability (such as permanent housing), these figures also displayed a high correlation with the amount of time in Israel. Eleven percent reported being "very content" with life in Israel, and 52 percent reported being "quite content" with life in Israel, but only 40 percent would recommend to others that they come to Israel.[19]

Along with the country's Arab citizens, the "Russians" have pioneered the "New Israeli." This new character is no longer a product of the "melting pot" that was supposed to create a uniform type, as described in chapter 3. Rather, this new image has been built on the model of ethnic-cultural pluralism, on the one hand, and individualism and personal and familial achievement,[20] on the other. Apparently, the ability for instrumental adaptation is paradoxically what contributed to the cultural and emotional inclination toward separateness of "Russians" in Israel.

In practice, the first wave of Russian-speaking immigrants began arriving sporadically in 1966 and gained the momentum of a mass im-

18. Zemach, Leshem, and Weinger, "Survey on Adaptation of Immigrants from CIS."
19. Zemach and Weisel, "Adaptation of Immigrants from CIS (1990–1995) in Israel."
20. Moore and Kimmerling, "Individual Strategies for Adopting Collective Identities."

migration beginning in 1971. Most of the immigrants came from peripheral areas partially annexed by the USSR prior to World War II,
such as the Baltic states and Moldavia, and from western Ukraine and
Georgia. Assimilation was relatively low in these areas, both because of
their remoteness from Moscow and because only a generation had gone
by since the coming of Soviet rule.[21] Immigrants' motives were thus
mostly religious or nationalist. Beginning in 1977, however, Jews from
centers such as Moscow, St. Petersburg, and Kiev also started to leave,
as did Germans, Armenians, and Greeks.

Of the 215,000 Jews who left the USSR between 1978 and 1989,
only 57,000 came to Israel. The majority, labeled "dropouts" in Zionist
terminology, went to the United States, Canada, Australia, and a small
number to Austria and Germany. The liberal immigration policies in
force during this period in the United States and Canada allowed for
these immigration patterns. These countries defined emigration from
Soviet lands from an ideological perspective and saw all those leaving
the USSR as political refugees entitled to asylum; thus they accepted even
immigrants who were not necessarily ideologically motivated.

The choice once again of North America as the main target for Jewish
immigration caused a great deal of tension between Israel and the United
States. Although North American Jews did not wish to deny Jews admission to the United States, Zionist lobbies worked to funnel the bulk
of Jewish immigration to Israel. In the end, the pressure bore fruit, and
on November 21, 1989, President George Bush signed what was called
the "Lautenberg Amendment," which greatly reduced the chances of
applicants not only from Russia but also from Vietnam receiving immigration visas to the United States.[22] The subsequent Russian-speaking
immigration to Israel thus became a "captive immigration," because
immigrants had no practical alternative, which apparently influenced
their attitudes and feelings (for better and for worse) toward the "absorbing society," their patterns of behavior within it, and their corresponding rage against the Americans.

Israel desired the immigration from Russia very much, not only for
ideological and sentimental reasons, but for instrumental reasons connected to the basic codes of its political culture, such as "demographic
balance" vis-à-vis the Arabs, "security," and "settlement" (mainly in
the occupied territories). The slogan invented in order to persuade

21. See Brym and Ryvkina, *Jews of Moscow, Kiev and Minsk.*
22. Beyer, "The Evolving United States Response to Soviet-Jewish Emigration."

veterans Israelis to receive the immigrants and this immigration with understanding, and perhaps even to make sacrifices for the sake of its absorption, was "From immigrant to immigrant, our strength is rising." Nonetheless, at the time, Israel was not prepared economically and socially to accommodate such large-scale immigration. One must remember that the standard of living in Israel was then far higher than it had been the 1950s and 1960s.[23] At the same time, the immigrants' expectations—ideological and instrumental—were high from the start, mainly given the human capital and the skills they possessed. So absorption under 1950s conditions was not acceptable to the immigrants or to society. The last thing that the Israeli state wanted was yet another potential focus for social unrest and protest, in addition to those of the oriental Jews and the Arabs.

The first wave of Russian-speaking immigrants was significant in its composition mainly on account of its ideological motives (which, as mentioned, characterized the majority), its selectivity, and a charismatic and amply crystallized leadership. Nevertheless, this wave alone did not possess sufficient critical mass or the segregationist ideology required to produce a "Russian" enclave within Israeli society. It was characterized by far more readiness to integrate into Israeli society than the wave that followed.[24] In the end, the two waves complemented each other. People of the first wave, primarily its elite, established the institutional and cultural infrastructure into which the people of the second wave were absorbed, indirectly enabling the creation of the "Russian" cultural and political enclave in Israel. Without the second wave, it is doubtful whether a sociocultural, ethnic, and, to a degree, also class-based enclave with such sharp boundaries would have been created, considerably contributing to changing the face of Israeli society. Thus the second wave especially contributed to an additional decline in the state's cultural homogeneity.

The two most important institutions created by immigrant activists and "Prisoners of Zion"[25] from the leadership elite of the first wave were the Russian-language press and the Zionist Forum. The latter was created in 1988 by Anatoly Sharansky and Edward Kuznetzov in order to

23. R. Cohen, "Israel's Problematic Absorption of Soviet Jews."
24. See Lissak, "Absorption Policy toward the Immigrants from the Soviet Union"; id., *Immigrants from the Commonwealth of Independent States between Segregation and Integration.*
25. "Prisoners of Zion" was the term used for men and women who suffered discrimination, imprisonment, or deportation because of their Zionist activities.

represent the interests of the immigrants, and as a mutual aid and support organization, and was substantially supported by the Jewish Agency. The Forum quickly became an umbrella organization, incorporating many national and local Russian associations, such as cultural centers and, particularly in Jerusalem, Russian lending libraries. By the time the second wave gained momentum in the mid 1990s, there were about forty different organizations aggregated in the Forum, numbering more than 50,000 members. The Forum also proved to be an efficient organization for mobilizing political activity, and essentially served as the infrastructure for the organization of the Israel B'Aliyah party in 1996.

By the time the second and third waves (a total of 750,000 people) arrived, the social system had already begun to absorb the changes that the flooding waves of immigration in the 1950s had brought about. The arrival of a large number of immigrants within a relatively short amount of time strengthened anxieties about the changing face of society, its identity, and the rules of the game. The bulk of the immigrants came from Russia proper (about 201,000), the Ukraine (about 200,000), and central Asia, Georgia, Armenia, and Azerbaijan (about 140,000), while about 115,000 immigrants arrived from the Baltic states, Moldavia, and Belarus. Despite the small number of children in this immigration (the rate of population growth among the Jews of the CIS is negative), the immigration was relatively young.[26]

The new large-scale immigration was immediately perceived as directly threatening a relatively large number of sectors within the veteran population. The oriental Jews, who had just begun to experience accelerated social mobility, and for the first time had even achieved a demographic majority over the Ashkenazim, felt threatened by the immigrants, most of whom were Ashkenazi and had higher educational credentials and occupational skills. About 58 percent of the immigrants of working age were classified as having academic professions (in comparison to 25 percent of the veteran Israeli population). Moreover, they feared that national resources that had in part begun to flow to the improvement of the situation and to affirmative action on behalf of the oriental Jews[27] would now be directed to immigrant

26. Although 13 percent of the immigrants were above the age of sixty-five, 35 percent were under twenty-four, 66 percent were younger than forty-four, and 75 percent were fifty-five or younger.

27. Such as neighborhood rehabilitation and building industrial factories in peripheral areas. See Hasson, *Urban Social Movements*.

absorption.[28] Arab citizens of Israel, who were also experiencing increased mobility and the creation of a new white-collar middle class,
also feared competition in the job market and threats to their political-
electoral power.[29] Because most of the immigrants were secular (and
often accompanied by halachically non-Jewish spouses), the immigration also threatened the political power of the religious parties and the
Jewish character of the state. Further complicating the situation, the
immigrants tended to have right-wing or "nationalist" opinions and
were thus seen as a political threat by many members of the Ashkenazi elite and the secular Ashkenazi middle class, who tend more toward the left as defined by Israeli political culture.[30] Most of these ap-
prehensions already existed prior to the second and third waves, but
with the appearance of the second wave of immigration, these anxieties increased, with each population sector fearing both short- and
long-term changes that would damage them and change the existing
rules of the game. These anxieties were fertile ground for attaching
negative stereotypes to the immigrants as individuals and as a collectivity. These stereotypes strengthened the immigrants' feelings of anger, foreignness, and alienation from the absorbing society and its culture, on the one hand, and internal "Russian" cohesiveness, on the
other.[31]

The ideological changes that had taken place in Israeli society also
changed the patterns of the relations between the state and the immigrants. As part of the customary patronage approach to implementation
of the "melting pot" ideology, immigrants of the first wave were still
subject to the close oversight, examination, and direction of state institutions. The second wave arrived in a society that more greatly emphasized individualist values (especially in 1992–96, during a period of left-
wing government), and championed less intervention of the authorities
in individual and family affairs (but also in their welfare). This ideological change translated to the "direct absorption" policy, in the framework of which the immigrants did not receive direct "absorption" services. Instead, the immigrant and his family received an amount of money
from the state that was equivalent more or less to the original "absorp-

28. Leshem, "The Israeli Population and Its Attitude to the Immigrants of the 1990s";
id., "Jewishness, Lifestyle and Opinions toward State and Religion among the Immigrants
from the Former Soviet Union."
   29. Al-Haj, "Soviet Immigration as Viewed by Jews and Arabs."
   30. See Horowitz, Between Three Political Cultures.
   31. Horowitz and Frenkel, "Immigrants in an Absorption Center."

tion basket" (including mortgages and loans). With this financing, the immigrants turned to the markets to acquire goods and services, including housing, according to their preferences. So, for example, they could choose between buying a private apartment or renting an apartment at a cost and a level that seemed appropriate to them. In the first stage, in the beginning of the 1990s, this policy seemed a failure, mainly given the large numbers of immigrants who overwhelmed the market with demands for apartments (which raised the costs of apartments in the entire market). In the longer term, however, it bore fruit.[32] Thus, about 86 percent of the immigrants who arrived in the early 1990s had obtained mortgages by 1996, and only 14 percent required public housing. Academic institutions, research institutions, and colleges that agreed to consider employing immigrant scientists were also subsidized.

In addition, this immigration highlighted the particularly problematic gap between the definition of "Jewish" according to the "Law of Return"[33] and the definition of "Jewish" according to the criteria of Halacha obligated by the laws of personal status that the state had adopted. While the "Law of Return" was interpreted broadly and charitably in the area of eligibility to immigrate to Israel, other issues of personal status, registration in the population registry, and identity cards were dealt with according to the strict and narrow criteria of the Halacha (see chapter 4). This interpretation considers as Jews only "those who were born to a Jewish mother or were converted according to Halacha" in the Orthodox version dominant in Israel. In this way, about a quarter of the immigrants—who had been unable to emigrate to Western countries as they had originally desired because they had been labeled as Jews in the Russian state and by North American immigration authorities— paradoxically found themselves considered "non-Jews" in the Jewish religious-national state. The definition of their independent collective identity was also shaped accordingly. When asked in polls to choose between "Israeli," "Jewish," or "Russian" identity, a large majority choose a fusion of Jewish and Russian, or "Russian-Jewish," while "Israeliness" is largely insignificant in their eyes. The difficulties experienced by many Russian-speaking immigrants with respect to marriages and burials according to Israeli law and custom are likely to contribute

---

32. Hacohen, *The "Direct Absorption" System and Its Implications.*

33. The Law of Return was the legal basis for issuing the immigration visas, immigrant status, and all the material benefits and the attendant civil rights that were bestowed upon these immigrants.

to the high rate of endogamy that helps perpetuate the "Russian bubble." The creation of separate educational institutions is another factor. Like other sectors of Israeli society, Russian-speaking immigrants tend to demand and enjoy cultural autonomy in the shape of segregated schools and colleges.

As mentioned, immigrants who arrived in Israel only a few years apart (for example, in 1989 as compared with 1993), seemingly from the same place, essentially left the same place only geographically. At the beginning of the 1990s, the socioeconomic and political structure in the large cities in Russia changed rapidly and almost completely. Young people in particular succeeded in acquiring skills that were not available to previous generations, undergoing formative experiences that were different, not only from those of their parents' generation, but even from those of their own age group who had emigrated three to four years previously from the Soviet state.[34] The skills were mainly "business" skills and also caused them to adopt a different system of values than those that constituted the cultural cargo and worldview of the immigrants of the end of the 1980s. Julia Mirski notes that "adolescent immigrants from the USSR were compelled to deal with sociocultural changes prior to immigration."[35] These changes, which occurred in the USSR at the end of the 1980s and the beginning of the 1990s, dramatically altered the political, social, and cultural structure of the republics of the disintegrating USSR, first and foremost in the reduction of the extent of their centralization. During the same period, a unique mix of post-Soviet culture was created, which included the underground rock music culture that flourished in Moscow, Leningrad, Sverdlovsk, and other cities. This culture, in the full meaning of the word, offered an aesthetic and moral alternative to the collapsing system of socialist realism and the American consumer culture that invaded the streets and squares of cities from the capital to the peripheries. "These changes give the individuation processes of adolescents in this society and the processes they undergo in immigration a unique hue," Mirski observes.[36] The youth who came of age during the social transformations and eagerly adopted their messages discovered for themselves that the gaps between them and their parents' generation were very large and barely

---

34. Mirski and Brawer, *To Make Aliyah as an Adolescent, to Become Adult as an Oleh.*
35. Mirski, "Psychological Adaptation of Students from the Former Soviet Union."
36. Ibid., p. 3.

bridgeable. Generally, the parents made few concessions to their children, but rather demanded that they act according to the formerly acceptable norms of their own generation.

The most conspicuous phenomenon of the Russian-speaking immigrants in Israel is the creation of a varied print media differentiated both from the Russian media in Russia and from the Hebrew press in Israel. The "Russians"—especially the intelligentsia that arrived from the Slavic and Baltic metropolitan areas—brought with them a developed reading culture. Something akin to a secular "holiness," similar to the reading of texts in traditional societies, is attributed to writing and reading in this culture. As a result, a great demand was created for various types of print media. In the beginning of the 1990s, the weekly circulation of all Russian periodicals consumed in Israel was estimated to have reached more than a million copies. These then included four national newspapers, nine local papers, twelve weekly journals that dealt with current events through translation and summary from other languages (mainly Hebrew, English, and French), five periodicals dedicated to culture and literature, and a weekly journal for children. Russian-language reporters, commentators, and journalists (especially in *Vesti*) receive noticeable attention and prestige in the Russian-speaking community of Israel, but the bulk of attention from a cultural perspective is directed not only inward but also toward events in Russia itself.

The Russian press, especially the widely distributed *Vesti,* to a great extent constructs the images of society and the Israeli state among Russian-speaking immigrants.[37] A conspicuously large number, even after having learned to read and speak Hebrew, prefer to receive information and commentary on world and national events through the interpretive prism of "their" newspapers, reporters, and intelligentsia. The press is certainly instrumental in critically decoding Israeli reality. The periodicals constitute a conduit for the transmission of information and advice from "veterans" (mainly people of the first wave) to "newcomers" on how to behave in the situations fraught with uncertainty that the new immigrant invariably encounters. In a poll of exposure to the media, it was found that 8 percent of the population of the second wave read the daily papers in Hebrew and 12 percent of them read weekend newspapers in Hebrew. In comparison, of those who immigrated in 1989–90, 11 percent were readers of daily newspapers and 17 percent of weekend papers. These percentages rise in direct relation to length of time in

---

37. Wertburg, "Russian-Language Press in Israel."

Israel.[38] The Russian press conducts something like a one-sided "dialogue" with the society and what it sees as the dominant culture in Israel. It brings translations and reactions to what is heard and printed in the mass and electronic media in Israel and engages in vigorous argument with it. Very much like the Orthodox, the national religious, and the Arab press in Israel, the Russian press has created something like a counterpress, constructing "Israeli reality" differently from the established Israeli press. The Hebrew media, however, have completely ignored and failed to respond to the "Russian discourse," and have thereby contributed unknowingly to its countercultural self-image.

The most noticeable expression of the segregated integration of the Russian immigrants is their success in converting their numbers and their organizational dexterity into political power through the establishment of an ethnic party within the first generation of the immigration. Already in the 1992 elections, there were attempts among the immigrants to come together as political group and to take advantage of the potential of approximately 250,000 voters. This potential was indeed exploited, although indirectly, and caused the change of governments in Israel. As mentioned, the Russian-speaking immigrants basically hold right-wing (or more accurately anti-left), "patriotic" positions and clear anti-Arab feelings. Nonetheless, the pragmatic approach that typifies them brought them to tilt their votes toward the Labor party, first and foremost given the American threat clearly perceived among the immigrants. The U.S. administration threatened that it would refrain from bestowing long-range loan guarantees (totaling $10 billion) for the purpose of the absorption of the immigration if the Israeli state directed resources and immigrants to the colonization of the occupied territories. The implicit rhetoric of the Labor party that the "Russians" would have to choose between allotting resources for the needs of the immigrants and financing the settlement of the occupied territories skewed the election results. The elections were decided by a relatively few votes to the advantage of what was called the "left bloc."

As already mentioned, the Israeli state (and mainly its national religious and nationalist elements) saw in the Russian immigrants considerable potential for bolstering the colonization of the occupied territories. Most of the immigrants, however, chose to settle in the three largest cities and their surrounding metropolitan areas and in a number of smaller cities within the boundaries of the Green Line, in which they

38. Fein, *Immigrants of the CIS.*

could create significant communities for themselves.[39] The "direct absorption track," which gave a great degree of freedom to the immigrants
in their choice of where to live, contributed to this trend.

By the 1996 elections, the situation had changed, as had the electoral
system.[40] This time the protest was directed at the left-wing government.
The immigrants already had a strong, organized institutional infrastructure, and the electoral system, under which votes were cast separately
for a party and for the prime minister, encouraged centrifugal processes
among other sectors in Israeli society as well. The accepted wisdom that
the fall of the Likud government in 1992 was caused mainly by the
immigrants added to their self-confidence and self-image. In this election
campaign, it was the right-wing opposition that succeeded in dictating
the public agenda. Based on this infrastructure, and in these conditions,
under the leadership of well-known personalities that were supported
by the Russian intelligentsia and press, Israel B'Aliyah was able to organize and expand rapidly to win 40 percent of the votes of the 400,000
eligible voters among these immigrants. This party won seven seats in
the parliament (while about 70 percent of their votes for prime minister
were given to the Likud candidate Benjamin Netanyahu, and were thus
largely responsible for his election), and joined the nationalist/national
religious/Orthodox coalition as an important partner. The great success
of the Russian-speaking immigrant party constitutes one of the indica-
tors of the deep changes happening inside the Israeli society and state.
"Russian" ethnicity, together with the other types of ethnicity and cultures, received legitimacy and institutionalization, very similarly to the
way, pinpointed by D. D. Laitin, that the "Russian-speaking (*russkoia-
zychini*) identity" of populations remained outside of the Russian state
after the disintegration of the Soviet Union.[41]

Paradoxically, the double message of the Israel B'Aliyah party—that
is, maximal integration into the political system, while using its rules of
the game in order to obtain maximal material means to preserve the
cultural-ethnic barriers—symbolizes more than any other phenomenon
the new polycultural, multivocal, multiracial Israeliness. In such a system, not all groups enjoy equal weight and power. Nonetheless,
the system precludes the possibility of a high degree of cultural and political hegemony, such as was established during the first two decades of

39. Such as Ashdod, Upper [Jewish] Nazareth, Kiryat Yam, and Carmiel.
40. See Kimmerling, "Elections as a Battleground over Collective Identity," pp. 27–44.
41. Laitin, *Identity in Formation.*

statehood. During the 1999 elections, the "Russian vote" was split between the more right-wing newly founded Israel Bieytenu ("Israel Is Our Home") party and Israel B'Aliyah, as a protest against the older party's perceived poor performance in protecting Russian interests. Israel B'Aliyah, however, conducted a very effective electoral campaign directed against the Shas party, which at the time held the Ministry of Interior, causing many difficulties to new immigrants whose "Jewishness" was questionable.

The Russian-speaking immigrants are very similar to the predominately Ashkenazi middle class, and, given the human capital they represent, these immigrants have already begun to be rapidly absorbed into that class as far as occupations are concerned. This class is in any case searching for political and demographic partners for class-cultural and political coalitions, in opposition to the Arabs, the non-Zionist Orthodox nationalists, and the Mizrahim, in particular. The Russians also feel threatened by these same segments and are in competition with them for a sectarian and symbolic place in the Israeli state. This suggests that the youngest generation of immigrants, and especially the next generation of the Russians, who in any case are experiencing growing generation gaps between parents and children, will be absorbed into the Israeli middle class. In this event, their uniqueness as a Russian cultural and social enclave would dissipate, and indeed a number of signs of this are already evident.

On the other hand, there is no certainty that the Russians will disappear in the next generation or will cease to exist in their current form or otherwise. The traditionalist Mizrahim of today and the Orthodox nationalists are only slightly similar to their parents' generations, yet even so the "bubbles" have been preserved and even strengthened in identity and boundaries. The degree and form in which Russian culture will be preserved as a separate culture of Russian speakers (fluent in Hebrew), depends on developments within Israeli and global society. If the class-cultural segmentation trends in Israeli society continue, there is no reason to think that the Russian Israeli will not be established as one of the types of Israeli and Israeliness, while continuing to transmit Russian language and culture from generation to generation. This could be accomplished by means of a partially separate educational system, an endogamous marriage market, the Russian press and other media, neighborhoods and cities with Russian majorities, and a distinct lifestyle. In addition, this trend is liable to be strengthened or weakened by contact with Russia itself and with other Russian (whether Jewish or not) immigrant communities in the world. If Russian cultural and economic contacts take place around the world, with Israel as a secondary center to Moscow and St. Petersburg, then the boundaries of the Russian collectivity inside the Israeli state will also continue to exist. This seems just as likely as Russian assimilation by the functional equivalent of the Zionist melting pot.

Another possibility is that a significant proportion of the Russian population will cling to their enclaves, without becoming any more "Israelified" either in their own eyes or in those of the public at large. The boundaries between them and the rest of the Israeli polity will in that case continue to be sharp, and their primary cultural and identity references would presumably be Russian and international, rather than Israeli.

Whatever the case, however, the Russian immigrant community in Israel has already undergone cultural, political, social, and demographic changes.

THE ETHIOPIANS

The Ethiopian Jewish immigrants to Israel are at almost at the other end of the spectrum from the immigrants from the USSR and CIS as far as their social characteristics and position in the system are concerned. Known as the "Beta Israel" or "Falashas,"[42] this group is relatively small, numbering only about 75,000, but its members are very conspicuous because of the deep-seated differences between them and the rest of the population and the low level of skills and meager human capital with which they arrived. The Ethiopians were brought to Israel in two dramatic "secret" operations—Operation Moses and Operation Solomon. Prior to Operation Moses, however, beginning mainly in 1977, about 6,000 Ethiopian immigrants (most of them from the Tigre region) had arrived in a sporadic and unorganized fashion. From the 1950s to 1977, only about 300 Ethiopians had arrived. In the framework of Operation Moses (1984–85), 7,000 Ethiopians were brought in by way of

42. "Falashas" is today considered a pejorative term for this ethnic group, but for many years this name was acceptable and neutral. "Beta Israel" ("House of Israel") is a relatively new identification and appellation and is considered politically correct for a religious and ethnic group that was called by many names in different Ethiopian contexts, particularly "Esrael" or "Esraelotz." "Beta Israel" is apparently a tradition and identity created in Israel in order to establish a direct connection between the Falashas and the Israeli state and society. In this book, they are referred to as "Falashas" in the Ethiopian context and "Ethiopians" in the Israeli context.

Sudan, and in between these two operations, another 11,000 immigrated to Israel. Also in the framework of Operation Solomon (in May 1991, toward the conclusion of the Ethiopian civil war), 14,300 Ethiopians were brought to Israel, and by the end of 1996, an additional 10,000 had been added. In addition, more than 12,000 Ethiopians have now been born in Israel, while about 1,000 have died there. As will be seen, there are significant differences in composition and qualities between the different waves of immigration (or operations).

The admission of these new dark-skinned Israelis, nowadays termed "Ethiopian Jews," was another step in the pluralization of the Israeli social system. Their appearance as a social category (and not only as individuals) transforms Israel into an even more varied society from an ethnic and national perspective and introduces into the system an additional social variable beyond the other societal hierarchies and boundaries—one that is almost insurmountable—the race boundary and color hierarchy.[43]

Acceptance of the Falashas as Jews was not self-evident, and in spite of two halachic verdicts that recognized their Judaism in principle, they were still required to undergo a ritual ceremony of conversion. Even today, their individual personal status is subject to the rulings of Orthodox rabbis who are recognized as experts and as authorized to rule on their issues, while their religious leaders (qessotch) are not recognized for the purposes of performing marriage, divorce, and burial. Although they are defined as Jews as a group, according to the Law of Return,[44] the Jewishness of every individual remains in question, "because according to the opinion of the rabbinate there is a question of a mixture of a minority of non-Jews in this Jewish tribe."[45] Originally, they were required to convert according to the strictest standards, including phlebotomy (symbolic circumcision) and immersion. Some of the people of the first wave (mainly those that came from the Tigre region) agreed to all the severe conditions of the Israeli rabbinate. Others (those from the Gondar region) were opposed to doing so and saw the demand for conversion as debasement and racism. In the end, this approach brought the Ethiopian immigrants into direct conflict with the rabbinate in a sit-

43. Before the arrival of the Ethiopians, the Mizrahi and Yemenite Jews were considered, and sometimes considered themselves, to be "blacks," which in most cases was used as a derogatory term. In Ethiopia, the Falashas were considered "reddish-brown," the color of the upper stratum in the local social hierarchy.
44. According to the determination of an interministerial committee in 1975.
45. Corinald, *Ethiopian Jewry*, p. 218.

in strike that lasted about a month in October 1985 and an even larger outburst in January 1996. In the face of the vociferous protest of 1985, the rabbinate was compelled to backtrack a little. It decided to recognize Ethiopian circumcisions and agreed to authorize a national marriage registrar to check each and every case of marriage registration among Ethiopians.

In September 1989, Rabbi David Chelouche of Netanya, who was known as an authority and a liberal, was appointed registrar of Ethiopian marriages. The Ethiopians did not, however, see this as an unequivocal resolution of their status and identity as Jews and as partners with equal status in Israeli society. The demand that they adopt family names[46] and Hebraicize their first names (which was done, at times, according to the whim of a clerk) was hurtful to their self-image and self-confidence. Despite considerable emotional preparation for adjustment to Israeli society on the part of the immigrants,[47] the Israeli system seems to have been challenged more by their absorption than by any other immigrant group.

This is a fascinating case of the "invention of tradition" and identity, albeit based on existing elements.[48] Although Orthodox and national religious activists and rabbis had lobbied for recognition of the (contingent) Jewishness of the "Beta Israel" and thus application to them of the Law of Return, the Orthodox rabbinical establishment discriminated against them on the basis of the "doubtfulness of their Jewishness." There have always been eschatological traditions in Judaism involving "discovering the lost tribes," embodying the promise of Israel's transformation into a (numerically) "great nation." The Falashas were perceived as having an unwavering Jewish religious identity, although their religious practices, albeit authentic, seemed naive and anachronistic, owing to their extended isolation from the central (mainly European) streams of rabbinical Judaism. The existence of communities in northern Ethiopia (in the areas of the Blue Nile, especially Gondar, Tigre, and Walqayit) who self-identified ethnically and religiously as Jews had been known since the fourteenth century. They possessed clear but highly

46. According to the first name in Ethiopian of the eldest adult man in the nuclear family (grandfather).
47. They had already acquired some idea of Israeli conditions from Ethiopians living in Israel or who had managed to emigrate to Israel earlier and to return to Ethiopia, often as emissaries of different organizations and institutions.
48. See Kaplan, *The Beta Israel (Falasha) in Ethiopia;* id., "History, Halakha and Identity."

selective Jewish traditional texts[49] and observed important central practices (the *mitzvoth,* or precepts) of pre-rabbinical Jewish religion, such as observing the Sabbath, the laws of ritual purity, circumcision, and so on.[50] In addition, in the eyes of Ethiopian Christians, they were for better or worse identified as Jews.

Until the fourteenth century, their main occupation had been agriculture. As the non-Christian communities were driven to the margins of the political-economic system, however, they lost their right to land ownership and were pushed into occupations considered degrading and impure, such as smithery, pottery, and weaving. Prior to the seventeenth century, the Falashas had had something like centralized self-government, and in the Samen region they were ruled by a monarchical dynasty. The dynasty and the self-government came to an end with their subordination to the Ethiopian Christians.

In addition to these political and social changes, the period from the beginning of the twentieth century to the mid 1930s was marked among the Falashas by what Shalva Weil calls an approach to "normative Judaism," through adoption of the religious corpus from the oral law to the attributes of rabbinical Judaism. Dr. Jacques (Yaacov) Paitlovitch, who arrived in Ethiopia in 1904, is considered the "inventor" of the Ethiopian Jews and as the person who introduced them into Jewish history by bringing their existence to the recognition of the Jewish world. Paitlovitch also brought the Falashas a certain knowledge of the Hebrew prayers, the lighting of Sabbath candles, and the use of the symbol of the Star of David. In the 1950s, the Torah Education Department of the Jewish Agency opened a seminar for teachers in Asmara, and many of the graduates of this seminar emigrated to or at least visited Israel. In the mid 1970s, school systems of the ORT network serving several hundred students were established in the Gondar region.[51]

Approximating central streams of Judaism and contact with emissaries of other Jewish communities in the world did not, however, mean that Ethiopian Jews gave up attributes common to them and their Christian neighbors, such as monasticism, animal sacrifice, and slavery. As a rule, throughout their known history, there were always partial overlaps and bidirectional religious conversions and intermarriages between them

---

49. For example, the *Orit,* a translation into Ge'ez, the local Semitic tongue, of the Hebrew Bible.

50. See Quirin, *Evolution of Ethiopian Jews.*

51. ORT is the Russian acronym for the Organization for Habilitation and Training, established in 1890 in Russia to provide Jews with vocational skills and training.

and the Christian (and perhaps also Moslem) communities among whom they lived. There had never been unequivocal divisions or social boundaries between the religious communities in Ethiopia. There were, and still are, Ethiopians who define themselves as both Jews and Christians, or as Jews who have also been baptized as Christians. These, the so-called Falas-Mura, frequently observe the rituals and commandments of the two religions simultaneously.[52] In the Ethiopian-African context, overlapping religious membership does not necessarily remove one from the group,[53] and it is even possible to find members of the same family who belong to different religions and observe different religious practices. D. L. Pankhurst notes that in the Ethiopian Jewish and Christian communities, the denominational-sectarian division was identical: priests, deacons, scribes, monks, and nuns even wore identical costumes.[54] The elite of the scribes and the priests of "Beta Israel" were accustomed to acquire their religious and literacy education in the schools of the Orthodox Christian community. Moreover, up until the fifteenth century, there was apparently no distinction made between Christianity and Judaism in Ethiopia, and only the appearance of Ayahud ("Jews") who withdrew from Christianity and proclaimed themselves to be "the real Jews," set them apart. They were persecuted for some time because of this, which created an even sharper separation between the Falashas and the other religious and ethnic communities in northern Ethiopia.

In any case, a sufficient historical explanation for the creation of an early Jewish community in Ethiopia that interrelates religion, historiography, myth, and theology is still lacking.[55] Christian Ethiopian legend, however, ascribes the origin of Ethiopian Jews as an ethno-national group to the union between the biblical King Solomon and the Queen of Sheba, who came from Axum, which according to tradition is the biblical Cush. The Ethiopian monarchical dynasties relate themselves to this genealogical tree, and the short biblical story has been expanded into a complete, detailed text in the *Kebra Nagast,* the national Ethiopian mythology.

Despite decentralization and extensive geographical dispersion, the social and sectarian structure of the Falasha villages remained more or

---

52. Falas-Mura is the name by which they are commonly known in Israel. See Friedmann, "Case of the Falas Mura."
53. Kaplan, "History, Halakha and Identity."
54. Pankhurst, "Beta Esra'el (Falashas) in Their Ethiopian Setting."
55. Kessler, *The Falashas.*

less identical after the priesthood (*qessotch*) replaced the institution of monkhood in both Ethiopian Christianity and Judaism in the twentieth century. In each village, the eldest men served as heads of the village or community in a sort of council of elders (*smaglotch*), which also functioned as a kind of court and arbitration forum. The priesthood was a scholarly merit position and not ascriptive. At the head of the clerical hierarchy was the priest (*qess*), who was surrounded by novice priests and assistants (the *debtera*). The *qess* would rule on religious questions (purity and impurity) and conduct collective or familial ritual ceremonies, such as the annual celebration of *Seged*. There was not a *qess* in every village, and they would travel from place to place according to need. After the *qessotch* came the literate, who were also the teachers of the children and mediators when necessary, particularly in contacts with the authorities, in which reading and writing were required, whether in Amharic or in the holy language, Ge'ez—an ancient Semitic tongue. The heads of the main households (*beta sab*) followed the literate in the order of hierarchy. At the bottom of the ladder were the remaining families and their members, differentiated according to property holdings, gender, and age. Gender role divisions were guarded carefully. The men dealt with all religious pursuits and work outside the household, including working the land (mainly as tenant farmers), whereas the women took care of the housework, domestic industries (pottery, basket weaving, and embroidery), and raising the young.

In spite of the recognition of the existence of this "lost tribe" during the first large waves of immigration to Israel, no effort was made, as was done for other Jewish communities around the world, to bring about their immigration. They were ignored, despite the longing of the Falashas themselves for "Zion" and Jerusalem. However, Jewish organizations, such as the American Jewish Joint Distribution Committee (AJJDC), acted to aid or strengthen the "normative" Jewish principles among them. The government of Emperor Haile Selassie was also very friendly both to Israel and to the Falashas, although in the mid 1960s he instituted a policy of Amharization and forcible assimilation of all ethnic and religious groups into one "nation." His regime began to falter at the beginning of the 1970s, and Ethiopia has since been beset by a series of revolutions and guerrilla and civil wars.

In 1974, a Marxist group, led by Mengistu Haile-Mariam, seized power in Ethiopia, which became oriented toward the USSR and the Eastern Bloc. The new regime abolished the religious character of the

Ethiopian state and bestowed equal civil rights on all citizens without difference of religion and ethnic origin. For the first time, young Falashas received a modern education inside Ethiopia and later even central positions in the administration. On the other hand, the regime's attitude toward ethnic and religious groups, which were all suspected of separatism, was extremely hostile. The sociopolitical and the economic situation greatly worsened, and so too did the living conditions of the Falashas. Their very existence came under uncertain threat. Against this backdrop, both the Falashas themselves and Jewish organizations in Israel and around the world began to call for aid in emigration from Ethiopia.

The regime change in Ethiopia had other effects on the Falashas. The new regime wanted to enlist Ethiopian youth in general and the Falashas in particular (who were not suspected of resistance to the regime) in the building of a "new socialist society." The youth were mobilized into the army and rural associations, and urban schools were opened to them (there were, however, also those who enlisted in various underground organizations). The revolution did considerable damage to the traditional Falasha society and family and undermined the traditional authorities, at least among those called the Beta Israel. These processes would recur in an even sharper and more explicit form among the refugees in Sudan and immigrants to Israel.

In 1984–85, civil wars, the forced conscription of tens of thousands of youths, and a severe drought and famine damaged the entire social and economic texture of Ethiopia. Hundreds of thousands of Ethiopians began to flee to Sudan, mainly from areas stricken by battles between government and various guerrilla forces. Among the Falashas, the crossing to Sudan had begun already in 1977, chiefly from the areas of Tigre and Walqayit. They joined the hundreds of thousands of Christians who had fled the terror of the revolution. By 1980, there were about 3,000 Falashas among the half million Ethiopian refugees in Sudan. In 1982, as a result of drought and increased fighting in the Gondar region, this flight of Falashas took on the form of a mass immigration. The decision to leave Ethiopia was made on the collective level of the village, and entire communities, among them educated youths with twelve years of schooling, hoarded food and planned their escape. By 1984, some 10,000 Falashas had crossed into Sudan, and another 4,000 had died of disease and the dangers of the journey—a walk of hundreds of kilometers. According to oral reports, agents of the Israeli Intelligence

Service (the Mossad) helped them both on the way and inside the camps in Sudan.[56] Today, the Ethiopians feel that the heroic story of their arrival in Israel has not been sufficiently included in the pantheon of Zionist Israeli heroism, and that this omission from Israeli collective memory reflects their marginality in Israeli society in general.

The stay in the camps in Sudan caused additional disintegration of the community, the family, and individuals' sense of identity. The dead could not be buried according to custom and tradition, and young women could not be married in the accepted manner and were exposed to rape and abuse. As a result, new patterns of relations were created in the camps that were known as "Sudan marriages," the legal status of which was unclear both according to Falasha tradition and to Halacha. The refugees in Sudan were largely compelled to conceal their Falasha identity and to present themselves as Christians. Families were separated and spouses split up without the possibility of relations between them. Reports of the high rates of mortality on the roads, in the refugee camps, and in the slums of Khartoum were frequently exaggerated by horrible rumors in the absence of real information. Men and women remarried, only to discover later that their first spouses were still alive.[57]

Operation Moses began at the end of November 1984 and continued for about two months under maximal secrecy. The transfer of the Falasha refugees from Sudan was made possible thanks to American pressure on the government of General Jaffar Numeiri. The emigration was halted in the beginning of January 1985 before its conclusion, apparently after information on the operation was published in the Israeli and world press, contrary to the stipulations of the Sudanese government. About 1,000 Falashas remained in Sudan, but were extricated within a short time by the Americans, and they too arrived in Israel. Between 1985 and 1989, about 2,000 additional Falashas, mainly from the Gondar region, exited Ethiopia legally by way of the Addis Ababa airport. In November 1989, with additional deterioration in the economic and security situation, the government of Ethiopia decided to renew ties with Israel (in the hope that this would help win American aid). As a result,

---

56. Parfitt, *Operation Moses*.

57. These and other natural and social plagues distorted and almost decomposed the Ethiopian family prior to arrival in Israel. According to 1996 figures, the structure of households was as follows: 31 percent were single persons, 20 percent one-parent families, 9 percent childless couples, and about 40 percent couples with children. See Benita and Noam, "Absorption of Ethiopian Immigrants in Israel"; Benita, Noam, and Levy, *Local Surveys of Ethiopian Immigrants*.

the Falashas began to migrate from their villages to the capital, Addis Ababa, where they were supposed to receive exit visas and be transported to Israel.

The conditions of the living quarters, the food, and the sanitation of the slums of Addis Ababa were difficult in spite of attempts to help by the Israeli embassy, the Jewish Agency, the AJJDC, and other Jewish organizations. Even attempts to organize a mutual camp and community life, to teach Hebrew, and to immunize against diseases had very poor results. Infectious and viral diseases, including jaundice and AIDS, very prevalent in Africa, infected many of the Falashas during their stay in Addis Ababa. Finally, when the rebels arrived on the outskirts of the capital and the regime fell apart, more than 14,000 Falashas, almost the entire community, were brought to Israel in an airlift that lasted approximately thirty-five hours (May 24–25, 1991). An unknown number of Falas-Mura, including many relatives of Ethiopians in Israel, were left behind.

With political, media, and "absorption bureaucracy" help, the Falashas succeeded in constructing an identity for themselves as "Beta Israel," connecting them directly with Judaism and Israel, but because of their dark skins, they have been labeled "blacks." In the Ethiopian context, the Falashas were considered relatively light-skinned and were termed "reddish-brown," the preferred color in Ethiopian culture. In the Israeli "color hierarchy," however, they found themselves ranked below the oriental Jews, the Yemenites, and even the Arabs. They were marginalized as a result of a combination three factors, any one of which would have assigned them a peripheral position in Israel: skin color; doubts about their Jewish origin—Jewishness being the most important common denominator in the highly ethnocentric Jewish state; and poor human capital. Their relatively small numbers are an advantage, making it possible for the state to devote appreciable material resources to improving their skills and occupational status. This could be accomplished by means of supplemental instruction programs in the elementary, middle, and high schools, as well as during military service, and in affirmative action in acceptance to institutions of higher education. The disadvantage in the relatively small number of Ethiopians in Israel is that they will not be able to constitute a significant voting bloc, but at most a moral lobby.

In a study that measured social distances, conducted in northern Israel, only about 40 percent of Jewish residents affirmed openly that they would not oppose the marriage of one of their children to an

Ethiopian.[58] From what is known from other societies, this percentage is likely to be even smaller when the situation is concrete. So it seems that intermarriage cannot be expected to blur the boundaries for generations to come. In the United States, for example, even in an era of flourishing American multiculturalism, mobility and a large improvement in the living conditions of some blacks, and the creation of an established African American middle class, did not abolish the social boundaries between them and whites. Improvement in the status of some blacks only created greater tension within the African American community and between it and white society, and, in particular, a highly alienated and belligerent black youth counterculture.[59]

The Israeli absorption institutions have been conscious, since Operation Moses, that absorption of the Ethiopians at the margins of Israeli society and the implications of this absorption for the image of Israeli society are socially explosive issues. This has been especially so since the 1970s, because hindsight has revealed severe errors that were made in absorbing the large-scale immigration of oriental Jewish immigrants, particularly those from North Africa. The patronizing and condescending approach adopted, which did not take into account their feelings and identity, was an obstacle to assimilation in the "melting pot," and protests broke out, which recurred with even greater fury in the third generation. On the other hand, to not take an interventionist approach and not provide intensive assistance for the Ethiopian immigrants would have meant their immediate frontal confrontation with a system whose rules they did not understand and whose values and institutions were foreign to them. The standard dilemmas faced in absorbing any group of immigrants were even more conspicuous in this case.

The secrecy entailed in Operation Moses predicated preliminary treatment of the immigrants as refugees, which initially alleviated this dilemma. They were brought directly from the airplane to a camp in Ashkelon, where they were provided with clothing and sorted (bureaucratically and medically). As mentioned, bureaucratic sorting included allocation to extended families, the giving of family names and Hebrew first names (close to 70 percent were changed to Hebrew names), and guessing at or reconstructing age. The method and giving of names was put together in consultation and with the active participation of veteran

58. Goldberg and Kirchenbaum, "Black Newcomers to Israel."
59. This is not to say that only black youths in America belong to such countercultures. Most of the purchasers of rap music, for example, are white.

Ethiopians immigrants, who also served as translators and guides. This was done in an attempt to build them up as leaders of the communities (largely at the expense of the elders and the *qessotch*). Even so, there was a considerable construction or invention of new kinship units that answered to the needs and rubrics of the Israeli bureaucratic system. At this stage, the refugee immigrants were in such a mental and physical state that it was possible to do with them whatever the Israeli bureaucracy wished.

In the next stage, every family received a tiny housing unit in an absorption center or hotel, basic household and kitchen tools, and a preliminary financial allocation. In addition, they were provided with an aide whose role was to instruct them on the Israeli lifestyle (including the use of running water and the like) and referred to a seminar for Hebrew instruction (*ulpan*).[60] Among this group, however, there were also literate young Ethiopians who had grown up and studied in urban centers and knew something about life in Israel. Most arrived without their families, and the place of the family was taken by the peer group with whom they had arrived in the Ethiopian town or city where they studied, traveling from there to Sudan and later to Israel. In the aftermath of Operation Moses, in whose framework about half of the immigrants that were brought in were young adults, teenagers, and children (under 18), there was an attempt to house them in predominantly religious boarding schools and youth villages.[61]

The preliminary intention was to house the refugees from Ethiopia in absorption centers for only a year,[62] both because there was a housing shortage and to give them time in order to adapt and to study the language and Israeli cultural and social customs. In practice, some of these absorption centers became permanent housing. Hebrew *ulpans* and subsistence allocations became shelter against entering the labor market, and a great dependence on the absorbing institution and its personnel was created. Most Russian immigrants quickly left the absorption centers, which were then turned into poverty housing for the Ethiopians.

---

60. The *ulpan* is usually a boarding school for fast and efficient learning of the language and for teaching the basic codes of Israeli culture and mores to new immigrants.

61. This was a result of both responsiveness to the political pressure of the religious parties and the conviction that they are indeed part of the religious-traditional population. The reason was that there should not be a repeat of the errors made in the years of the large waves of immigration in the 1950s, when, according to claims, "children were taken away from their religion" (see chapter 3).

62. Herzog, "Bureaucratic Absorption of Ethiopian Immigrants in Israel"; id., *Bureaucracy and Ethiopian Immigrants;* Holt, "Culture Cluster."

The authorities began to buy or to rent apartments for the Ethiopians in an effort to disperse them to different places in Israel and to prevent concentrations that could become new enclaves and ghettos. By the end of 1987, about 2,000 families had moved to permanent housing in medium-sized and large Israeli cities; 1,400 families remained in the original absorption centers, but the conditions of paternalistic tutelage had been eliminated.

The army built an enlistment framework for Ethiopians,[63] and even the universities began to absorb Ethiopian students. The most serious bottleneck of all, however, was finding appropriate work for them. As mentioned, in Ethiopia, most of the Falashas had worked in agriculture and related crafts—occupations little sought after in the Israeli labor market. Programs were prepared for professional retraining and for learning new skills, but the majority of Ethiopian men encountered great difficulties in absorption into the Israeli labor market, and chronic unemployment remains high among them. According to surveys in the 1990s, fewer than half the immigrants of employment age (22–64) were employed, and only a third of these in professional jobs,[64] but the employment rate among the male Ethiopian population rises with the number of years in Israel until it almost equals that of the general population. The type of work offered in the Israeli labor market did not correspond to the Ethiopians' self-image, and only a few had the skills to acquire professional jobs. Contrary to expectations, the women tended to agree more to work in service industries and households. The departure of the women to work outside the house, and their transformation in many cases into the main and even sole breadwinner, was absolutely contrary to Falasha tradition and caused great tension within families.

The destruction of donated blood perhaps most vividly illuminates the situation of the Falasha in Israeli society and the difficulties the Israeli system had in adapting to their presence. Hagar Salamon has explored the subject of blood as a key symbol around which collective identity among the Falashas and their relations with Christians were organized in Ethiopia.[65] He focuses primarily on three areas: menstruation, animal slaughter, and eating. These differences between the Falashas and the Christians demarcated cultural boundaries between them, contributed

---

63. Shabtay, "Identity Construction among Soldiers Immigrated from Ethiopia."
64. Also see Benita and Noam, "Absorption of Ethiopian Immigrants in Israel."
65. Salamon, "Slavery among the 'Beta-Israel' in Ethiopia"; id., "Between Ethnicity and Religiosity."

to the shaping of their collective identity, and were everyday subjects of argument and debate. During their menstrual period, Jewish women in Ethiopia were completely distanced from the community and spent seven days in a "blood house," which was fenced off and located outside the village.[66] Among their Christian neighbors, however, menstruating women are not considered impure and continue to live in their homes, to cook, and to perform other accepted female roles, excluding conjugal relations. The Falashas describe animal slaughter as professional work, done by specialists, using the sharpest knife and taking care that blood (identified with the soul) does not remain in the body of the animal. According to the testimony of the Falashas, Ethiopian Christians, however, are even prepared to eat meat from animals that have not yet been slaughtered. Conversely, the Christians regarded the slaughtering customs of the Falashas as a symbol of the killing of Jesus and a breach of the covenant between them and God through violation of the prohibition against bloodshed. Therefore, even when members of one ethnoreligious unit invited members of the other to a meal, they would let the invited party slaughter the animal themselves according to their own customs, and even refrained from eating meat side by side. Blood thus symbolized the separation and marked the boundary between the Falashas and their Christian neighbors, ironically in a situation in which there were also great similarities and other blurred boundaries. It is thus not surprising that after their arrival in Israel, they sought to mix their blood with the blood of other Jewish Israelis by means of blood donations, and that there was an enormous rupture in relations when it was bluntly and unequivocally rejected. In the end of January 1996, it became known that the blood bank administered by the Magen David Adom organization (the Israeli equivalent of the Red Cross) was destroying Ethiopian donations of blood without any testing. Theirs was the only "high risk group" whose contributions were accepted, but they were not used out of fear that they carried the AIDS virus. On January 28, 10,000 protesters gathered opposite the Prime Minister's Office. According to the media, this was "one of the stormiest demonstrations in the annals of Israel,"[67] and it quickly turned to serious violence, during which sixty-one people (forty-one of them policemen) were wounded.

66. This was also a powerful control mechanism of the community over the women, whose husbands were away for long periods of time, as well as over unmarried young women and girls. In Israel, Ethiopian women were found spending their menstrual period outside their homes (*Maariv,* January 30, 1996).

67. *Maariv* and *Yediot Achronot,* January 29, 1996.

There is no doubt that, as important as the subject of the blood contributions was to them, the eruption of the Ethiopians resulted from feelings of long-standing discrimination and their inability to integrate into Israeli society, as discussed above. The media was filled with retrospective items on dozens of cases of discrimination, on unwillingness to allow them to live in a number of cities, on the resistance of parents to their children learning together with Ethiopian children, and mainly on the lack of recognition of their full status as Jews. On both sides, the identification "Beta Israel" disappeared, and the terms "Ethiopian" and "black" were used.

An immediate analogy was drawn between treatment of the oriental Jewish immigrants of the 1950s and that of the Ethiopians. Two days later, in a session of the Absorption Committee of the Knesset, Addisu Messele, chairman of the United Ethiopian Jewish Organization,[68] declared:

> [I]t is unbelievable that the sovereign state of Israel would treat us in the most primitive and the most debasing way. They would require our leader to drop his pants in order to examine his sex organ. For all the failures, there are always explanations. For the DDT affair, there were also logical explanations from their perspective. For the affair of the Yemenite children too.[69] You did not learn any lessons. You should be ashamed of yourselves.[70]

An Ethiopian doctor at the Hillel Jaffe hospital said: "[I]f a sick person did not want to be treated by me, I would understand him." Researchers interviewed by the media praised the demonstration outside Prime Minister's Office. "[T]his is a stage on their way to integration," the anthropologist Shalva Weil said. "In this fashion they create an identity for themselves and come together." Intellectuals, mainly oriental

68. The UEJO united umbrella organization was formed by seven different immigrant organizations under the strong encouragement of the Jewish Agency. In 1996, Messele was elected to the "immigrant slot" on the Labor party list, and he served until 1999 as the first Ethiopian member of parliament. During the 1999 primaries, he did not receive a realistic spot on the party list (i.e., stand a chance of being elected).

69. One wound still open in Israeli society is the mysterious disappearance of several hundred Yemenite children during the early 1950s. According to authorities, most of them died in hospitals, and their parents were not identified at the time, while others were given away in bona fide adoptions. Many Yemenite parents suspected or felt that their children had been kidnapped by private or official agencies for various reasons. Several investigation committees have since been appointed, but none have reached any conclusive or convincing conclusions.

70. *Yediot Achronot*, January 30, 1996. He referred to the immigrants that arrived in Israel in the 1950s and were regarded as potential carriers of diverse diseases and "disinfected" upon arrival with DDT. This entered into the collective memory of the immigrants from Arab and Muslim lands as a major humiliation.

Jews, such as the novelist Sami Michael, were also interviewed and challenged. "[W]e said that we learned the lesson of the 1950s," Michael said. "We lied to ourselves and led them astray. With the welcome, we labeled them in advance—the immigrant women from Russia are prostitutes, the immigrants from Ethiopia have AIDS." A more optimistic writer told of a middle-class couple consisting of a (white) Israeli man and an Ethiopian woman, both in liberal arts professions. At the same time, it was discovered that the Ethiopians excommunicated individuals and families among them who carried the AIDS virus and blamed them for their marginal status in Israeli society.[71]

Unlike their Russian new immigrant counterparts, the Ethiopians initially wanted to be completely absorbed into a homogeneous Jewish ethnicity and to undergo a fast process of acculturation and assimilation.[72] As time passes, however, they and other Israelis are becoming increasingly aware that this expectation is difficult to fulfill. It is highly predictable that the Ethiopians will remain a separate and relatively marginal group within the collectivity. Their high salience and visibility will persist even as the Ethiopians as individuals and as a group considerably improve their economic and class positions and bridge the gaps between themselves and veteran Israelis. This small group of new Israelis is challenging two contradictory inherent premises of Jewish nationalism. One is the myth that all the world's Jews are descended from a common ancient ancestor. The other is denial of the presumption, mainly rooted in racist Nazi ideology, that the Jews are one genetic or racial group. The immigration of the Falashas to Israel, based on the Law of Return, was supposed to provide the ultimate proof of nonexistence of any racial elements in Zionism and Judaism, and at the same time to demonstrate—if it was ever needed—that the Jews themselves are far from being a single-race collectivity. Nonetheless, doubts about their Jewishness—a necessary condition for their acceptance as members of equal standing in the collectivity—have marginalized and alienated the Ethiopians.[73]

71. *Yediot Achronot*, February 9, 1996.

72. Weil, "Collective Denominations and Collective Identities among Ethiopian Jews."

73. The younger generation of Ethiopians has already begun to form a protest counterculture related to the African American and global black protest cultures.

THE NONCITIZEN WORKERS

Among the territories occupied by Israel in 1967 were the Gaza Strip
(previously under Egyptian rule) and the West Bank (annexed by Transjordan in 1950), two overpopulated areas that had been part of British
colonial Palestine. At the time of their conquest, the population of these
regions numbered about 505,000 on the West Bank and 389,700 in the
Gaza Strip. By the early 1980s, however, owing to one of the highest
birthrates in the world,[74] the population of the occupied territories
reached about 748,000 on the West Bank and 476,000 in the Gaza Strip.
Their total population was estimated at close to 2 million in the late
1980s, despite continuous emigration, mainly of Christian Palestinians.
With the exception of the metropolitan area of the old city of Jerusalem,
these territories were not officially annexed to Israel. For all other purposes—economic, military, and territorial—they nonetheless became a
part of the Israeli state's control system.[75]

The "permanent temporary" long-run status of these areas as "administered territories," whose populations were under absolute Israeli
control but lacked citizens' rights, reopened the frontiers of the settler
state. The West Bank and Gaza Strip became available for Jewish settlement and the state's territorial expansion without annexation.[76] These
territories and their populations also became outlets for Israeli domestic
products and merchandise. Most important, however, the territories
served as reservoirs of inexpensive and highly flexible unskilled and
semi-skilled labor. Almost from the moment the territories were opened,
an influx of Palestinian male commuter workers began to flow into Israel
(women laborers, mainly working for textile manufacturers, were usually used by Israelis through local subcontractors). From about 75,000
in 1982, the total number reached 109,000 in 1987. Palestinians from
the occupied territories employed in the Israeli labor market constituted
more than 7 percent of all registered employed persons in Israel at the

74. The annual birthrates for the Gaza Strip and the West Bank respectively were then
around 2.7 percent and 2.4 percent, but declined slightly during that period. Women had
an average of seven children or more. However, the rate of population increase was moderated by a 1 percent annual emigration rate during most periods.
75. See chapter 2 and Kimmerling, "Boundaries and Frontiers of the Israeli Control
System."
76. Annexation would have meant granting citizenship and citizens' rights to the Palestinian population, increasing the demographic ratio in favor of the non-Jewish Palestinian population, raising the appalling possibility of a binational state.

time.[77] Together with unregistered workers, the total number reached 130,000. As with underclasses in other industrialized states, the Palestinian commuter workers constituted a segregated ethnic minority, and they were paid considerably less than Israeli citizens in comparable occupational categories. They were employed mainly in construction, agriculture, sanitation, workshops (such as garages), and industrial plants. Usually hired by the day, they lacked most welfare and social security rights (such as pensions or life and unemployment insurance and children's allowances), with the exception of worker's compensation, employer's bankruptcy insurance, and maternity leave.

For the Israeli regime, this was a very convenient arrangement. The Palestinians were not immigrants who might threaten to settle down permanently in the country. Unlike the Third World migrant workers flooding European countries, they did not pose the threat of incrementally seeking naturalization, which could challenge the whole concept of citizenship.[78] Nevertheless, the backdrop of the Jewish Palestinian conflict and pressures from employers' lobbies caused them to be permanently suspected of being "terrorists."

Even after the outbreak of the Palestinian popular uprising in December 1987, the numbers of Palestinian frontier workers in the Israeli labor market did not considerably decrease, but this occurred during a series of terrorist attacks in the urban Israeli heartland in late 1993 and early 1994. The attacks were a result of the Islamic armed opposition to the Oslo Accords between al-Fatah and Israel.[79] They aroused panic and caused extended closures to be imposed on the Palestinian population, preventing most of them from commuting to their places of work. The security situation made the noncitizen Palestinian labor force highly unstable.

Following pressure from employers, the authorities opened up the country to legal migrant workers from Asian and African developing countries (including Thailand, the Philippines, Sri Lanka, and Nigeria) and poorer eastern European or Balkan countries (like Bulgaria, Romania, and Turkey). In fact, the first wave of foreign workers was

77. Zakai, *Economic Development in Judea and Samaria and Gaza Strip, 1985–1986;* Semyonov and Lewin-Epstein, *Hewers of Wood and Drawers of Water.*
78. Soysal, *Limits of Citizenship;* Jacobson, *Rights across Borders.* For the Israeli state's inability to deal with non-Jewish immigrants, see Shafir and Peled, "Citizenship and Stratification in an Ethnic Democracy."
79. See Kimmerling, "Power-Oriented Settlement."

authorized in 1989, at the same time as the dramatic increase of the immigration from the Soviet Union. From about 10,000 licenses to import guest workers in 1993, these authorizations grew to about 80–100,000 by 1996–98. According to the Central Bank of Israel's report in 1997, a total of 128,000 authorized and unauthorized workers were employed in Israel, consisting of 6 percent of total employed workers. An additional 48,000 noncitizen Palestinian commuter workers were also employed.[80] Together, foreign and noncitizen Palestinian workers totaled close to 10 percent of the total civilian labor force, making Israel relatively speaking one of the largest employers of noncitizen laborers in the world.

At the time, this policy was regarded as a temporary measure and limited in its scope. The official and ideological orientation was and remained avoidance of any permanent settlement of such new populations in Israel. Nonetheless, they soon became a permanent and large-scale social and economic phenomenon. As local employers "discovered" these sources of cheap, safe, unprotected, and permanent labor and migrant laborers "discovered" the Israeli labor market, their influx as registered and legal as well as unregistered or illegal workers inevitably became hard to regulate and control.[81] To the abovementioned numbers, one can add about 50–100,000 unregistered and illegal workers. Moreover, many women guest workers, legal and nonlegal, opened up additional new occupations, previously almost unknown in Israel, providing personal services as maids, housekeepers, and caretakers of the old and disabled—jobs never held by Palestinian workers.

The foreign workers constitute a paradigmatic challenge to the Israeli state and its raison d'être. The founding principle of the Jewish community was that it be built on the policy of "only Hebrew labor" (i.e.,

80. Bank of Israel, *Annual Report, 1997*, p. 99. This report also mentions that the Ministry of Labor and Social Affairs estimates the number at about 190,000. However, its seems that this wide range in estimating the number of noncitizen laborers is rooted, not only in the difficulty of accurately accounting for them, but mainly in the "politics of numbers." The lobbies interested in their increase tend toward low estimates, while those aspiring to an exclusively Jewish state (for religious, nationalistic, or ethnic reasons), tend to overestimate their numbers. See Rozenhek, "Migration Regimes, Intra-State Conflicts, and the Policy of Exclusion and Inclusion."

81. Unregistered or illegal workers commonly enter the country as tourists or pilgrims. As a tourist country committed to providing free access to holy sites of all faiths, Israel cannot apply a harsh entrance policy at ports and airports. Other foreign workers simply remain in the country after their work permits and visas (usually granted for two years) expire. Owing to increasing unemployment in Israel during the late 1990s, Ministry of Interior supervisors tried, without great success, to "hunt down" illegal workers in order to repatriate them. About 400 were located and coercively repatriated.

exclusively by Jewish labor). An essential part of "healing the Jewish nation" was to be by physical work and the creation of a large working class, in order to counter the common anti-Semitic myth that Jews were mainly merchants and "unproductive" classes. The major challenge of the foreign workers, however, goes beyond this. It exposes Israel's character as an immigrant society, but exclusively for Jews and their first-order relatives. This situation led to the highly embarrassing declaration by a senior official of the Ministry of Labor and Social Affairs that "Israel is not an immigration country."[82] Any other kind of immigration or potential immigration is perceived as a direct violation of the cosmic order created by the regime, even after the collapse of hegemony. Thus, the state tried for both economic and ideological reasons to impose severe restrictions on foreign workers and their employers. Their visas are usually limited to two years. They are not entitled to bring any family members with them, and—unless they are Palestinians—they are not beneficiaries of any public or state-supplied services or rights. Their minimal medical insurance is supposed to be covered by their employers through private insurance companies. Just as with the Palestinian non-citizen workers, the Israeli labor unions avoid granting them any union protection.[83] Thus, the entire sphere has been depoliticized and located in the private sphere of employer-employee relationships. Israel does not even recognize the guest workers' states of origin as entitled to provide consular or any other type of protection for their subjects in Israel with the status of foreign workers.

Despite this highly restrictive and exclusionary policy, small *gemein-schaftlichen* (origin-based) foreign workers' communities, including families with children, were established, mostly by African illegal workers. These communities are salient mainly in the Tel Aviv/Jaffa metropolitan area, where such workers are concentrated. These small communities constitute a mosaic of cultural "bubbles" and extend and diversify the slum areas and the homeless phenomenon in Israel. As the center of concentration of undocumented workers, the Tel Aviv municipality feels responsible for providing health care (or at least preventive medicine) and educational services to these workers and their families. The municipality's interest in preventing epidemics and crimes in the city

82. See Rozenhek, "Migration Regimes, Intra-State Conflicts, and the Policy of Exclusion and Inclusion," p. 60.

83. Various nongovernmental voluntary organizations try to provide foreign workers with some legal and humanitarian protection, yet they are still harshly exploited, underpaid, or not paid at all by their employers.

puts it in conflict with the interests of the statist agencies. Still, most children of foreign workers who attend school go to schools run by Christian churches in Jaffa and Jerusalem.

Researchers studying the influx of noncitizen Palestinian commuter workers into the Israeli labor market have concluded, in the words of Moshe Semyonov and Noah Lewin-Epstein, that the "rapid growth of the subordinate ethnic groups was related to upward mobility of all [citizen] groups higher in the ethnic hierarchy. Furthermore, when more than one ethnic group stood to benefit from entry and growth of a subordinate group, the group on the top benefited more from the change in ethnic composition [of the labor market]."[84] Thus, the major beneficiaries of the ethnic restructuring of the labor market were the Ashkenazi Jews. They benefited more than the Mizrahim, although both were pushed upward and enjoyed occupational and social mobility. Israeli Arab citizens also experienced some occupational mobility as a consequence of the entry of noncitizen Arab laborers, but far less than did the Jewish ethnic groups. Additionally, economic and social gaps between them and other Jewish groups were enlarged.[85] The research explaining this phenomena, conducted in the mid 1980s, referred only to the social consequences of the influx of noncitizen Palestinians and not to the larger numbers of foreign workers, a different but similar category. However, based on the queuing model, which presumes that ethnic groups are ordered on the basis of their desirability to employers, and that an increase in the relative scope of a subordinate ethnic minority leads to both greater disadvantages for that group and increasing mobility for the most advantaged ethnic groups,[86] a similar if not greater impact should be expected following the appearance of great numbers of foreign workers.

During the past decade, the Israeli economy has been undergoing a rapid process of restructuring, from low-tech and skilled manual labor toward middle and high-tech industries, demanding different kinds of skilled workers.[87] This restructuring has displaced thousands of skilled

84. Semyonov and Lewin-Epstein, *Hewers of Wood and Drawers of Water*, p. 63.

85. The researchers explained this by the political weakness of Arab citizens of Israel, the closure of most public and governmental positions to them, and their inability to convert material resources into cultural capital. See the above section of this chapter and Semyonov and Lewin-Epstein, *The Arab Minority in Israel's Economy*.

86. See, for example, the case of black migrants from South to North in the United States compared with white immigrants from Europe. Lieberson, *A Piece of Pie*; Hodge, "Toward a Theory of Racial Differences in Employment."

87. Some of the remaining low-tech manual plants (such as textiles) are expected to be transplanted to places where labor is cheaper, such as Jordan.

and semi-skilled workers from the labor market, creating an unemployment rate of approximately 7 percent among the domestic population
(about 10 percent among new immigrants). This rate of unemployment
has increased social and political instability and prompted political rhetoric about the necessity for "expulsion" of foreign workers in order to
free jobs for domestic laborers.[88] Nonetheless, it is quite clear that most
of the jobs presently occupied by guest workers cannot be filled by domestic labor.

Today, the guest workers are politically, socially, and culturally completely excluded from the Israeli state. Economically, however, they
seem to constitute an irreversible factor, and their numbers and presence
are continuously increasing. It seems unlikely that this economic phenomenon will not incrementally spill over into other spheres and contribute to the rapid pluralization of the Israeli state.

CONCLUSIONS

The general phenomena that constitute a necessary background to the
analysis of the subdivision of the Israeli polity into seven cultures, countercultures, and other populations, unexpected by traditional Zionism,
are a direct consequence of the rupture within the hegemonic cultural-
political regime. This regime's version of a secular, somewhat Western
"Israeliness," was that of the historical labor movement as presented
and analyzed in chapter 3. The major consequence of this rupture was
the appearance of a number of subsocieties, which, despite their inter-
dependence, were almost autonomous and separate from one another
within the framework of the Israeli state. This process took place
through the slow and incremental empowerment of population groups
that in the past had been situated on the margins or excluded from the
Israeli polity, and through the appearance of new populations (as in the
case of the Russians and Ethiopians). These populations became critical
masses that translated into political power, aided by high birthrates and
immigration, as well as by acquisition of new political and social skills.
Previously existing social boundaries were sharpened, and new social
boundaries—located in the new or renewed group identities—were created and established. These boundaries and identities create, recon-
struct, and reinscribe historicity and particularistic collective memories

---

88. But in contrast to most western European countries, this demand has not yet been
articulated in real political parties or movements.

that retell the history both of the state in general and of the group itself, and its place within the whole, in a different way than had been previously accepted.

A marriage market common to all Israelis—or even just Israeli Jews—is almost nonexistent. Owing to different boundaries and degrees of Kashrut certification, there is no "common table" that makes it possible for different Israelis to dine together. Housing is almost completely segregated, and patterns of consumption, lifestyle, and apparel are identifiably separate. Languages, dialects, and codes of speech signal the boundaries of separation or are part of the boundaries themselves.

These cultures also rest on separate institutional and sociopolitical systems, such as schools, houses of worship, religious or civil beliefs, marketing networks, charity funds, and alternative media (print and broadcast) unique to each specific culture. Each culture not only has its own inner codes, which at times are expressed by the existence of a separate system of justice that obligates the community, but also holds different perceptions of the rules of the game and of the desirable division of state resources. Thus, a number of separate Israeli cultures and identities have been created: (a) national religious; (b) Orthodox nationalist (Jewish but non-Zionist); (c) Sephardic traditional; (d) Israeli Arab; (e) middle-class secular, (f) Russian-speaking; and (g) Ethiopian. The addition of the Russians and Ethiopians (not to mention foreign guest workers) to Israeli society has intensified the heterogenization of the Israeli system. For the first time, new immigrants have contributed to a profound change in the system more than the Israeli system has changed the new immigrants.

No sooner had it been created than the state established a civilian and military bureaucratic mechanism that, backed by nonstate bodies and mechanisms that it co-opted, infiltrated the peripheries of Israeli society and exerted tight oversight and control of them and their mobilization for state ends.[89] In addition, the state created a new secular bourgeois middle class of veterans, the third generation of which has given its complete loyalty to Israel regardless of the prevailing government or regime, even through the end of the fifth decade since its establishment. Over time, this class has absorbed Mizrahi groups and individuals, and even Arabs, both as individuals and families. It includes administrative, economic, professional, and cultural elites, and is essen-

---

89. Such as some of the political parties, the Jewish Agency, the Jewish National Fund, and the all-encompassing labor union, Histadrut.

tially the context in which the hegemonic "Israeli culture," Israeli civil identity, and what I have called "Israeliness" were constructed and cultivated. Recently, both this class and the power of the state have been in relative decline, and it is rapidly losing its hegemonic cultural dominance, but it has still succeeded in preserving its centrality as a class. It still maintains primary control of large businesses, commerce and industry, the media establishment, and the upper echelons of the armed forces and of higher education, although its dominant position has begun to be eroded in these areas as well. At times, there has been a partial overlapping among the different groups and cultures, but for the most part the boundaries have remained sharp and impermeable, and the differences are greater than the commonalties. Moreover, opinions as to the best way to handle the Jewish-Arab conflict and relations (see chapter 7) are partially overlapping, cutting across, and regrouping the cultures and countercultures discussed in this chapter.

Thus, when national religious Judaism succeeded in breaking the secular socialist national hegemony and in moving to the center of the social arena, it also unintentionally paved the way for the establishment of other autonomous cultures, with different degrees of separatism within the Israeli state. It also enabled the expansion both of the autonomy and of the increasing participation of Arab citizens in the state. A path was opened that allowed for institution-building by different cultures, without the development of an ideology that legitimized multiculturalism. At the same time, the formation of these cultures did not undo, and perhaps even strengthened, the identity and primordial loyalties of extensive segments of the Jewish population. The elections of 1996 and 1999 erased any doubt that may have existed about this. The new electoral system not only reflected the existence of, but also politically strengthened, central sectors of the autonomous cultures, which because of their high dependence on the state cannot be regarded as independent civil societies, despite having some traits in common with such entities. It also emphasized the extent of a common Jewishness and ethnocentrism, although expressed to different degrees and in different ways in each of the Jewish cultures.

However, when the Labor party regained power following the 1999 elections, owing to the massive support of the Arab citizenry, in his anxiety to establish the legitimacy of his government, the party's new leader again excluded Arabs from the foci of power. Later, when a violent new crisis erupted between Israel and the Palestinian authority (the so-called al-Aqsa intifada), and Arab citizens demonstrated in solidarity with the Palestinian struggle, the Israeli police overreacted in their response, using live ammunition. Thirteen Arabs were killed and several hundred wounded. This outraged the Arab population, who saw it as yet another massacre of Arabs by Jews, like those that had occurred at Dier Yassin in 1948 and Kafar Qassam in 1956. Arab anger and frustration only increased when the Israeli authorities and most of the Jewish public showed themselves completely indifferent. Most Israeli Arab citizens boycotted the February 2001 elections as a result, denying Labor party leader Ehud Barak their community's traditional support. For the first time, the Arab electorate acted independently of the rest of the Israeli electorate.

Some analysts have interpreted the boycott as the withdrawal of the Israeli Arabs from the state, from their Israeliness, and from the political arena. However, the meaning of this collective act was quite the opposite. The aim of the boycott was to indicate to the Israeli state, especially the political left (namely, the Labor and Meretz parties) that the support of Arab voters can no longer be considered self-evident, and that they demand an equal voice in the Israeli polity's critical decision-making.

CHAPTER 6

The Cultural Code of Jewishness

Religion and Nationalism

Despite the segmentation of the Israeli state into seven cultures and countercultures, two common metacultural codes or narratives remain intact for at least most Jewish citizens of the state. The first code is the power-oriented "securitistic" one, which is analyzed in chapter 7. The other is a local Israeli version of "Jewishness." The main characteristic of the social and political order in Israel is its definition as a "Jewish state," in large measure blurring the boundaries between nationalism and religion in many societal spaces. This situation is expressed in a taken-for-granted equivalency between the Jewish religion, on the one hand, and Jewish, as well as Israeli, nationalism and its expressions in the cultural, political, and judicial system, on the other. These codes are common to both the right and the left, to Ashkenazim and Mizrahim, to the poor and the rich, to women and men, and to the religious—in their various degrees and hues—as well as to the secular.

Even after the all-encompassing secular Ashkenazi nationalistic hegemony and social order was dismantled, two initial components of the original hegemonic "basket" still persisted. Moreover, because most other ingredients of the hegemonic situation vanished, those that remained became more salient. The present chapter analyzes one of the most significant components, namely, Jewish primordialism and its institutional and legal consequences. This component is usually found above public debate and outside it; a social situation that is unchallengeable, because there are not yet even terms and concepts by means of which to characterize and question it. The cultural, social, economic, and constitutional conditions of primordialism reinforce one another, raising the "Jewish consensus" above all other conflicting cultures. Thus, this order is accepted and comfortable to all those within the boundaries of the consensus.[1]

In daily behavior and self-identification, most of the Jewish population of Israel is secular. There are even those who wage cultural (or religious) war on state imposition of religious behavior or halachic rules. Nevertheless, in terms of collective national identity, the great majority of the Jewish public in the Israeli state relate to an identity defined, as previously demonstrated, in large part by terms, values, symbols, and collective memory still anchored in the Jewish religion, as it was constructed before the constitution of the state and Israeliness.[2] In other words, there are secular Jews and secular cultural life in Israel, but it is highly doubtful whether a secular Israeli Judaism exists or could be constructed. Judaism as constructed and developed in Israel and secularism have been mutually exclusive. At the same time, however, the state is also administered by universal and secular codes drawn from what is called "Western culture." Without these codes, it would be impossible to administer a modern state and to maintain Israel's military might, a relatively developed economy, and all the other mechanisms of a strong, highly developed state. These values do not necessarily stand in contradiction to the "Jewishness" of the state, despite the constant tension between them. The two conflicting value systems are usually managed by compartmentalization and the application of different values in different contexts and social spheres.

Israel is thus, in fact, a democracy only within the parameters fixed by a particular interpretation of "Jewishness," and the Israeli state fluctuates between secular liberal democracy and nationalist theocracy. Only those outside the "Jewish consensus," such as Arab Israeli citizens, a few secular Jewish women, and a handful of secular Jewish men, can fully appreciate this (see chapter 5), and lacking meaningful common ground with the occupants of the Jewish bubble, they are unable to

1. Israel is also by no means a "consociational democracy," as has been suggested by some social scientists. Representatives of separate ethnic, religious, or national segments make no major decisions with regard to matters of common concern. For the general concept, see Lijphart, *Democracies in Plural Societies*. For a recent application to the Israeli case, see Dowty, *The Jewish State*, pp. 32–33.
2. See Kimmerling, "Between the Primordial and the Civil Definitions of the Collective Identity."

communicate with them. The situation can be dramatically demonstrated by analyzing the position and the legal status of women in Israel.

THE CONSTRUCTION OF WOMANHOOD

Women do not constitute a separate culture or counterculture in Israel.
Each of the seven cultures and countercultures surveyed in chapters 4
and 6 of this volume has its own gender cleavage. In fact, women are
the subjects of a double socioeconomic hierarchy: hierarchy between the
cultural groups and hierarchy within the cultural group. Women in most
modern societies (except perhaps in Scandinavia) are, albeit by different
measures, still an underprivileged sociological minority, a situation that
has fueled feminist movements and social theories worldwide. Data on
the condition of women in the labor market indicate that gender inequality in the socioeconomic sphere in Israel resembles that in most
Western states. Occupational segregation of men and women is apparent
in both the public and the private sectors, and women participate less
than men in the labor force. In 1995, 45.5 percent of women worked,
compared with 62.2 percent of men, while 7.9 percent of all women
were unemployed, as opposed to only 5 percent of men.[3] There are also
major differences between the work patterns of men and of women.
Many women hold part-time jobs. In 1994, 72 percent of those who
regularly worked part-time were women. Of all working women, 38.4
percent regularly worked part-time, while the figure was only 20.6 percent for men.[4] Women work an average of 33.7 hours a week, compared
with men's 45.5 hours. Homemaking remains a woman's role and is,
indeed, classified by statutory definition in Israel as exclusively female
for purposes of national security.[5] The second-shift syndrome explains
the female patterns of late entry into the labor market, intermittent labor
force participation, and part-time work.

The average male employee's monthly income in all branches of the
Israeli labor market during the years 1992–93 was 1.7 times higher than
that of the average female employee. In other words, women's average
monthly income was less than 58 percent that of men.[6] This is partly
explained by differences in average weekly work hours. However, the

3. Israel, CEDAW report, p. 126; Israeli Women's Network, "Status of Women in
Israeli Law."
4. Israel, CEDAW report, p. 130
5. Raday, "On Equality," p. 4; Izraeli, "Gender in the Labor World."
6. Israel, CEDAW report, p. 139.

data showed that there was also a wide gap in average hourly income, which was 1.25 times higher for men.[7] In other words, women's hourly income was 80 percent that of the men. Women also constitute 80 percent of workers at the minimum wage level.[8] Although employers are required to pay the legal minimum wage, enforcement is not effective and many women are, in practice, doing full-time jobs for less than minimum wage.

The number of men and women in managerial positions is related to the so-called "glass ceiling" aspect of inequality of opportunity in the workplace. According to the 1995 figures, 6.9 percent of all working men in Israel were managers, while only 2.2 percent of working women were managers, and only 19.5 percent of all managers were women.[9] In the civil service, although the women made up 59.4 percent of all public employees in December 1995, they accounted for only 10.5 percent in the top four grades. The underrepresentation of women in the higher ranks is accentuated, not only by their overrepresentation in the lowest grades, where they constituted 64.2 percent, but also by the fact that they have a higher average number of years of education than their male co-workers.

In most so-called Western liberal democracies, men and women at least formally share equal legal citizenship. In the Israeli immigrant settler state, it is different. Beyond the "usual" discrimination, women in Israel are subject to explicit legal discrimination, directly deriving from the definition of the state as "Jewish" and the unique institutional and constitutional consequences of this. Personal status laws are under the jurisdiction of the rabbinical courts, which rule not according to the laws of the state, but based on the patriarchal Halacha code and its interpretations by Orthodox *dayanim*.[10] Nonetheless, just like the verdicts of state courts, their verdicts are imposed by the state's authority.

Halachic laws and their interpretations blatantly discriminate against women in matters involving marriage, divorce, alimony, support, guardianship, the legitimation and adoption of minors, the property of persons who are legally incompetent, and wills and legacies. Women are not allowed to appear as witnesses in rabbinical courts, although in

7. Raday, "On Equality," p. 67.
8. Efroni, "Trends in the Israeli Payment System."
9. Israel, CEDAW report, p. 139.
10. That is to say, according to the Law of Rabbinical Court Judgment (Marriage and Divorce), 1953, and the Law of Dayanim, 1955. A *dayan* (plural, *dayanim*) is a rabbinical court judge.

recent years some women have been permitted to enter pleas in these courts. The orthodox worldview regards a woman as her husband's property.[11] Given the biblical imperative "Be fruitful, and multiply," she is an instrument for reproducing her husband's individuality and his family and ethnic community (read: the nation). The second-century Mishnaic codification of the Jewish religious canon, which is still held to be valid, states that a woman becomes her husband's property in marriage in one of three ways: by a payment, by contract, or by coition. Mixed marriage in Israel between a Jewish man or woman and a gentile is not possible, unless the gentile has converted according to the strict Orthodox tradition.[12] Mixed marriages contracted abroad are recognized, but if the female partner of the couple is not Jewish, the couple's children are not considered to be or registered as Jews.

Recently, secular family courts have been established to deal with some of these issues, but their authority is limited. They do not have the power to grant divorce or marriage, which remain the prerogative solely of the rabbinical courts. During the colonial period, a person could bypass his religious community (the *millet*) and turn to the civil adjudication of the secular state. Since the establishment of the Jewish nation-state and the transformation of a religious community into a national majority exercising sovereign control by means of its elected institutions, this option has been excluded.[13]

The religious courts and diverse religious cultures of Israel do not, however, reproduce this autonomous concept of womanhood. The sociologist Nitza Berkovitch has analyzed the Israeli parliament's legislation and jurisprudence and legal discourse during the state's formative period and reached the conclusion that women have been constructed, not as equal individual citizens, but first and foremost as mothers and

11. Even today the Hebrew word for "husband" is *baal,* equated with "owner," and the standard and legal term for sexual intercourse, which assumes an act carried out by a male on any female (even if she is not his wife, or even in the case of rape), is "to own" (*li'bol*).

12. Some other marriages are also excluded, such as marriages between male members of the mythical ancient noble priestly tribe (*Cohanim,* or virtually any Jewish male who bears a name such as "Cohen" or "Khun") and a divorced woman (who is considered "impure"). A marriage between any Jew and a person defined or suspected of being a "bastard" (born following a woman's adultery) is also forbidden. These are only a few examples.

13. Recently, increasing numbers of couples have chosen to live together under a civil "marriage contract" (or without any official or contractual commitments) or to marry in neighboring Cyprus. Israeli civil courts recognize civil marriages performed abroad, as well as the inheritance rights of longtime cohabitating unmarried couples.

wives.[14] Even when the legislation has been protective and appears to take affirmative action for women, it takes into consideration mainly their biological reproductive roles and their roles as children-raising mothers. Thus, motherhood has been legally constructed as a public role with great national significance.

Jewish primordialism and the Israeli-Arab conflict reinforced each other in the establishment of the statuses of women and Arabs within the collectivity. In the context of the conflict and overall relations between Arabs (and, in particular, Palestinians) and Israelis, the demographic asymmetry between the two groups became a central factor in both sides' thinking. In Israel, both external (Jewish immigration) and internal (high birthrates) growth became a national imperative. Along with attempts to limit abortions, an intensive policy of family expansion incentives was adopted.[15] The family became a core state value, blurring the boundaries between the private and public spheres.[16]

Berkovitch focuses her analysis on two laws, the Defense Service Law (1949) and the Women's Equal Rights Law (1951). The Defense Service Law, sparsely amended since 1949, imposes universal compulsory service on all physically eligible citizens of the state, with the exception of married or pregnant women, women with children, or women who plead reasons of conscience or religious conviction. The law does not provide the same rights for men to be exempted as fathers or because of religious or conscientious objections. However, it gives the minister of defense discretion to exempt from the draft any individual he sees fit.[17] Only about half of the women of relevant age have been drafted over the years (some have opted instead for "national service," an option not available to males). In practice, too, drafted women have never filled

14. Berkovitch, "Motherhood as a National Mission."
15. This was done mainly by according increased social insurance grants to (Jewish) immigrant families with numerous children. In the early 1950s, Prime Minister David Ben-Gurion offered a special monetary prize on the occasion of the birth of a thirteenth child. Slowly, this demographic policy was abandoned, for essentially internal reasons: the tendency for big families was concentrated among Mizrahi lower-class and Orthodox families, while the Arabs (with the greatest internal natural increase) also demanded equal rights and social welfare benefits in this field. See chapter 5 and Yuval-Davis, *Gender and Nation*, pp. 29–30.
16. See Kimmerling, "Yes, Back to the Family."
17. Accordingly, Muslim and Christian Arabs have never been drafted. Bedouins are allowed to volunteer. Druse are drafted compulsorily. Until 1977, a limited number of Yeshiva students were exempted, but following a later coalition agreement, all ultra-Orthodox youngsters were defined as "Yeshiva students" and were exempted from the service. During early 2000, following increasing secularist protests, some attempts were made to regulate this arrangement.

the same roles as men, although there is no provision for this in the law. They have not been incorporated into combat units and have historically held only traditionally female jobs, serving as secretaries, nurses, teachers, and in other auxiliary roles.[18] Women's military service in Israel, long presented as major sign of their equality and liberation, is in fact just another mechanism for reproducing the traditional gender-based division of labor. "Whoever is worried about Jewish demography should worry about the [Jewish] family," one member of parliament said. "We cannot afford to draft married women, because it will decrease the birthrate."[19]

The Women's Equal Rights Law of 1951, which deals directly with the state's duty to provide equal rights for all women, begins with the preamble that "from the beginning of the movement to return to Zion, the Jewish woman was *a loyal companion* to the early immigrants and settlers" (emphasis added). Women are thus considered to have been merely companions to the founding fathers, not "pioneers" themselves. Presenting the Equal Rights Law, the Ministry of Justice declared that "in fulfilling her duty and privilege as a Hebrew mother cherishing the young generation and educating them . . . the Hebrew woman and mother continues the great tradition of the Israeli heroine."[20] Following the passage of the law, the status of women in Israel actually improved considerably. For example, women's equal rights as parents, including guardianship rights, were recognized. The total loss of a woman's property rights upon marriage was also abolished. Still, the Israeli legal scholar Pnina Lahav asserted that the law "looked at the woman [only as] a mother and a wife."[21] Since then, there have been many other laws passed and court decisions issued favorable to women, but the Israeli state's basic attitude to women's citizenship has continued to emphasize their biological and sociological role as mothers and wives.

---

18. During the 1948 war, a few young women participated actively on the battlefield. Recently, more semi-combatant roles were opened to drafted women (such as in armored units and as artillery instructors). In an unprecedented High Court decision, the military was obliged to allow women to be trained as fighter pilots. See *Miller* v. *Minister of Defense et al.*, 49 (4) P.D. 94. HC 4541/1994.

19. Berkovitch, "Motherhood as a National Mission," p. 610.

20. Ibid.

21. Lahav, "When the 'Palliative' Just Spoils Things."

THE CONSTRUCTION OF A DEMOCRACY

Israeli and Western scholars generally consider Israel to be a democracy. Over the past fifty years, dozens of books have analyzed it as such, although recognizing "imperfections" and limitations, especially as regards the inequality of Israel's Arab citizens and the oppressive treatment of the Palestinian inhabitants of the occupied territories.[22] These "imperfections" have very conveniently been attributed mainly to external and situational factors, such as Israel's protracted conflict with its environment. It has been presumed that once the conflict is terminated, these major deviations from the liberal democratic model will be corrected. All these scholars have emphasized the existence of structural conditions for a viable democratic regime in Israel. For example, Israel has a government established as a result of free elections and universal suffrage and a pretty good separation of powers between the executive, legislative, and judicial branches of government. Israeli citizens (mainly Jewish citizens) enjoy innumerable civil rights and liberties, resembling those in the most "perfect" liberal democracies in the Western world.

The aim of this chapter is to analyze the Israeli state's cultural-constitutional regime more closely in the historical and ideological context of its national identity, in order to examine the limits of its democracy in some crucial areas. Some researchers have called the Israeli regime an "ethnic democracy," in which the dominant ethnos (i.e., the Jews) enjoy collective rights, while minorities have rights only as individuals.[23] The assumption is that as citizens of a Jewish nation-state, Jews in Israel are entitled to "collective rights," whereas Arabs are only entitled to rights as individual citizens. The closest approach to mine is Oren Yiftachel's definition of the Israeli state as an ethnocracy. He suggests that in an ethnocracy, one ethno-nation attempts to extend or preserve its disproportional control over contested territories and rival nation(s). This also typically results in the creation of stratified ethno-classes within each nation. Notable examples comparable to Is-

22. Under the Emergency Regulations inherited from the British colonial regime, anyone suspected of subversive action or intention can be detained for an infinite period without trial, his or her property can be expropriated without any justification being provided by the state, and his or her house can be demolished. Israeli political culture has permitted the government to use such measures only against Arab citizens, but this is also highly indicative of the regime's nature.

23. See Smooha, "Minority Status in an Ethnic Democracy"; Peled, "Ethnic Democracy and the Legal Construction of Citizenship." In his book *The Idea of Judaism as a Culture*, Eliezer Schweid uses the term "Jewish democracy."

rael, according to Yiftachel, are Malaysia, Sri Lanka, Estonia, Latvia, Serbia, and Slovakia.[24] This characterization, however, only partially diagnoses the sociocultural and constitutional nature of the Israeli state, where ethnicity and nationalism are inseparably intermingled.

In fact, the term "democracy" has no one conclusive theoretical definition or even agreed-upon set of empirical manifestations.[25] According to all existing definitions, no actual political regime can be classified as a "complete" or "pure" democracy; rather, regimes are located on a continuum between the poles of democracy/nondemocracy. Moreover, multiple paths to democracy exist. Nonetheless, classification of any regime as "democratic" demands five *necessary* (although not sufficient) *conditions*. These conditions seem to include:

1. Periodic free elections, including the possibility of changing the ruling political elites or parties through such elections.

2. Sovereignty of the people, exercised through a legislative system constructed by a parliament, according to which the judicial system operates.[26] No independent or parallel legislative and judicial system can be created by the state.

3. Equal and inclusive citizenship and civil rights.

4. Universal suffrage where every vote is equal.

5. Protection of the civil and human rights of minorities from the tyranny of the majority.

Given the nature of the Israeli "reality," as described in this book (see also chapter 5), it is easy to conclude that only one of the five necessary conditions for considering Israel a democracy is present. Despite attempts in the 1960s and 1970s to define Israel as a liberal democratic and socialistic state, the conditions described above make apparent the difficulty in applying the liberal democratic model to Israel. The main reason for this is the historically inherent inability to separate religion from nationalism and nationality implicit in the "Jewishness" of the Israeli state.

24. See Yiftachel, "Israeli Society and Jewish-Palestinian Reconciliation."
25. See Collier and Levitsky, "Democracy with Adjectives"; Dawisha, "Democratization and Political Participation."
26. If the parliament decides to give up its sovereignty over certain domains of the public sphere to another legislative body, the act is interpreted as giving up democracy by "democratic means."

The Israeli state is one of the strongest in the world in terms of control of its material resources and its ability to enlist the population in times of war and emergency; these conditions have remained the same since its constitution (as demonstrated in chapter 2). In addition, the basis of belonging and the criteria for measuring enjoyment of rights in the state is ethnic-religious, as argued throughout this book. The state is defined as belonging, not only to its citizens, but to the entire Jewish people— a major deviation from any acceptable definition of liberal democracy. Rights within the state are determined more according to ethnic-national religious belonging than according to citizenship.

Israeli political culture and most of its academic analysts, however, systematically and compulsively deny the basically undemocratic nature of the Israeli regime. This is, of course, understandable, not only because Jewish Israelis' self-image identifies Israel as a Western democratic nation, but also because being seen as democratic is a powerful mechanism for generating legitimacy, both internally and externally.

STATE AND ETHNICITY

At least three basic laws,[27] and one additional regular law, state the dual commitment of Israel as a "Jewish and democratic state." However, the definition of its "Jewishness" that the state itself has adopted makes these two concepts, "democracy" and "Jewishness," mutually contradictory in some respects. Much of Israeli practice hardly conforms to usually accepted notions of Western liberal and enlightened democracy. Israel inherited what is known as the *millet* system from both the Ottoman Empire and the British colonial administration.[28] This system provided that "religious-ethnic" communities enjoy a degree of auton-

27. See "Basic Law: Knesset," "Basic Law: Freedom of Occupation (1992)," and "Basic Law: Human Dignity and Liberty (1992)." The additional "regular" law is the Parties' Law. A basic law is one passed by a special majority of the Knesset and intended to be incorporated in any future written constitution (Israel lacks a written constitution at present).

28. Since 1948, the Israeli government has recognized certain established religious groups, whose leaders are granted special status, even when they are tiny minorities. These communities are entitled to state financial support and tax exemptions. Under Israeli law, all residents must belong to a religious denomination, whose rules they are obliged to follow with regard to marriage, divorce, and burial. British colonial rule recognized Islam, Judaism, and nine Christian denominations as *millet*. The Israeli state recognized the Druse in 1957, the Evangelical Episcopal Church in 1970, and the Baha'is in 1971. Muslims have not been officially recognized, but their religious courts de facto have similar authority to a *millet* institution. All other groups, from Conservative and Reform Jews to new sects (i.e., cults), are not recognized.

omy from the state and sole jurisdiction in matters of personal status litigation. Even before it was established as a sovereign entity, the founders of Israel decided to preserve this institution and construct a *millet* form of citizenship. Citizens were thus subjected to two legal and judicial systems, which are separate and operate according to different, and even opposing, principles. One is secular, "Western," and universalistic; the other is religious, primordial, and patriarchal, and is mainly run—as far as Jews are concerned—according to the Orthodox interpretation of Halacha. The minorities, who were thus defined ab initio as religious minorities, were also forced to conduct their "autonomous" lives in accordance with this dual system.

The Israeli parliament (Knesset) has to this extent given up its authority to legislate in crucial areas and recognized a parallel legal and judicial system outside its control. In fact, the state obligated itself to treat Halacha, Shari'a (Islamic law), and diverse Christian denominational rules as if they were its own laws.

Jewish religious elements have been incorporated into other areas of legislation as well, such as the "Work Hours and Days of Rest Law," the "Freedom of Occupation Law," and the like. In contrast to these, the "Law of Return" and "Law of Citizenship," immigration laws intended to establish a sort of "affirmative action" (or corrective discrimination) on behalf of world Jewry after the Holocaust, were relatively liberal ordinances as far as Jews were concerned, but highly discriminatory both against the Palestinians who fled or were forced to flee from the territory that fell under the rule of the new state and against those who remained and who were for the most part denied family reunification.

Although the laws of Return and Citizenship are based on the theological definition of Judaism,[29] in practice these ethno-national affirmative action laws grant Israeli citizenship (and define the boundaries of Judaism) more or less in accordance with the broader definition of the Nazi Nuremberg Laws. The logic underlying this was internally consistent and justified, as these laws were intended to enable the granting of citizenship to almost everyone who suffered persecution as a Jew, mainly during the Holocaust and World War II, even if those concerned

---

29. A Jew is defined as one born to a Jewish mother or "converted according to Halacha." However, the law does not include this crucial last phrase, thus allowing non-Orthodox converts (abroad) and even family members who are not converts to enter and enjoy the privileges granted by the Law of Return.

did not fall under the halachic definition of Jewishness. If the laws of Return and Citizenship have been among the most problematic laws in Israel until now, they nevertheless preserved relatively open "Jewish" boundaries. The recently proposed Conversion Law, which provides that the state recognize only Orthodox conversions to Judaism, is apparently intended to give Jewish Orthodoxy a monopoly on determining the boundaries of the collectivity.

Complementing the laws of Return and Citizenship is the Law on the Status of the World Zionist Organization (of the Jewish Agency), which also facilitates the granting of particularistic benefits only to Jewish citizens of the state. For many years, too, the Social Security Law was complemented by a set of welfare laws under which the only eligible beneficiaries were former soldiers and their families, unsubtly constructing a broad separation between Jewish and Arab citizens. Similarly, the agreement between the Jewish National Fund and the Israel Lands Authority prevents the leasing of state lands, which are 93 percent of the territory inside the Green Line,[30] to non-Jews. A recent unprecedented ruling of the High Court of Justice challenged this situation, but the challenge has not yet had any institutional consequences.[31]

One must also take into account the long-term role of the courts and the High Court of Justice. Although they have taken much care, especially in recent years, to promote a proper, "enlightened," law-governed state, this has been done only within the framework of the Jewish social and political boundaries of the state. Thus, in the 1950s and 1960s, the courts were one of the most active mechanisms for the dispossession of Arab citizens from their lands and afforded no relief to the victims of the infamous military administration.[32] The High Court of Justice ruled that its jurisdiction also extended to the acts of the Israeli authorities in the occupied territories. In the great majority of cases brought before it, however, whenever the authorities have claimed that "state security" was involved, the High Court has tended to accept this claim without

30. The 1949 armistice line agreed between Israel and the Arab states following the 1948 war.

31. This happened in the "Katzir affair" (2000), in which Adel and Iman Qadan, a couple from Baka al-Garbiya, sought to purchase a plot of land for the purpose of building their home in the settlement of Katzir in Wadi Ara, south of Hadera. The council clerk of Tel-Eiron refused to sell them the land, because official policy prohibits selling land to non-Jews. The petition was filed in the name of the Association for Civil Rights in Israel. The president of the Supreme Court, Aharon Barak, tried to avoid ruling, as in other "sensitive" cases, and suggested that the sides try to reach an out-of-court settlement.

32. From 1948 to 1965, Arab citizens of Israel were subject to a permanent military curfew and needed special permits to leave their immediate locality (see chapter 7).

examining it and without attempting to define the meaning and content of the term "security." Thus, its jurisdiction has extended to everything except whatever the state has defined as a security-related issue.

Perhaps the most conspicuous example of this is the systematic sanctioning by the High Court of Israel's blatant violation of international law in allowing Jewish settlement of the occupied Arab territories.[33] International law forbids an occupying power to make any substantial changes in the status of occupied territories, except for reasons of security. Accordingly, in the present situation, from the perspective of the High Court, all the settlements in the occupied territories were built for security reasons. This is an astonishing and problematic expansion of the concept of "security." The same justification was used by the High Court when it permitted individual and mass deportations and the use of torture during interrogations.

All this has taken place at the most institutionalized level, which allows one to consider it as the constitutional level. The general political culture, too, has also set a number of norms not usually considered pillars of a democratic political culture. For example, a government coalition that includes parties defined as "Arab" or a piece of legislation that depends on "non-Jewish votes" is widely considered "illegitimate." Such a perspective constitutes a gross violation of the basic principle of "one person, one vote."

AN IMMIGRANT SETTLER
SOCIETY IN SEARCH OF LEGITIMACY

However, even the absence of the distinction between religion and nation is not the primary cause of the difficulty in regarding Israel as a liberal democracy, which lies in the basic nature of the Israeli state. Israel was founded as an immigrant settler frontier state and is still an active immigrant society, engaged in a settlement and territorial expansion process down to the present day. Despite the constant rapid transformation of Israel, institutionally and culturally, it remains a settler society, living by the sword because it needs to make space for itself in limited terrain.

33. Article 49 of the 1949 Fourth Geneva Convention states that "the occupying power shall not deport or transfer parts of its own civilian population into the territory it occupies." For a more detailed discussion of this issue, see Hofnung, *Law, Democracy and National Security in Israel*. Recently, the UN redefined such population transfer as a war crime.

Zionism, the national movement that motivated a part of the Jewish immigration and settlement, and was also formed by it, was sophisticated enough to distance itself from the global colonial context, which was the matrix out of which it was born. Zionism emphasized the uniqueness of the "Jewish problem," anti-Semitism, persecutions, and later the Holocaust, and presented itself as the sole realistic and moral solution to these. Thus, the Jewish immigration movement was successfully represented as a "return to Zion," correcting a cosmic injustice that had lasted for thousands of years, and as totally disconnected from the movements of European immigration to other continents.

The fact that Jewish immigration and settlement were construed in Zionist terms does not, however, change the fact that Israel is a society established mostly by immigrants whose ethnic, religious, and cultural background differed from that of the broad local population. Moreover, it saw (and sees) itself as "Western." In the political culture of the postcolonial world order, this is a society plagued by the problem of existential legitimacy. It has repeatedly had to explain to itself and to the international community why it chose Palestine, retitled "The Land of Israel," for settlement. It was not chosen for its fertile soil, its natural resources, the cheap labor to be found there, or its potential markets; rather, it was chosen for ideological-religious reasons.[34] This fact turned the Zionist project, not only into a venture that was not self-supporting from an economic point of view, but also into an essentially religion-based project, unable to disconnect itself from its original identity as a quasi-messianic movement. The essence of this society and state's right and reason to exist is embedded in religious symbols, ideas, and scriptures, even if there has been an attempt to give them a secular reinterpretation and context.

SECULARIZATION OF A NATIONALISM

In order to understand this unusual phenomenon, one must dig deep into the history of the Jewish national movement. Looking at Zionism from a macroscopic perspective, it is possible to locate two central goals: (a) the reconstruction or reinvention of Judaism as an essentially modern and secular national movement, rather than a religion or civilization, thus defining the "Jewish problem" in political, national, and secular terms; and (b) the need to recruit and optimally concentrate Jews within

34. See Kimmerling, *Zionism and Economy* and *Zionism and Territory*, ch. 7.

a territorial framework to enable the establishment of an independent political entity. From the very beginning, there were contradictions and tensions between these two goals. These contradictions and tensions led to the constitution of a social order—the shape of the society and state, political culture, and the general culture of Israel, as we know them today—that can be characterized as mixing democracy with theocracy. The national religious system and the secular liberal democratic system in Israel are incompatible, but at the same time complement each other—the one cannot exist without the other.

Most of the forerunners and builders of the national Jewish movement as an idea and as a social and political movement were secular. Figures such as Leo Pinsker, Theodor Herzl, Max Nordau, Jacob Klatzkin, and Micha Joseph Berditschevsky adopted strong secularist ideologies, because at that time it was only in those terms that one could think of modern nationalism.[35] Their nationalism was generally not purely constructed, but was intermingled with other ideologies, such as classical liberalism and varieties of socialism, including communism.[36] It is necessary also to remember that the beginnings of Jewish national thought and activity were shaped at the end of the colonialist era, when Jewish migration was intertwined with large-scale intercontinental population movements. That was the era when the formation and construction of immigrant settler nations was still at its height. European colonialism was the dominant world order, and Eurocentrism was the hegemonic cultural approach.

Jewish religious nationalists, or people who came to Zionism with a religious outlook, were a negligible and marginal minority within the Jewish religious collectivity, because religious principles did not permit "forcing the End,"[37] or achieving collective redemption without divine intervention. Despite this, the religious worldview looked positively on ascent (aliyah) to the Holy Land. Still, the religious-national mixture was a relatively marginal phenomenon, which demanded very great intellectual interpretive and reinterpretative efforts. Even today, its theological standing within Judaism is shaky and problematic.[38]

35. See Avineri, Making of Modern Zionism; Laqueur, History of Zionism; Vital, Origins of Zionism.

36. See Kimmerling, "Between the Primordial and the Civil Definitions of the Collective Identity."

37. See, for example, Ravitzky, Messianism, Zionism, and Jewish Religious Radicalism, appendix.

38. Friedman, "The State of Israel as a Theological Dilemma."

Thus, for example, the first rabbi who can be classified as a "Zionist," Samuel Mohilever, was more concerned with persuading secular Jews to consider the sensitivities of fervently observant Jews than he was with the theological problems of a return to Zion in his day. Practically speaking, Mohilever failed in his mission to achieve an understanding among the founding fathers of Zionism, and he played a part in the split that started between the religious and secular components of the movement. With this, the foundations were laid for the beginnings of the Mizrahi (short for *mercaz ruchani,* spiritual center) movement, which in 1902 incorporated the group of Rabbi Isaac Jacob Reines.[39]

The appearance of Zionism as a political movement forced the great and mighty camp of the *haredim*[40] to organize politically, too. They began to come together in eastern Europe and even in the west (especially in Germany) as a political party, which could hold its own against Zionism and secularization in the general political (gentile) sphere. Agudat Israel was founded in 1912 in Poland and in Germany (and even ran in elections to the Polish parliament) in order to represent the "true Jew in the world" through the modern and democratic means that emancipation had provided. The other major aim was not to abandon the political arena to assimilators and secularizers—and even worse, to the carriers of false messianism, which Zionism was considered to be. Agudat Israel was the largest organized Jewish political force in Europe until the Holocaust and also represented Jews who were not completely Orthodox but had not disconnected from religion and tradition and wished to demonstrate their patriotic loyalty to the land of their residence. In this way, the lifestyle of secular intellectuals like Moses Mendelssohn, a "German (or Pole) of the Mosaic religion," distinguishing between public and private spheres, made its way into the Lithuanian and Hassidic courts.

But when the secular thinkers and activists of the national Jewish movement sought to define the territorial framework in which the national collectivity would be established, they were compelled to choose

39. Isaac Reines (1839–1915) was an Orthodox rabbi of the community of Lida who called for some adaptation of Halacha to the modernizing world, in order to prevent the secularization of the Jews. He first joined the Lovers of Zion movement and later Herzl's "political Zionism." His major approach was that Zionism should be a genuine religious movement.

40. Plural of *haredi,* referring to the heterogeneous Orthodox and ultra-Orthodox currents in Judaism.

Zion, the religiously sanctified Eretz Israel (Land of Israel). This was done despite the many potential alternatives apparently available to them, including nonterritorial and supraterritorial alternatives, and despite their being clearly secularists and even socialists. In effect, the territorial aim was determined at the fetal and apolitical stage of the Jewish national movement, in the Hovevei Zion ("Lover of Zion") period, prior to its consolidation as a modern national political movement. This choice was not taken for granted from the beginning, but was also not accidental. The territorial goal was forced on them, in practice, because the "Land of Israel" was the only territorial space that from the start had a value and an emotional attachment among a critical mass of Jews. This attachment to the "Land of Israel," or the "Holy Land," was mediated by the host of traditional religious associations and symbols they embodied.

It quickly became apparent to the secular visionaries of the Jewish national idea that it was only to the "Holy Land" that it would be possible to enlist Jews for emigration in search of *collective redemption,* as opposed to emigration to lands such as the United States or Argentina for the sake of individual salvation. Only the dialectically desanctified "Holy Land" had significance within the Jewish conceptual framework. Universalistic ideologies such as communism, socialism, and liberalism challenged this approach, offering participation instead in movements supposed to redeem the entire "world" through emancipation, democratization, and assorted industrial or sociopolitical revolutions, and promising a solution to the "Jewish problem" as a by-product. Moreover, from the beginning, there was a preference among the Jewish collectivity for seeking *individual redemption* in the form of emigration to North America.

Emigration to America did not demand ideological or theological decisions or dilemmas, and the personal cost was thus less. It even carried within it a multiplicity of options. Emigration to North America made it possible, at least in principle, for Jews to maintain an Orthodox religious lifestyle and to be absorbed once again into a local, supportive, and partially segregated traditional community. Conversely, it made possible Jewish political movements on the basis of universal ideals.[41] Finally, they were able to come out "into the light"—to enlightenment and modernity. Moreover, they could even go completely outside the boundaries of Judaism and become completely embedded in non-Jewish

41. See Peled, *Class and Ethnicity in the Pale.*

society through a change of personal and collective identity, which was required in any case in the course of emigration.

. . . AND THE SECULARIZATION OF A NATION

It is also important to remember that the Jewish religion preceded its law and in its various versions and incarnations included clear proto-nationalist principles.[42] But these historically manifested themselves only in millenary movements, such as Shabbateanism, that adopted a "false messianism" confusing concrete, present time and place with transcendental time and place.

The construction of Judaism as a nationality, giving it historical depth and analyzing it systematically according to nineteenth-century European national concepts, should be credited to historians like Heinrich Graetz and, later, Simon Dubnow. The historiographical projects of these two historians had tremendous influence in the construction of collective consciousness and of a coherent collective identity and memory, which are necessary conditions for thinking and acting in national terms. Although both Graetz and also Dubnow saw Judaism essentially as a "civilization," and not as a national entity, their contributions to the construction of Judaism as nationalism were decisive. Both Graetz and Dubnow, who used Jewish (especially religious) and non-Jewish sources and texts equally, took as a given invented Judaism as an ancient nationality. They included, among the expressions of this nationalism, the religion that was, according to both, a national preservation mechanism in a state of deterritorialized nationality and absence of sovereignty. Dubnow, however, thought that the Jews had been transformed into a European nation, and that it was incumbent upon them to demand the status of a national minority within the European and American nation-states.

Some writers of the Jewish enlightenment movement also made weighty, even if indirect, contributions to the consolidation of the Jewish national consciousness, notably Abraham Mapu, who in his well-known novel, in the French Romantic spirit, *The Shepherd-Prince* (1845) suc-

---

42. For example, most of A. D. Smith's argument about the ancient nuclei of nationalism (see his *Ethnic Origins of Nations*, "Myth of the 'Modern Nation' and the Myths of Nations," and "Zionism and Diaspora Nationalism") as contrary to the thesis of its being a modern invention (as argued by Ernest Gellner, in, e.g., *Nations and Nationalism*) is based on the "Zionist case."

ceeded in creating the sense of Jewish everyday life in the framework of the legendary Jewish kingdom in the Holy Land.

Zionism therefore adopted some central ingredients of the Jewish religion, but gave them different meanings and put them in another context, which included:

1. The definition of the boundaries of the collectivity as including all of world Jewry in one single imaginary community.[43]

2. The target territory, Palestine, viewed from the a priori perspective that emigration from Europe and establishing a society on another continent and amid other peoples was an acceptable and legitimate practice in the context of the European colonial world order.

3. Components selectively taken from among the religious symbols of Judaism, including the holy tongue, Hebrew, and the attempt to secularize and hierarchize it and transform it into a modern everyday language.[44]

4. Expropriation and historicization of the Bible, especially the books of Joshua, Isaiah, and Amos. The Book of Joshua provided the muscular and militaristic dimension of conquest and the annihilation of the Canaanites and other ancient peoples that populated the "Promised Land,"[45] as mentioned in chapter 1, while the books of Isaiah and Amos were considered as preaching social justice and equality, equated with a kind of proto-socialism.

Judaism as a religion and a civilization, as it developed in "exile," was distanced from the biblical texts and focused instead on creating different bodies of knowledge and culture, in particular the Babylonian

43. At the time that meant only European and American Jewish communities. The Jewish communities in Arab lands were a minority among world Jewry (about 6–8 percent) and were outside the consciousness of European Zionists.

44. Ironically, the daily (European) secular "Jewish" language, Yiddish, and its rich and multifaceted culture were rejected and became the symbol of those principles of Judaism as a civilization that should not be taken seriously, but rather rejected. The adoption of the holy tongue and religious symbols was nothing revolutionary. The previous generation of the Jewish enlightenment movement had already created a body of knowledge and a body of culture that, while it was greatly inferior in richness and variety to the Yiddish culture, was able to provide the combination of the holy and the profane that Zionism needed.

45. The Book of Joshua contains one of the most ancient descriptions of ethnic cleansing.

Talmud and Responsa literature of the rabbis (*poskim*). The rabbis—a great innovation in Judaism—were the source of a new type of knowledge that allowed complete adjustment to the place, the time, and the context of Jewish existence within non-Jewish power frameworks, even those hostile to Jews and Judaism. Thus a new culture was created, and law and order were established within the community. New interpretations were given, not only to Judaism, but also to the entire cosmic order, through emphasis on the local culture and institutions, while "all of Judaism" was transferred to the abstract plane. The majority of rabbis, in fact, drew their authority from general knowledge of theology and often also of mysticism (the Kabbalah), but the source of power was usually anchored in the local community, of which the rabbi was the guide.

The Bible, whose birth and construction was in the land from which the Jews were exiled, not accidentally had a marginal place in rabbinical culture and theology. Its relevance to actual Jewish life and "continuity" was minimal, despite its being, among other things, a moral-religious text. And if use was made of it, it was a chance, selective usage, mainly of the tales of the Pentateuch, particularly as a textbook for small boys attending the *heder*.[46] It is no wonder, therefore, that Zionism adopted the Bible, redefined it as a national historical text, and tried to transform it into the primary mythical infrastructure for a new historiography of Judaism as a nationality. Despite its secularization, the Bible remained a religious morality text based on a binary opposition between those "who do good in the eyes of God" and are rewarded and those "who do evil in the eyes of God," and receive their due punishment.[47]

Rachel Yannait Ben Zvi, one of the few Zionist founding-mothers, says that immediately upon her immigration to Palestine, her socialist-secular Ha'poel Hatzair buddies took her on field trips to "holy" sites. With Bible in hand, they tried with great emotion and religiosity to locate and recreate the biblical geography of the country.[48] In the mid 1960s, Dr. George Tamarin, a social psychologist, pointed out that one of the results of uncritical study of the Bible in the state schools in Israel and the efforts of the educational system to create a "Jewish conscious-

46. The *heder* is a traditional religious elementary school for boys aged 5–8 years old, mainly teaching the basics of the Hebrew alphabet and the moral stories of the Chumash (or Pentateuch).
47. There may nonetheless be "a righteous man and evil befalls him," as in the Book of Job, as well as the reverse.
48. Yannait, *We are Ascending.*

ness" was radical Jewish ethnocentrism among young Israelis.[49] Tamarin based his conclusions on the approach of Piaget, which relates to the development of moral judgment at different stages of maturation. He took as an example the chapter from the Bible that talks of the brutal conquest of the land of Canaan by the legendary military leader of the Hebrew tribes Joshua bin Nun, which was fully approved by most of the students ("that was the accepted behavior at that time") and barely received any moral condemnation. In contrast, the very same actions, when switched to the context of the building of an imaginary ancient Chinese empire, and attributed to a Chinese warrior, were defined by most of the students as genocide, although supposedly occurring at the same historical time.

TOWARD AN ATHEISTIC JUDAISM?

The people of the first wave of contemporary immigration to Palestine (ca. 1882–1900) from Russia and Romania were mainly very devout, modern Orthodox Jews, and their meaningful social unit, alongside the colony (*moshava*), was the traditional family. They intended to establish religious moral communities in the "Land of Israel" and to "worship the Lord" while working the land (see chapter 1). Most of the groups were careful to bring with them three professionals—a rabbi, a ritual circumciser, and an agronomist. Prior to building their own houses and establishing their farms, they erected a synagogue and a ritual bath (*mikveh*) for the good of the collectivity. The people of the second and third waves of immigration (ca. 1904–30) were already different from them by most criteria. They were young immigrants without family responsibilities, without private capital, and espoused more or less established political worldviews. Their social vision was materialist, and they regarded themselves from the beginning as an avant-garde social elite. They established political parties and communal groups, and at least some of them saw themselves as involved in the upcoming world revolution. They rebelled against their parents, and part of this rebellion found expression in active secularism, even atheism. In addition, in their very act of emigrating to the "Land of Israel," with all that this implied, most of them regarded themselves first and foremost as Jews and saw their actions as a national revolution, which for them was often more central than its socialist-universalist context.

49. Tamarin, *Israeli Dilemma*.

They were educated, but were not necessarily of sufficient intellectual stature to be able to articulate for themselves the essence of their secular-nationalist-socialist Judaism, as opposed to the religious Judaism of their parents' generation. Aharon David Gordon, an influential charismatic spiritual leader of the Ha'poel Hatzair faction, tried to create an alternative mix of religion with secular religion for the young immigrants, the so-called "religion of labor." He asked in 1921: "Has the accepted idea [of secular labor Zionism] been sufficiently examined and analyzed critically—is it sufficiently founded in logic and in the human spirit—that with the loss of the basis for blind faith, the basis for religion has also been destroyed?" He proposed to distinguish between "blind faith" and a flexible, selective, and critical religious faith, and to retain Yom Kippur, for example.[50]

In thoroughly examining the cultural baggage that the people of the second and third immigration waves brought with them, and their relationship with the Jewish religion, a complicated picture arises. Their "grievance list" condemning Judaism's petrifaction and blindness had already been presented by some of the enlightenment writers.[51] The chalutzim ("pioneers") themselves and the settlers in Palestine were already a sociological generation removed from the "grievances," and, to a certain extent, even something of a reaction to them. Since most of them were the first generation out of the ghetto, they were mostly still anchored in the traditional religious elementary school (the heder). If not one's father, then at least one's grandfather (and it is more difficult to rebel against grandfathers than against fathers) had been what we would classify today as an Orthodox Jew. The writer Micha Josef Berdichevsky eloquently expresses their sense of "the split heart." Berdichevsky emphasized Nietzschean individualism and completely rejected tradition and religion, calling them the work of Balaam and frenziedly reproaching the Talmudic legends and Hassidic court. It may be difficult to regard

50. Gordon, "Our Account with Religion," p. 127. Berl Katznelson, the major practical ideologist of the local Zionist Labor movement and legendary editor of its organ Davar, on the other hand, called for the preservation of Passover and the fixing of Tisha B'Av (the day of both Temples' destruction) as a day of remembrance.

51. Mordechai Zeev Feuerberg, Yehuda Lev Gordon, and Peretz Smolenskin, three well-known writers of the period, all feared the excessive radicalism of the Enlightenment, which they thought was liable to bring about complete assimilation. Moshe Hess praised the literature of the haskalah but warned that it threatened to turn Judaism back into a religion (which, like other religions, could be reformed), rather than a nationality. Hess had been a close collaborator of Karl Marx's, but after the publication of the Communist Manifesto, he dissociated himself from Marx's revolutionary activities and deterministic historicism and adopted a mild socialist attitude, mixed with Jewish nationalism.

Berdichevsky as a full-fledged "Zionist," but he expressed the problematic of his time forcefully, and he and his ideas were well known and read among the "immigrants to Zion."

THE PRE-STATE JEWISH COMMUNITY

The problem of the specific character of the regime and its institutions in the Zionist collectivity (or future state) when it was consolidated into an autonomous entity was not a central issue in the discourse and ideology of Zionism. It appeared as such only some time after the establishment of the sovereign state. It is possible to enumerate several primary reasons for this absence. First, as long as great political, military, social, and economic problems impeded the establishment of this entity, discussion of the character of the regime seemed like "putting the cart before the horse." Second, most of the thinkers, statesmen, and implementers of practical Zionism had, in truth, some kind of initial image of the desired characteristics of the administration of internal affairs, decision-making, allocation mechanisms, and regulation of future internal conflicts.

Thus, the liberal wing of Zionism, as in the case of Herzl or Nordau, envisaged an enlightened, tolerant secular meritocracy. Among the varied socialists, it was envisaged as an egalitarian regime under the guidance of a "proletarian" avant-garde and an elite representing a mixture of class-sectoral interests. These interests were supposed to overlap more or less with the national interest as a whole (through a transition, according to David Ben-Gurion's slogan, "from a class to a nation"). Among the nationalist streams, first priority was given to building national institutions (especially economic and military ones) and myths.

Only later, when some of them became marginalized with regard to the diffusion of political power within the Jewish community, did the problem of "democracy" arise—that is, the question of the mechanism by which different factions would be included, not only in the processes of decision-making and nation-building, but also in the allocation of prestige and of the material resources of the collectivity.

In the religious Zionist stream, aside from the existence of mechanisms for allocating material resources "justly," there was not much interest in the secular regime, since the final objective—even if utopian— was the building of a collectivity ruled as far as possible according to Halacha. This objective at that time was perceived as completely unrealistic by the vast majority of the Yishuv collectivity.

A third reason for the supposed lack of interest within the Jewish collectivity in the nature of the political regime was that this kind of discussion would arouse internal conflicts and enflame the antagonisms and tensions built into the collectivity since its inception. Also, only a minuscule minority of the leadership and the Jewish Zionist population in the territory had any kind of experience of participation in any kind of democratic regime. And, finally, the common "Jewish" basis seemed to promise the construction of a society with a wide social consensus, within which discrimination on the part of Jews (others were not even taken into account) seemed irrelevant, especially vis-à-vis the Arab community.

Moreover, although Jewish immigration to Palestine during the colonial period was limited (relative to that expected and desired from the Zionist perspective), most immigrants were in need of direct or indirect subsidies from the "national funds." Because of this—and because of the pseudo-voluntaristic principles that in essence determined membership in the collectivity—there was a need for tools for the allocation of resources and the determination of rules for such allocation that would more or less win approval from the different elements of the system. This was important, especially on the level of the elites who stood at the heads of the different sectors.

In order to legitimize the rules of the game and the criteria for allocation of resources, the Jewish political system resorted to elections to "national institutions," as well as intraclass and intraorganizational elections, such as the elections to the Histadrut and other ethnic political institutions (such as municipalities).[52]

---

52. The Histadrut, or "Labor Society," was a Jewish labor union. It was not, however, based on restrictive European and American concepts of "unionism," because it had two other purposes. First of all, it aimed at establishing an autonomous "workers' society" that would be self-sufficient from a material and cultural standpoint. As such, the Histadrut operated industrial plants, agricultural and other cooperative enterprises, banks, newspapers, a health insurance company, an employment exchange, and publication houses. For a long time, it was one of Israel's major employers. See Grinberg, *Split Corporatism in Israel*. Second, the Histadrut played a key role in the Jewish-Arab conflict, excluding Arab labor from the Jewish labor market, and, until 1937, running the Haganah, the semi-underground Jewish militia of the colonial period. See Shafir, *Land, Labor and the Origins of the Israeli-Palestinian Conflict*. In elections to the Histadrut Conference in 1927, the Achdut Ha'avodah party won an absolute majority. In 1930, it united with Ha'poel Hatzair and became the Mifleget Poalei Eretz Israel (Mapai) party, which lost its majority in the Histadrut only in the 1994 elections. In 1933, Mapai won a majority in the elections for the Zionist Congress and became the ruling party in the World Zionist Organization. Attempts by the British mandatory authorities to hold general elections for an advisory council encountered opposition first from the Arab side and later from the Jewish side as well.

These elections gave the Jewish system the partial appearance and some of the external trappings of democracy. This was a sort of procedural democracy, lacking most other conditions and freedoms of a liberal democracy,[53] but it was rationalized in terms of the fact that it lacked sovereignty. Along with access to material resources, these quasi-consensual arrangements also gave autonomy to different social elements in the Jewish community. Within this autonomy, individuals found protection and support in the frameworks of different sociopolitical groups, which often took the form of political parties. Thus a sort of internal autonomy was granted to the urban and rural middle classes and to a variety of religious groups, as well as to the political-economic and cultural complex of the "Labor Society" (the so-called *hevrat ovdim*), of course.

Democracy in any Western liberal sense was in any case irrelevant in the context of the British colonial regime, even as moderated by its mandatory status. Jewish Palestine was an immigrant settler society, at least partially mobilized to fight the local Arab population, with a collectivist orientation, and under the leadership of the pupils of various stages of the successful Bolshevik revolution in Russia. Within the Jewish framework, there was also a need for "external groups,"[54] and these were the various "outsiders," or those defined as such, such as the non-Zionist Orthodox, the communists, and later the revisionists. A borderline case was that of the Sephardi "old Yishuv," the Jewish nobility of the Ottoman period, who declined with the change in rule. They could be "inside" or "outside," almost as they chose.

In this fashion, an ethnic communalism was created that more or less answered the needs of most members of the community. The boundaries between "Jewish" identity and "Zionist" identity (as opposed to "Diaspora mentality") were blurred, not only as collective identities but also as organizing principles for the protection of the different rights of the members of the community. These were not universal civil rights, but rather communal, not necessarily egalitarian, rights. They guaranteed specific rights that differed from community to community, but included collective external representation (vis-à-vis British rule and the Arab majority) and granted protection against injury to person and property. To a certain degree, these communal rights guaranteed work, minimal

---

53. Shapiro, *Formative Years of the Israeli Labor Party.*
54. In addition to those that in any case were external to the Jewish society, such as the Arabs and the British.

support and aid systems, and health and education services (generally separately for each group in the community).

The reason for constructing these rights was not only concern for the members of the community but the aspiration of the Jewish community to reach maximal autonomy and independence from the British colonial state. Thus, a state within a state was constructed in the context of the triangular relations among the British, Arabs, and Jews. Since the Zionist movement did not succeed in creating a Jewish majority in Palestine, it was necessary to create parallel mechanisms and institutions ("the state in the making") that in time would be able to replace the British colonial state mechanisms and bureaucracy.[55] The Palestinian Arab community did not feel obligated to this institution-building process, since, as the majority population, they expected to inherit the colonial state's institutions and bureaucracy, as had occurred in most of the new nations liberated from colonial rule.[56] The meaning of local Judaism, between religion and nationality, was not a topic that needed to be decided at that historical stage.

This was not the case with the establishment of the sovereign state of Israel, which was intended to be a nation-state and the self-appointed representative of all the world's Jews. On June 19, 1947, the Jewish Agency sent a letter to the non-Zionist Agudat Yisrael asking for its support and full participation in the declaration of state (the sending of the letter was preceded by relentless informal bargaining). In this letter, which even today is accepted as the basis for the so-called status quo and as one of the cornerstones of the political culture in Israel and state-church relations, the head of the Jewish Agency, David Ben-Gurion, made three commitments: (a) Shabbat would be the state's legal day of rest, (b) Kashrut, the Jewish religious dietary laws, would be observed in all public and state kitchens, and (c) "everything possible" would be done to meet "the deep needs of the religious public" on personal status issues. The letter also promised full autonomy to every "educational stream." At the same time, the letter rejected the demand—which had been raised in contacts behind the scenes— that Halacha be proclaimed the constitution of the Jewish state. Agudat Yisrael's saw the rejection of this demand as justified only by a phony and formalistic constraint— supposed external pressure and fear of refusal by the United Nations to accept the establishment of a completely theocratic state. The impression

---

55. See Kimmerling, "State Building, State Autonomy, and the Identity of Society."
56. See Kimmerling and Migdal, *Palestinians*.

is given that had it not been for these pressures, Jewish society would have been prepared to take upon itself the "yoke of the Kingship of Heaven" immediately upon the establishment of the state. In an aside, it was noted that there would also be non-Jewish citizens and that it would be necessary to guarantee equal rights for them as well. This also served as a rationale for not establishing the Halacha as the constitution—another example of external pressure. Agudat Yisrael praised the letter and saw it as an "important document," but noted that there was still not enough in it to meet its demands and suggested the continuation of face-to-face negotiations.

THE NONSEPARATION OF STATE AND RELIGION

The wording of Israel's 1948 Declaration of Independence created difficulties, but the solution was signaled: "[T]he Land of Israel was the birthplace of the Jewish people. Here their spiritual, religious and national identity was formed. Here they . . . created a culture of national and universal significance. Here they wrote and gave the Bible to the world." While the state itself was declared on the basis of "natural and historical right" and on the basis of the decision of the United Nations General Assembly, it was also supposed to be simultaneously based "on the precepts of liberty, justice and peace, [as] taught by the Hebrew Prophets." These were primarily religious teachings. The state "will uphold the full social and political equality of all its citizens, without distinction of race, creed, or gender" (but not nationality). And all this was signed "with trust in the Rock of Israel," in order not to mention God explicitly, but at the same time not to ignore him.

The issue here was defining Israel's identity and the source of its legitimacy as an immigrant settler state. The sublimated tension between the religious foundations ensconced in the declaration and the aspiration to give it secular universalistic validity by mentioning some of the secular rights and freedoms of its citizens in the style of the French and American revolutions and constitutions is clear. The solution already signified, then, was the blurring of the boundaries between religious principles and secular ones, between religion and nationality. But here perhaps it ought to be added that even in the cradle of the idea of the separation of church and state—in the United States of America and its Constitution—this separation never fully succeeded and was never fully enacted.

Sooner or later, the topic of separation of religion from nationality was brought before Israel's Supreme Court, which, in several rulings that set precedent, not only determined the accepted interpretation of the laws, but also reflected the insoluble cultural, historiosophical, and sociopolitical situation. The best-known verdict on the issue was of the registration of Benjamin Shalit's children as Jews. Judge Zvi Berenzon wrote in the majority ruling, in the spirit of moderate liberalism: "The concept 'nationality' should be given a regular meaning appropriate to the spirit of the time and reflecting the opinion acceptable to the enlightened portion of residents of the country." (But he did not say which segments of the population were enlightened.) Furthermore, "there should not be injected into the concept of nationalism, which according to the recognition of most human beings is separate from religion, the strictures of the Jewish *halakhah* . . . [Therefore] the view of the *halakhah* on the issue of the nationality of a resident of the country cannot serve as a basis for a ruling of the civil courts in the state of Israel." In contrast, Judge Moshe Zilberg declared in a minority opinion well anchored in Israeli political culture: "Jewish nationalism should not be detached from its religious foundations. Jewish religious belonging is necessary for Jewish nationalism. There is still no Israeli Jewish nationalism, and if it exists, it is not necessarily secular nationalism." Judge Shimon Agranat added: "In the history of the Jewish people, the racial-national [*sic!*] principle was joined with religious uniqueness, and between these two principles a connection was formed that cannot be broken. During the long history of the Jewish people, and at least until the modern era, it carried a national religious character . . . according to the historical Jewish view, the principles of nationality and religion are bound up one with the other and cannot be separated."[57]

Even more fascinating was the approach of the court to the demand of Oswald Rufeisen (also known as "Brother Daniel") to be registered

57. Supreme Court Decision 68/58. The ruling in the Shalit matter brought about a change in the Law of Return (Amendment No. 2, 1970). Until January 1960, the practice (inaugurated by Interior Minister Bar-Yehuda) was that the declaration of anyone who came to the Ministry of the Interior for the purpose of registration to obtain an identity card or passport and who declared his Jewishness would be accepted. On January 10, 1960, however, Interior Minister H. M. Shapiro issued guidelines that "in the matter of registering religious and national details in the population registry," a person would be registered as a Jew who had been either: (a) born of a Jewish mother and did not belong to another religion, or (b) converted according to Halacha. This brought about Shalit's petition, resulting in a change in the Law of Return in the spirit of the guidelines established by the new interior minister. The demand that conversion be "according to Halacha" was dropped. Prime Minister David Ben-Gurion saw this subject as so significant as to be beyond the scope of parliamentary legislation and took counsel with "Forty-Five Sages of Israel" (October 27, 1958) in the country and the world. Thirty-seven responded and only three suggested separation of religion and nationality.

as Jewish despite having converted to Christianity.[58] The problem at
hand was the meaning of the term "Jewish" as determined by the Law
of Return. In a paradoxical fashion, the decision in this case rejected the
principles of Halacha, which states that one who is born a Jew (that is,
to a Jewish mother) continues to be a Jew even if he willingly converts.
The court rejected the plea and distinguished between the secular meaning of "Jewish" under the Law of Return and its religious meaning under
the laws of personal status administered according to Halacha. This
ruling did not, in truth, enter into a discussion of the existence or nonexistence of a Jewish nationality separate from religion. Instead, it ruled,
as if by way of common sense, that, according to the "commonly accepted" meaning of the term "Jewish," a Jew who became Christian "is
not called 'Jewish,'" despite the halachic rule. Thus the ruling created,
perhaps unintentionally, a definition of "Jewish" according to the (perhaps secular) "accepted norm," as opposed to the halachic form. Here
there was another unflinching declaration by the Supreme Court: "Israel
is not a theocratic state, because it is not the religion that orders the life
of the citizen, but the law." This assertion is weird and puzzling, taking
into consideration that within the very same ruling, the court had accepted that the laws of personal status are under the jurisdiction of the
rabbinical courts. In the opinion of certain religious thinkers, the most
outspoken being the late Yeshayahu Leibowitz, this has made for the
bureaucratization of religion, turning it into the "slave of the state."[59]
Religion has lost its autonomy, and those doing holy work have lost
their religious source of authority and become government clerks. This
claim certainly deserves to be separately examined in depth. However,
it does not change the facts of the existence of the rabbinical courts and
of national and local legislation intended to impose halachic mores on
all Jewish citizens of the Israeli state.[60] Two types of explanations are
generally put forward to elucidate this anomaly, especially the topic of
the transfer of state authority to religious institutions in the areas of
personal status. The first explanation is the normative one already hinted
at in the letter to Agudat Israel—the threat of a schism in the people

58. Supreme Court 62/72. Shulamit Aloni, the leader of the Civil Rights Movement
party, suggested an amendment to the Law of Return to define as a Jew "anyone who
declares in good faith that he/she is Jewish and has tied his/her fate to that of the Jewish
nation, and who has one Jewish parent," but this was rejected.
59. See Leibowitz, *Judaism, Human Values and the Jewish State.*
60. The same problem faces non-Jewish communities in Israel. The state compels its
Muslim citizens to be subject to Shari'a law and Christians to their own religious denominational courts.

(see chapter 4). If two or more sets of rules for marriage and divorce were created, a person committed to Orthodoxy would never be able to marry a non-Orthodox Jew.[61] Following this reasoning, marriages performed by Conservative or Reform rabbis or congregations in Israel are not recognized, an issue that is the major battlefield between the majority of American Jewry and the Israeli state.[62] The second explanation is political—since no party in Israel has achieved an absolute parliamentary majority, the large parties are in need of the "religious votes" and parties in order to establish governing coalitions. In concession, they have put through legislation that at least partially imposes a halachic way of life on the entire Jewish population of the state, as well as granting the religious parties other privileges.[63]

The second explanation is accurate in some cases, but not in all. In any case, it cannot provide an explanation on the cultural and general societal level, where we seek causality beyond the mechanics of daily political life. The parties, groups, and individuals connected to the "religious" public domain provide a certain kind of legitimacy in an immigrant settler society that has never resolved the tension between the diverse elements of its collective identity.

WESTERNIZATION AND STATIZATION

In the course of the establishment of the Israeli state, when the Eastern and Western blocs were being demarcated in the international arena, and the nascent Cold War was developing, it was incumbent upon Israel to decide which bloc to belong to. Although it seems obvious in hindsight today, in the perspective of that time, it was not entirely clear what the character of the state and its international orientation would be— two issues that were bound up one with the other. The dominant political and social forces in the state defined themselves as socialists, and some of them were clearly oriented toward the Soviet Union.[64] In the

61. Since then the Orthodox and other religious factions have threatened to maintain separate genealogy bookkeeping of marriages, divorces, and births. This will prevent any religious man or woman from marrying any Jew who is not inscribed in this genealogy book. However, out-marriages in these groups are very rare in any case.

62. See Kimmerling, "Between 'Alexandria-on-Hudson' and Zion."

63. Another highly controversial and contested privilege granted mainly to Ashkenazi Yeshiva students is their exemption from the compulsory military draft (see chapter 5).

64. Like Mapam, for instance, and, of course, the Communist party, which was reestablished immediately after the founding of the state and had deep historical roots in the Jewish community of Palestine.

period after World War II, communism and the Soviet Union seemed to symbolize the "world of tomorrow,"[65] while colonialism and Western capitalism (and their liberal regimes) seemed a world in decline, against which (in its British incarnation) the Jewish undergrounds of the Jewish community in Palestine had fought.

Even after the Holocaust, eastern Europe was still the largest reservoir for Jewish immigration. On the other hand, the U.S. government and American society were suspicious of the "socialist" Jewish state, whose trademarks were agricultural communes (the *kibbutzim*), dominant socialist parties, and an all-embracing trade union (the Histadrut). During the 1948 war, the U.S. government and its allies declared an embargo on arms shipments to the Middle East, the perceived principal victims of which were the Jews. In contrast, Eastern Bloc nations (mainly Czechoslovakia) were a primary source of weapons and even provided training sites for the Jewish forces fighting in Palestine. It must be supposed that the Soviet Union originally hoped that the Jewish state would become its ally in the region and saw a reasonable chance that it would come under its aegis.

In the end, as we know, the new state aligned itself with the Western Bloc. As an organized community, American Jewry would be able to influence the U.S. government and seemed likely to be Israel's most reliable source of political and economical support in the long term. The price of a split with American Jewry was perceived as too high—more than the Jewish state could or wanted to pay. Moreover, visiting the United States for the Biltmore Hotel Conference in May 1942, Ben-Gurion had been deeply impressed by American society's power and diversity, and he did not share the opinion that it was a society in decline. Finally, despite the fact that the signing of armistice agreements at the end of the war aroused hopes of the end of the Arab-Israeli conflict, it became clear that the Arabs were in no hurry to recognize Israel. Given Israel's expansion and the uprooting and expulsion of about 750,000 Arab Palestinians, its recognition by the Arab states in the short term was, in fact, out of the question. A siege mentality began to develop within Israel, apparently to the benefit of the political and cultural establishment.

As has been emphasized several times in this book, the ruling elite in Israel did not want the country to be assimilated into the backward

---

65. Communist revolutionaries had defeated the Kuomintang in China, and even France and Italy seemed to be striding toward communist rule.

Levantine Middle East, especially after having been forced by ideological pressures to absorb such a large number of immigrants from the Middle East and North Africa (see chapters 4 and 5).[66] Israel hoped to be attached to the European Community, whose visionaries had even then already begun enthusiastically to discuss the goal of establishing a United States of Western Europe.[67] Geopolitically, economically, and culturally, the Jewish elite in Israel saw itself as part of Europe, and not of the Middle East. The more the conflict with the Arab environment worsened (with the refusal of Israel to accept the return of Arab refugees, while at the same time absorbing masses of Jews), the more the seeds of a legitimacy problem for a Jewish state in the region developed.[68] This problem became even more acute after the 1967 war.

Ironically, Israel's legitimization in the postcolonial age was found in an increasingly religious interpretation of the state. The persecution of the Jews, the Holocaust, the ascetic heroism of the Zionist enterprise, the results of the 1948 war, with the victory of the "few against the many"[69]—all appeared to help legitimize building a Jewish state at the expense of the Palestinians. This construction and interpretation of the past, near and far, was accepted by most Jews who survived the Holocaust. This was also a political, cultural, and, in a certain sense, theological victory for Zionism as a social movement and as a social and political idea.

The ultimate answer, however, was locked in the very same original symbols and values through which the Zionist movement succeeded in recruiting some elements of the Jewish masses and obtaining the political support of others. These were clearly religious sentiments, symbols, and values. The Jewish state and Jewish society were not and could not be a theocracy, but they needed Judaism, and those who represented or claimed to represent Judaism, for the "final" legitimization of Zionism. Secular Zionism was incapable of relinquishing the active inclusion of the "religious" (and the more religious the better) in the Jewish national project. This inclusion could never have happened if Israel had aligned itself with the atheist communist powers. An orientation toward the Eastern Bloc would also have immediately changed the balance of forces

---

66. See Rejwan, "The Two Israels."

67. See Kimmerling, Zionism and Economy.

68. The Israelis made considerable efforts to construct this demographic transformation of Palestine as a "population exchange" of the Arabs of Palestine for the Jews of Arab lands, but the international community refused to accept this interpretation.

69. See Kimmerling, "Social Construction of Israel's National Security."

in the internal political arena. It might have created a favorable political atmosphere for Mapam—Mapai's main rival for hegemony within the labor camp—and might have even created the basis for an alliance between Mapam and the Jewish segments of the Israeli Communist party.

Since the 1960s, the decision to align with the West has been connected with commitment to a democratic, multiparty regime, at least in the formal and declarative sphere, as opposed to communist "popular democracy." From an institutional perspective, the tools for establishing a liberal democracy—parties, a parliament, free elections, and an autonomous judicial system—were there or were created in a short time. But in addition to this institutional basis, there was a need to create ideological mechanisms and a political structure that would "balance" democracy and guarantee the continued rule of Mapai and its allies. For this reason, some sectors of the society demanded a "statist" approach, as discussed in chapter 2.

CONCLUSIONS: THE LIMITS OF DEMOCRACY IN ISRAEL

To understand what is happening in the Middle East today, it is necessary to note the existence of a number of social and political limits to Israeli democracy, which paradoxically also serve, by reason of their multiplicity, to present a sort of pluralist façade and thus provide the Israeli state with a veneer of democratic legitimacy. It is possible to distinguish five main, partially overlapping limits:

The limitation of halachic rule. It is customary to consider Israel a "full," enlightened liberal democracy. However, given the constitutional admixture of religion and nationality, the nonreligious sections of Israeli society—the majority—are subject to a legislative and judicial system that is not based on fundamental democratic assumptions. Thus, even privileged strata of Israeli society, such as the Ashkenazi middle class, lack full democratic rights. The dual judicial system, which gives the rabbinical courts jurisdiction over personal status law, creates a basic inequality between religious and secular Jews, as well as between men and women.

The limitation of Jewish female citizenship. As has been shown, Halacha is basically an archaic patriarchal legal doctrine that consistently preserves the superior status of male over female.[70] This is one of the most systematic and notable violations of the right of freedom from religion, which mainly limits the citizens' rights of women, even if they

70. See Raday, "Religion, Multiculturalism and Equality."

belong to the upper privileged veteran Ashkenazi classes and culture. The state's legislation also tends to construct a separate and different kind of citizenship for women, stressing their roles as wives and mothers.

The limitation of Israeli citizenship. This includes both Jews and Arabs (or Palestinians) in Israel. With the previously enumerated limitations, Arabs in Israel, and other minorities, are granted citizens' rights equal to those enjoyed by the Jews, but on an individual rather than a collective basis. Thus, for example, Orthodox,[71] national religious, other religious and perhaps even secular Jews are allowed group educational autonomy, but not Arabs. As for the principle of equal suffrage, Arab votes cast in Israel for parties defined as "Arab" are, in fact, partially "wasted," because no substantial decision made by the parliament based on "Arab votes" is considered politically and morally legitimate.

The ethnic limitation. This includes everyone defined as belonging to the "Jewish people," both those living in Israel and those in the Diaspora. Potentially, and with only a few reservations, the Israeli state "belongs" to anyone defined as a Jew, wherever he or she may be, even if he or she has never considered immigrating to Israel or requesting citizenship. The first and third categories can be further subdivided into Jews according to the halachic Orthodox definition and Jews accepted as such according to a political and/or any other social definition. However, even Jews who meet all the halachic Orthodox criteria of belonging are, in practice, divided by an additional social boundary into three main "castes": the secular, national religious, and *haredi*.

The limitation of the Israeli control system. The Palestinian population in the occupied territories is even today, after the setting up of an autonomous Palestinian national authority (following partial implementation of the Oslo Accords), still included within the force field and economic system of the Israeli state. As long as no final settlement is reached, and as long as no sovereign Palestinian state has been established, there will be no essential change in this situation. But even if and when a Palestinian state is set up, it is difficult to see how it will be possible to separate the two entities, because they are so interwoven with each other geopolitically, and the economic, military, and sociocultural asymmetry between them is so great. After twenty-nine years of direct, coercive Israeli rule, control over the Palestinians has, for the time being, been divided between the Palestinian National Authority and Israel. This

---

71. However, it must be said that it is easier for those women who belong to more privileged segments to skirt such limitations.

rule continues to be implemented by military, police, and economic means, as well as by colonization. The network of Jewish settlements on the West Bank and in the Gaza Strip, and the military protection they are given, constitutes a direct expansion of the Israeli state. In any event, even today, the West Bank and Gaza Strip cannot be considered as outside the boundaries of Israeli military and economic control, even if the level of control has declined or has been passed to a subcontractor.[72] It is not a usual colonial situation, but a kind of internal colonialism, because (among other reasons) according to the basic perception of each side, neither of them has another homeland.

At first glance, we would seem to be dealing with three different, separate issues. The first is the transfer of some of the universalistic Israeli state's legislative and judicial powers to the particularistic realm of halachic religion, but as interpreted by only one of the denominations within Judaism—Orthodoxy. In so doing, the state delineates its collective identity, and the criteria for membership in it, according to noncivic criteria. From this perspective, the Israeli state is not just Jewish, but *Jewish Orthodox*. The handing over of these powers to the religious legal-judicial framework turns Israel into a partial theocracy, which cannot be reconciled with any definition of liberal democracy. This regime places severe limits on women, secular citizens, and citizens who identify themselves as Jews but are not classified as "Jews" according to Orthodox interpretation of halachic rules. The second issue is the discrimination, entrenched in law, against the non-Jewish minorities within the boundaries of the state. The third issue is the holding of over two million human beings under occupation for more than a generation and the creation of a control system to keep them there. The Israeli state is expanding its boundaries beyond the limits of its legitimate authority by effectively incorporating the occupied territories and their population as a subsidiary economy, while at the same time encouraging its underdevelopment.[73] Although they continue to find themselves trapped within the economic and political force field of the Israeli state, most Palestinians lack even the rights enjoyed by those of their compatriots who are Israeli citizens.

72. According to the various agreements, Area A (initially the densely populated areas of the urban centers and refugee camps) was passed to "full Palestinian control" (but not sovereignty). Area B was designed for Palestinian "civilian responsibility" and full Israeli "security control." Area C, including all of the Jewish settlements and bypass roads to them, remained under full Israeli rule.
73. See Kimmerling, "Boundaries and Frontiers of the Israeli Control System."

CHAPTER 7

The Code of Security

The Israeli Military-Cultural Complex

In a well-known eulogy for Roy Rothberg, an Israeli frontier settler who was killed in May 1956, Moshe Dayan, then chief of staff, said:

> We are a generation of settlers, yet without a helmet or a gun barrel we will be unable to plant a tree or build a house. Let us not be afraid to perceive the enmity that consumes the lives of hundreds of thousands of Arabs around us. Let us not avert our gaze, for it will weaken our hands. This is the fate of our generation. The only choice we have is to be armed, strong and resolute or else our sword will fall from our hands and the thread of our lives will be severed.[1]

Although a professional soldier uttered these words, they reflect a basic element of Israeli culture, which in some measure is relevant even on the eve of Israel's peace-making attempts with its Arab environment. For this reason, Dayan's eulogy remains branded into the national collective memory. Deconstructing texts concerned with contemporary Israeli culture and cultural orientations provides a point of departure for understanding the impact of long-term Arab-Jewish conflict on Jewish mainstream Israeli society and culture. This society and culture results from a combination of that conflict with other constructs of traumatic "Jewish experiences," including exile, long years of persecution, and the

---

1. Teveth, *Moshe Dayan*, p. 240.

Holocaust, as well as cultural codes such as ethnocentrism, chauvinism, anxiety, and politicized messianic religion, all mixed with the universalistic values of democracy and human rights (as described in chapter 6). All these conflicting primordial and civic values have been absorbed into the Jewish Israeli collective identity and condensed around the cultural code of a civilian militarism.[2] At the same time, however, absorption/acceptance of the conflict as a crucial part of collective identity has also been accompanied by a search for an overall peaceful solution.

These contradictory trends have created three intersecting political orientations within Israeli society, cutting across and partially overlapping the major cultures of the Israeli state. These orientations are based on a common denominator in the form of a statist power discourse, including in different degrees all the cultures defined as Jewish, but excluding the Arabs. In fact, all that remains of the original Israeliness of Israel, apart from the entire population's vested interest in the continued existence of the state, are its militaristic values, while the Jewishness that previously existed has been marginalized and counterbalanced. These militaristic and power-oriented values have a common "organizing principle"—the perceived need for institutional violence, requiring permanent preparation for both full-scale war and occasional use of limited violence—and form a military-cultural complex. A mixture of institutional arrangements, including the military and economy, with distinctive cultural traits, expresses this complex.[3]

Uri Ben-Eliezer traces the origins of Israeli militarism back to the response of the first young native generation of Zionist immigrant settlers to the great Arab revolt in Palestine of 1936–39. Despairing of a peaceful acceptance of Jewish immigrant settler society by the Arabs, this generation concluded that only a clear-cut and decisive military decision would ensure the existence of the Jewish polity in the region, and that any attempt at reconciliation with the Arabs was hopeless. The Zionist leadership adopted this power-oriented ideology long before 1948, and since then the Israeli state has pursued a systematic militaristic

2. See Kimmerling and Backer, *Interrupted System.* The roles of the military and militaristic culture were long blurred in the discourse of Israeli social science, as were other issues linked with the Jewish-Arab conflict and Jewish-Arab relations. Ideological and value considerations made even the use of the term "militarism" taboo in Israel until the appearance of Uri Ben-Eliezer's *Making of Israeli Militarism.* See also Kimmerling, "Patterns of Militarism in Israel."

3. Here I am expanding the traditional meaning of the well-known term "military-industrial complex" (MIC) into the cultural field too.

policy that has avoided any peaceful solution to the Jewish-Arab conflict.[4]

How exactly did the rejection of the Jewish immigrant settler society by the Arab inhabitants of the region lead that society to develop the specific brand of militaristic culture that divides the Israeli state into three different segments, imbricating each of the seven cultures and countercultures surveyed in chapters 4 and 5?

Each of these orientations provides an alternate narrative for an active immigrant settler society engaged in total conflict[5] against a "local" people (the Palestinians are construed as "local" rather than "native," a category reserved in Zionist discourse for "sabra-ized" Jews)[6] over a territory to which both entities claim exclusive rights and title. The process of making conflict and war into a self-evident and routine part of everyday life is an especially pervasive trend at the institutional level.[7] This is reinforced by the accumulation of combat experience within Israeli society, making it a polity able to mobilize itself at a moment's notice. This mobilization advances two interconnected goals. First, enlistment of reserve soldiers (who serve along with regular conscripts and army career professionals) effects a rapid military advantage and creates a regional superpower. Second, mobilization of the "home front" in a manner that compensates for the enlistment and departure of the vast

4. Ben-Eliezer, *Making of Israeli Militarism.* However, Ben-Eliezer ignores the strong militaristic impulse of the immigrants of the second and third waves. For example, from the very beginning of the second wave of immigration, a secret society called Bar-Giora (named for a legendary hero of the Jewish revolt against the Romans) worked to establish a nucleus of military power to conquer the land, under the slogan "In fire and blood Judea fell; in fire and blood Judea will rise." In 1912, Bar-Giora set up a semi-clandestine organization called Hashomer with the immediate goal of defending the Jewish colonies, but the ultimate aim of forming a Jewish militia in Palestine. See Avigur et al., *The History of the Hagana,* vol. 1, bk. 1.

5. Total conflict means the existence of arrangements for the potential recruitment of. optimal material and human resources of a collectivity in conflict management and the conduct of war, as well as the constant preparation for war. The final result of war is perceived in terms of "the worst case analysis"—total annihilation of the society. There is no spatial or cognitive distinction between the "front" and the "rear," and each member of the collectivity, regardless of role, age, gender, or class carries the conflict within him or herself. Usually, perception of war as "total" characterizes ethnic conflicts. It should be stressed that the indirect influence of the conflict, just as that of economic change, may be enormous, but it is very difficult to isolate the role of one single factor, such as conflict, from other major variables. This argues that a discussion of the conflict must therefore take into account all other major characteristics of Israeli state and society, such as territorial smallness, ethnic and national heterogeneity, and heavy dependency on foreign aid. See Kimmerling, "Social Construction of Israel's National Security."

6. See Kimmerling and Migdal, *Palestinians.*

7. See Horowitz and Kimmerling, "Some Social Implications of Military Service and Reserves System in Israel."

majority of adult males accomplishes the complementary goal of maintaining operation of the domestic social economy (although the level of performance drops and supply of many broad social services is deferred).[8] Although this capacity for rapid mobilization has not been tested since the 1973 war, it is still an important component of the legend of Israeli might.[9]

This process of routinization does not end with the absorption of the conflict into the institutions of society. The impact of war and protracted political-military conflict on Israelis is central to the self-understanding of the society and the formation of its social, military, domestic, and foreign policy doctrines. Institutions not explicitly designed for waging war and conflict management have played crucial roles in shaping Israel's militaristic metaculture and have in turn been deeply influenced by that culture and the conflict.

One institution, the school system, has been mobilized from its inception for the purpose of nation-building. The schools from the outset sought to create the "New Jew," a productive pioneer who would "conquer labor" (i.e., take jobs from Arab workers), settle the land (taken from the Arabs), and "guard" (*shmira*) the community (against the Arabs). Even after these aims became largely obsolete, the school system continued to be one of the major socialization agents of the militaristic-survivalist worldview that dominates Israeli society in general and, to a greater degree, the conflict-oriented groups.[10] Most of the academic and research centers that deal with national security also belong to this military-cultural complex, and they generally serve it slavishly and uncritically.[11] The judicial system, too, has always operated under the conflicting demands of security and of its Western, universalistic orientation, usually giving priority to security requirements, thus becoming an in-

8. See Kimmerling and Backer, *Interrupted System.*
9. The ability to mobilize reserves quickly is challenged by long-range missiles, such as the Scud. On the other hand, the annual cohorts of recruits have become large enough to allow for extended reliance on regular soldiers in an emergency.
10. Bar-Tal, *Rocky Roads toward Peace;* Bar Gal, *Moledet and Geography during a Hundred Years of Zionist Education;* Firer, *Agents of Jewish Education.* See also Gertz, "Security Narrative in Israeli Literature and Cinema."
11. Hebrew University nuclear physicists refused, with very few exceptions, to take part in an Israeli nuclear weapons development program in the mid 1950s, but the state found other collaborators, mainly from Tel Aviv University, for this task (see Aronson, *Israel's Nuclear Programme,* p. 18). Most of the academics dealing with national security are former high-ranking officers, who form an "old boy network" with other ex-officers in the economic and bureaucratic fields and officers still in service (see Keren, "Israel's Security Intellectuals").

tegral part of the defense establishment.[12] The nuclear family, with its
gender division of roles, is also influenced by security and conflict orientations, notably with respect to the socialization of children.[13]

A comparison of Israeli political and economic institutions shows that
primacy is consistently given to political over economic considerations
in decision-making. It would be intriguing to find out what, if any, is
the precise role of the three security orientations in this phenomenon.
With regard to the state, several scholars have commented on the high
degree of "stateness" in Israeli society, arguing that the Israeli state is
one of the strongest in relation to its society, with a formidable capacity
for rule-making and law enforcement.[14] One of the major components
of the state's strength is its monopolistic control over land resources,
which is directly attributable to security and conflict considerations.

THE CIVIL RELIGION OF SECURITY

A research team on national security and public opinion in Israel summarized part of its findings as follows:

> The "religion of security" is a metaphor for considering the phenomenon of
> security in Israel. Just as a child is born into a certain religion, so too the
> Israeli is born into a very difficult geopolitical world with its attendant di-
> lemmas. Just as a child accepts unquestioningly the religion he was born into
> and some basic answers he receives . . . so too the Israeli child absorbs at a
> very early age the basics of the core-belief of national security.[15]

This socialization is so deep that when samples of youngsters were
asked in the early 1990s whether they would volunteer for service in the
Israeli armed forces if this were to become completely voluntary, 86
percent of male respondents expressed their willingness to serve. In
1988, 62 percent expressed willingness to be drafted into combat units,[16]
but in the 1990s, a general tendency of "declining motivation" to serve
in the armed forces was detected among secular youth, and this figure

---

12. Dowty, "Use of Emergency Powers in Israel"; Hofnung, *Law, Democracy and National Security in Israel*; Barzilai, "The Argument of 'National Security' in Politics and Jurisprudence." See also Kimmerling, "Legislation and Jurisprudence in the Immigrant Settler State" (forthcoming).
13. See chapter 6 above and Herzog, "Women's Status in the Shadow of Security."
14. Migdal, "State Making and Rule Making in Israel."
15. Arian, Talmud, and Herman, *National Security and Public Opinion in Israel*, p. 83.
16. Gal, "Portrait of the Israeli Soldier," pp. 61–62.

had fallen to 52 percent by 1994.[17] The issue has stimulated hot public debate, although unconditional readiness to serve among Israeli young-sters remains the highest in the world. Moreover, actual volunteering rates for special units or officer courses that involve high risk and phys-ical and mental stress and hardship (such as the paratroopers, recon-naissance, or commandos) are always higher than the actual needs of the armed forces and remain unaffected by other reported changes in motivation.

Israeli individual (Jewish male) and institutional preparedness for war remains the highest in the world by any criteria. Usually, most people take the issue of militarism out of its general context. War preparations of the potential adversary are clearly defined as "militarist"; "our own" military activities, however, may not even be counted as war prepara-tions. They are more likely to be seen as part of a "defense" or "deter-rence" policy, the professed aim of which may be to avoid war rather than to fight it.

An ambivalent attitude toward power in general and toward power wielded by Jews in particular is reflected in the writings of such figures as Micha Yosef Berdichewsky, Max Nordau, and Y. H. Brener.[18] A sim-ilar trend has been detected in contemporary Israeli literature by the cultural critic Yitzhak Laor.[19] A kind of counterhistory has developed around this ambiguity—a view perceiving the deployment of power by Jews as a normalizing trend, making the Jews "like all other nations." At its extreme, contemporary Jewish writers such as Eliezer Schweid and Emil Fackenheim utilize the example of extreme Jewish vulnerability—especially during the Holocaust—to legitimize Israel's deployment of unrestrained violence against "the gentiles."[20]

Once militarism penetrates the cognitive dimensions of a culture, it suffuses both the structural and cultural state of mind of the collectivity. This situation is liable to be reflected by full or partial institutional or cultural expressions; yet, the main expression remains *latent*. Both

17. Ezrahi and Gal, *High-School Student Worldview and Attitudes towards Society, Security and Peace.*
18. See Shapira, *Land and Power.*
19. Laor, *Narratives without Natives.*
20. See, e.g., Fackenheim, *Jewish Return to History,* and Schweid, *Israel at the Cross-roads.* An intriguing review of ambivalent Jewish responses to the responsibilities and vagaries of power and force since the emergence of a modern Jewish national movement, and then later with the establishment of the Israeli state, can be found in Biale, *Power and Powerlessness in Jewish History.*

civilian leaders and their constituency regard primary military and strategic considerations as self-evidently the only or the predominant considerations in most of their social and political decision-making. Usually,
such an acceptance is unconscious. This militarism is what Steven Lukes
characterizes as the "third dimension of power."[21] In such a situation,
the entire social nexus, in both institutional (economic, industrial, legislative) and cognitive terms, is oriented toward permanent war preparation (of course) in order to defend the collectivity's very existence. Such
preparation becomes part of social routine and is no longer considered
a matter of public debate or political struggle.[22] Even when military
performance or other measures taken by the armed forces are publicly
criticized, as often occurs in Israel, this criticism is made in terms of
"military expertise" and reinforces militaristic orientations and discourse.

Israel's system may be characterized as "total militarism," mainly
because it encompasses most of Israel's social institutions and is accompanied by the perception that the people participate in war preparations
and possess military expertise, and that the majority are involved in
active combat. Civilian militarism in many ways stands in contradiction
to the "professional militarism" of the military itself.[23] Professional militarism limits the role of the military to its most restricted instrumental
tasks,[24] while civilian militarism expands the boundaries and roles of
the military far beyond the notion of preparation of the armed forces
for future war(s) with the best available material and human resources.

The civilian government, civilian elites, and most of the members of
the collectivity all function as agents of civilian militarism. With respect
to this type of militarism, it is not necessary that the military, as an
institutional structure, govern the political sphere, nor is the military
necessarily stationed at the center of a statist cult. Civilian militarism is

21. Lukes, *Power*.

22. This definition bears a resemblance to that in Michael Mann's "Roots and Contradictions of Modern Militarism," but it is less sweeping than Mann's view that "militarism [is] a set of attitudes and social practices which regards war and preparation for
war as a normal and desirable social activity."

23. See Janowitz, *Professional Soldier*; Johnson, *Military and Society in Latin America*; Huntington, *Soldier and the State*; Abrahamson, *Military Professionalization and Political Powers*.

24. For example, during the 1987–91 Palestinian uprising, the Israeli chief of staff,
Lieutenant General Dan Shomron, declared a policy of making the military "slimmer and
smarter," and the slogan of his successor, Lieutenant General Ehud Barak, was "that
which does not shoot must be cut." See Cohen, "Peace Process and the Impact on the
Development of a 'Slimmer and Smarter' Israeli Defence Force."

systematically internalized by most statesmen, politicians, and the general public as a self-evident reality whose imperatives transcend partisan or social allegiances. The gist of civilian militarism is that military considerations, as well as matters that are defined as national security issues, almost always receive higher priority than political, economic, and ideological problems. Thus, dialectically, making peace is also a military matter (for example, during the 1996 and 1999 elections, the alternatives with which the voters were presented were "Peace with Security" and "A Secure Peace"). Moreover, while professional militarists perceive war as an end in itself, civilian militarized politicians perceive war as a Machiavellian "continuation" of diplomacy and domestic policy.

Military and national security considerations constitute a considerable part of the central organizing principles of the Israeli collectivity. In fact, most nonmilitary considerations are liable to be subordinated to national security rationales and discourse.[25] Israel thus serves as a clear example of this type of militarism. This characterization is amply underscored by the overt and latent social significance that is attributed to military service, and by the way in which the society orients itself toward constant preparation for war, a kind of "militarism of the mind." In this case, the sociopolitical boundaries of the collectivity are determined and maintained by participation in military service and manipulation of the collectivity to sacrifice in order to support the spheres classified as belonging to national security.[26]

THE BASIC ORIENTATIONS

Three orientations have developed and were institutionalized, each of them offering a different image of civilian militarism: (1) the security orientation, (2) the conflict orientation, and (3) the settlement, or peace, orientation. These orientations are aggregates of interests, perceptions, norms, customs, identifications, and social practices that set some individuals and groups apart from the larger society to which they belong. Sometimes one of these orientations is more likely to be associated with one or other of the seven cultures described earlier, but they largely cut across most of these cultures.

25. Lincoln, *Discourse and the Construction of Society.*
26. In this case, there is usually a tendency to incorporate many spheres and issues under the umbrella of national security, such as education (to supply better human power for military or technological development) and welfare (for the "nation's strength").

Periodic eruptions of violence, full-scale or limited wars and perpetual, severe conflict have dogged the Jewish immigrant settler society in the Middle East from its very beginning. The intensity, patterns, and scope of these conflicts and wars, as well as the parties involved, have changed from time to time, but the permanent external threat and self-perception of a besieged society remains. The need to manage this conflict is inherent in the nation-building process and to stratification and subgroup formation in Israeli society.

With time, larger amounts of material and human resources have been mobilized, accumulated, and invested directly or indirectly to cope with the conflict. One aspect of Israel's response to the conflict was the establishment of a vast variety of institutions and organizations specifically designed to deal with it (e.g., the armed forces, reserve system, settlements, military industries, and R&D projects). Other institutions purportedly serving quite different purposes (such as the family, with its gender division of roles, the educational system, religious institutions, youth movements, immigrant absorption organizations, cultural organizations, and the mass media) have from time to time also been mobilized, adapted, and transformed in order to handle problems arising from the conflict.

Another facet of this situation of perpetual threat has been the development and adoption of a value system—that is, the rules of the game implied by culture, values, mores, folklore, and myths—that tends to support the real and artificial needs created by warfare and a perceived siege situation. This value system has, however, also tended to diminish or even deny the centrality of conflict management, routinizing and trivializing it by fostering the image of an explicitly civilian and nonmilitaristic culture. Thus, as institutionalization of the use of force and violence increased, and more and more resources were allocated to conflict management, the employment of traditional militaristic symbols such as parades, public demonstrations of military might, and cults of personality surrounding military commanders and war heroes (which flourished particularly after the 1967 war) decreased. At the same time, the military's prestige diminished following the fiasco of the first stages of the 1973 war, which had a profound impact on Israeli society, serving as the primary catalyst for the crystallization of the compromise and conflict-oriented orientations, as discussed below.

Three principal sociopolitical orientations have been created over time, each with very different perceptions of Judaism, Israeli society, and the nature of the Jewish-Arab conflict, based on different social

strata and constituencies. Several marginal groups and segments of Israeli society do not belong to any of these orientations and do not behave
in accordance with them. These are mainly members of the Israeli underclasses: the underprivileged, Israeli Palestinian citizens, other minorities (including some traditional religious women and ultra-Orthodox
Israelis),[27] and new Russian immigrants who are developing their own
"bubble" culture (see chapter 5). Many of those who do not belong to
one of the orientations do not serve *as a group* in the military, and have
thus been defined as outsiders in Israeli society.

THE SECURITIST ORIENTATION

The "securitist" (in Hebrew, *bitchonist*) orientation is highly heterogeneous and is the political culture of most "mainstream" social groups.
This orientation is expressed politically in votes for the two largest parties, Likud and Labor, and the smaller Tzomet party, which existed up
until the 1999 elections. The major premises of this orientation are that
the Jewish state is involved in a battle for survival with its Arab neighbors, and that a major military defeat would mean its annihilation. The
primary means to prevent this destruction is maintenance of absolute
and permanent Israeli military superiority in the region, and the supreme
duty of every member of this society is to give his or her utmost in
military service. The Israeli state is regarded as the ultimate authority
for determining the organization, location, duration, and purpose of
military service in general, and for the role of each draftee in particular.
This authority is not entirely unconditional, however, as the state is
expected not to abuse this readiness for self-sacrifice and to use the military only for what are believed to be matters of survival. During the
large-scale phase of the war in Lebanon in 1982–85, for example, there
was debate about whether the state had violated this "social contract."[28]

27. One of the most important recent transformations of Israeli society is the convergence between parts of the ultra-Orthodox religious groups, who in the past were considered as non- or even anti-Zionists, and "hawkish" national religious groups, especially
the settlers of the occupied territories. The "nationalization" of the ultra-Orthodox groups
has been accompanied by their participation in intensive political parliamentary and extraparliamentary activities. Their participation was especially salient in the period of the
demonstrations against the Oslo Accords and during the 1996 elections. In the latter, they
played a major role in bringing about the change from a Labor-Meretz government to the
coalition government of Likud and the religious parties led by Netanyahu, which was
marketed under the slogan "Good for the Jews."

28. For the alternative view, see Begin, "War of No Choice and War by Choice"; Yariv,
"Wars by Choice—Wars by No Choice"; and Kimmerling, "Most Important War."

Either way, the concept of "security" has been used and abused as one of the central codes of Israeli society.[29]

Israeli society and state are indeed committed to other, complementary social goals, such as welfare, education, internal law and order, equality, democracy, economic development, civil liberties and human rights, and humanitarianism, as well as to the fulfillment of Zionist goals, such as the immigration and absorption of Jews, protection of Jews all over the world, and the "Judification" of Eretz Israel. Nonetheless, because human and material resources are scarce and limited, the basic societal choice is seen as being between "guns or butter." As long as the collectivity's existence is threatened in any way, all other social and private goals are subordinated, although not completely disregarded, to the maintenance of security.[30] In principle, the achievement of peace and legitimacy in the region is desirable and attainable in the distant and unpredictable future, if and when "the Arabs" understand that the Jewish state is indestructible. When that happens, there will be peace, and another Zionist goal, the complete "normalization" of Israeli society, will be attained. Concomitantly, the Palestinian problem will be solved without endangering Israel's security.

"Security" is interpreted in its wider meaning, which includes factors other than the resolution of military threat. One of these factors is Israel's demographic makeup.[31] Another is its international position and

29. The first crude manipulation of security-related symbols transpired on July 5, 1961, when a small rocket ("Shavit 2") was launched a few days before a national election. The missile's purpose was defined as "weather research," but in the pictures released to the public, emphasis was placed on the presence of the prime minister and defense minister (Ben-Gurion), who wore a military uniform, as well as on the chief of staff (Major General Zevi Tzur). The timing of the destruction by Israeli aircraft of the Iraqi nuclear reactor in 1984 was also surely a part of the ruling party's electoral campaign. For a long time, however, the most important abuse of "security needs" was military censorship of the mass media. This excuse was employed many times between the 1950s and 1970s for purposes of political censorship. See Goren, Secrecy and the Right to Know.

30. Moshe Dayan expressed this approach very well, by labeling it "the two banners." One banner was security and the other banner, all "the rest" (welfare, education, social and ethnic equality, etc.). One way of overcoming this constructed zero-sum situation between "security" and other social desiderata was to create a linkage among them. That is, to assert that education and science "contribute to security," or that social welfare is "part and parcel of national strength."

31. At least ideologically, the whole of Likud, the direct inheritor of the ultranationalist Herut party, and considerable portions of the activist branch of Labor (mainly the former Achdut Ha'avodah faction) are committed to annexing the entire territory of "Greater Israel." The "Greater Israel Movement" was initially founded after the 1967 war by mainstream Laborites. When in power, neither of these parties, however, declared annexation, owing to the "pragmatic reason" of not wanting to include within the Israeli

image, especially with reference to the United States. Since the 1987–91 Palestinian uprising, Israel's policy has also been to avoid using the military to perform major policing tasks that may diminish its strength. Following the 1987–91 Palestinian popular uprising, another form of reasoning has been introduced into the "security equation": avoid using the military to perform major policing tasks that can diminish its strength. Beginning in 1991, too, the Intifada started to creep past the Green Line,[32] intensifying guerrilla warfare and increasing the burden of "immediate security" (*bitahon shotef*) on both the armed forces and the civilian population. These pressures have made the continued holding of the densely populated occupied territories a real threat to security at the strategic level, especially after the renewal of violence following the deadlock of the Israeli-Palestinian talks of 2000–2001.

Classical sociology and social psychology argue that external stress—in Israel's case, war, the threat of war, and conflict—tends to reinforce internal cohesion and integration of the "in-group" and to intensify the solidarity of the collectivity.[33] This is the case, however, only when the collectivity copes successfully with the external threat. If not, the disintegrative trend will increase, and the external threat becomes "dysfunctional" for the group. This seems to be the kind of argument advanced by Arnold Toynbee: when the "challenge" is proportional to the ability of a society, the challenge is "good," the response will be successful, and the society will develop and grow; if the challenge is too great, however, the society will collapse. In retrospect, we can see that such a theory is tautological (i.e., any outcome can be held to prove it). In the Israeli case, the outcome remains ambiguous. Although both suicides and strikes apparently correlate with the conflict's salience,

---

state about 1.5–2 million Palestinian Arabs, who would demand full citizens' rights, transforming the state into a de facto binational entity. Instead of formal annexation, both parties opted for maintaining direct military control over the West Bank and Gaza Strip and complementing it with civilian colonization. It thus seems that Israel's original reason for signing the Oslo Accords was to establish indirect control over the occupied territories by subcontracting security there to the Palestinian Authority. This basic situation will not change, even if some form of autonomy is granted to the Palestinians in the territories. Even if Israel's armed forces leave populated areas, the real power will still remain in Israel's hands. Only the transfer of real authority to another sovereign entity will put an end to the coercive control over the Palestinians that has persisted since 1967. See Kimmerling, "Power-Oriented Settlement."

32. The border under the 1948–49 cease-fire agreements between Israel and neighboring Arab states.

33. See Coser, *Functions of Social Conflict,* following Georg Simmel.

suicides tend to multiply with its perceived intensity, while strikes and labor conflicts decrease.[34] Likewise, in his examination of the influence of the conflict on Jewish emigration from Israel, Yinon Cohen found that, although the burden of annual reserve duty does apparently induce emigration, contrary to what one might have thought, the *perceived* intensity (i.e., salience) of the conflict attenuates emigration, inasmuch as it tends to enhance social cohesion and integration.[35]

The armed forces and universal military service are the major institutional manifestation of the securitist orientation.[36] People participate in the military more as members of a nuclear (or slightly extended) family or a primary group (as husbands, daughters, sons, first cousins, in-laws, school class or youth movement buddies) than as individuals. When a member of a family serves, the whole family is "recruited." The specific content of this institution varies from cohort to cohort, or from one sociological generation to another (e.g., the Palmach, "Six Day War," "Yom Kippur War," and, recently, Intifada generations). Each of these generations acquires its own experiences, developing its own slang, jargon, and worldview, either as "fighters" (which is itself a cultural attribute), as part of a primary group of which only some directly participate in conflict, or through the mass media and folklore.[37]

Another institutional embodiment of the securitist culture is the rise of an economic and bureaucratic "defense" establishment, an Israeli military industrial complex, which has led to economies of scale that have restructured the entire economy.[38] This is an immense institutional conglomerate, including private and public weapons and military tech-

34. See Kimmerling, "Anomie and Integration in Israeli Society and the Salience of the Arab Israeli Conflict."
35. Cohen, "War and Social Integration."
36. Since the state's establishment and through the present day, military service has been obligatory (today, the length of service is three years for men and two for women). Yet the minister of defense retains the authority to release any person or group from service. Upon such authority, so-called "declared" religiously observant girls, students of traditional Jewish religious academies (*Yeshivot*), and all Arabs, with the exception of Druse and Circassians, have been exempted. Christian Arabs and Bedouins can volunteer for service. Many young Druse see military service as a good career opportunity and a means to social mobility. The subject of being included or excluded in the framework of universal and compulsory military service has sometimes also been a cause for bargaining between the military authorities and sociopolitical pressure and interest groups. See Kimmerling, "Determination of the Boundaries and Framework of Conscription."
37. Lomsky-Feder, "Youth in the Shadow of War, War in the Light of Youth"; Lieblich, *Transition to Adulthood during Military Service.*
38. See, e.g., Mintz, "Military-Industrial Complex"; id., "Military-Industrial Linkages in Israel"; Mintz and Ward, "Political Economy of Military Spending in Israel"; Bichler, "Political Economy of Military Spending in Israel."

nology industries, research and development institutions devoted completely or partially to military purposes, military elites of junior active and reserve officers, and the political circle based in the Ministry of Defense and the Prime Minister's Office (which is in charge of many security and intelligence branches not run by the military). Over the past decade, however, partially owing to changes in the world order and a decrease in the world market for Israel's military products, the scope of the MIC and the economic infrastructure of the "security sector" have been drastically reduced. Direct military expenditure, which comprised about 40 percent of the state's budget in the middle of the 1980s, decreased to 32 percent at the end of that decade, and to about 16 to 20 percent in the 1990s—still among the highest levels of military expenditure in the world.

THE CONFLICT ORIENTATION

The conflict-oriented group is best characterized by contrasting its basic assumptions to that of the compromise-oriented group. The major assumptions of this orientation are that the Jewish-Arab conflict is just another incarnation of traditional anti-Semitism. Given the current world order and Israel's encirclement by Arabs, no peaceful settlement with its neighbors can be attained in the foreseeable future. Periodic wars are inevitable, and the most important goal of the collectivity is to win any war. All other collective or private goals are subordinate to this, and pursuit of them detracts from it. Power and military strength are the only consideration in relations between different national, ethnic, or religious groups. The only difference in relations between Jews and non-Jews in the present Israeli and Zionist context, in comparison to other historical periods, is that now Jews have some advantage in the regional power game; the foremost priority is to preserve this superiority.

Holding on to as much as possible of Eretz Israel, whose boundaries are not precisely defined, but change with political circumstances, is seen not only as a strategic necessity (see chapter 4), but mainly as a moral, sacred, and religious-nationalistic imperative.[39] The collectivity is a

---

39. The ideal of Eretz Israel is construed in terms of the biblical "promise" of Yahweh to Moses, the legendary founding father of the nation, as running "from the Euphrates River to the Rivers of Egypt" (probably meaning a small river in the eastern part of the Sinai Peninsula, but there are broader interpretations). Today, the boundaries of colonial British Palestine are the reference point. More pragmatically, however, the boundaries move according to political and military ability to hold them. As one central rabbinical

moral community based on primordial and ethno-religious ties, which
are the only relevant criterion for membership.[40] Equality, justice, welfare, and mutual aid are meaningless beyond the boundaries of the Jewish primordial collectivity. Opponents are found not only outside the
boundaries of the Jewish collectivity but also inside it.[41]

Both the conflict-oriented groups and their alter ego, the compromise-
oriented groups (discussed below), especially at their hard-core nuclei,
tend to demand intensive involvement from their members, often in
highly politicized parliamentary and extraparliamentary bodies, such as
political parties, protest movements, the Chabad messianic movement,
and even settlement organizations, such as the Council of Heads of Jewish Settlements of Judea, Samaria, and Gaza (see chapter 4) and the
Amana.[42] Both orientations are elitist by nature, being overrepresented
in artistic and media circles. Some elements of their hard ideological
nuclei tend to circumscribe the unconditional authority of the state, because both claim to express "true Zionism" more faithfully than the
official version, suggesting in part an alternative social order. The conflict orientation is based on a model of an ethnocentric Jewish collectivity that grants priority to halachic law (as they interpret it) and other
particularistic orientations over the modern, Westernized legal and
"democratic" system.[43] While this may legitimize extralegal activities,
the state and the military are central components of this orientation's
symbolic system.

Despite the diversity of types and motivation for settlement and the
social origins of the settlers, a distinct kind of sociopolitical system has
developed among them in the occupied territories of the West Bank.[44]
This system seems to be the nucleus of the conflict orientation and
its institutional infrastructure. It is a community and lifestyle (under

---

figure, Rabbi Abraham Shapiro, put it, "Everywhere the IDF is present is the Land of
Israel; any place outside of IDF rule is the land of gentiles" (N. Shragai's report, *Ha'aretz*,
November 25, 1996). IDF is the acronym for "Israel Defense Forces," the official title of
the Israeli military.

40. See chapter 6 above and Kimmerling, "Between the Primordial and the Civil Definitions of the Collective Identity."

41. Such as the "self-hater" infidel "leftist" Jews, who are completely detached from
their own people, heritage, and interests. For an American echo of this highly simplistic
attitude, see Hazony, *Jewish State.*

42. Amana is the Gush Emunim state-supported settlement organization.

43. They label "democracy" as a foe and as an external worldview and sociopolitical
order to that of Judaism, as they interpret it.

44. The settlers in the Syrian [Golan] Heights belong more to the securitist-oriented
group in terms of their social and ideological origins.

partial siege) based on extended social networks (both locally and with the population of Israel proper) and special relations with the armed forces and the surrounding Palestinian population. The settlers possess their own leisure institutions and other institutional arrangements (e.g., shopping, transportation, and local defense). Their society has its own division of family roles, a school system, local community-based groups and organizations, and an emerging local and supraterritorial leadership. It is also faced with its own internal social, ideological, and religious cleavages and tensions.

THE COMPROMISE ORIENTATION

The guiding principle of this orientation is essentially the diametrical opposite of that of the conflict-oriented group: achieving peaceful resolution to the Jewish-Arab (and especially Palestinian) conflict, which is seen as no different from any other negotiable dispute and unconnected to the persecution of Jews in the past, because it is unrelated to traditional Jewish-Gentile relations. The conflict is framed mainly in terms of material interests, such as territorial resources, markets, boundaries, and water. Peace, democracy, and "normalcy," the most desirable collective goals of the Israeli state, are perceived as linked to compromise, and the achievement of peace as a necessary condition for the attainment of all other aims, such as a more egalitarian society, economic growth, welfare, technological, scientific, cultural, and artistic progress, and so on. Above all, the core of this orientation is that peace—which is equated with Israel's acceptance as a legitimate state and society in the region—is security.

Society and state are seen, in this orientation, as having a universal civilian basis; membership accords with citizenship, regardless of non-universalistic attributes (i.e., religious, ethnic, or racial affiliations). Citizenship is conditional, however, depending on the fulfillment of mutual obligations. The state must provide its citizens with law and order, protection from external threats, well-being, and all other generally accepted civil and human rights. In turn, citizens are mainly obligated to obey the state's laws, to perform military duties (if needed), and to pay reasonable taxes. The existence of the state and membership in the collectivity itself are not of ultimate value, but are conditional on the quality of life that the state offers its citizens.

On the one hand, the compromise-oriented worldview subscribes to the civilian-oriented rules of the game, including the supremacy of democratic law enforcement and judicial systems. Yet, on the other hand, it anxiously perceives advocates of the other orientations as abusing the law, the state, and the consensus about the necessity of universal military service to impose their own political will and programs. This leads to a peripheral phenomenon of conscientious objection, in which conditions are laid down in return for willingness to perform military duties.[45] But the most important institutional embodiment of the compromise-directed orientation is its fragmented protest movement and huge journalistic, literary, and general cultural output, which highlights its elitist nature and social basis mainly among the Ashkenazi upper-middle-class strata of Israeli society, expressed socially by the secularist (mainly Ashkenazi) culture (see chapter 4) and politically by the Meretz party.[46]

Adherents of this viewpoint to a great extent express their political orientation through their professional activity as media personnel, essayists, poets, educators, singers, artists, university professors (or students), and so forth. Yitzhak Rabin was added posthumously to their pantheon. Paradoxically, the concentration in these sectors only emphasizes their alienation and detachment from the rest of society. If the hard core of the conflict orientation is mainly geographically segregated, the hard core of the compromise-oriented strata lives in a social ghetto. The boundaries between these two orientations are clear and impermeable.

Arab citizens of the state are excluded not only from the securitist and conflict orientations but also from the compromise orientation. Peace, like war, is perceived as exclusively "Jewish business." Thus, most "Peace Now" activists proudly use their military ranks and expertise in their debates against their political rivals, and their arguments and rhetoric are usually formulated in militaristic terms. Most of them tacitly agree that it is better to leave Arab citizens out of the debate and the political battle over the future of the state. Some, for tactical reasons, do not want to be suspected of supporting the "Arab cause" or depending on "Arab ballots"; others are convinced that conflict-related issues are indeed "internal Jewish matters." All this despite the fact that Arab

45. See, e.g., Helman, "Conscientious Objection to Military Service as an Attempt to Redefine the Contents of Citizenship."

46. The national daily newspaper *Ha'aretz* is a very important institution of this orientation owing to its style, editorial policy, contributors, and chain of local weeklies. Another relatively informal "center" of this orientation is Tel Aviv's downtown area, known in current Israeli slang as "Sheinkin [Street] culture."

citizens of Israel originated the formula for peace common to the most of these groups: "Two states for two nations."[47]

Some members of peripheral groups of the compromise orientation have demonstrated their strong political and moral commitment as conscientious objectors by refusing to perform military service (whether as enlisted soldiers or reservists) in the occupied territories (or in Lebanon during the 1982–85 war). They become the heroes of this orientation when they are imprisoned or "martyred," as was the case with Emile Greenzweig, a student killed during a demonstration of the "Peace Now" movement. Refusal to serve in the military, however, is still anathema to the majority of the members of this orientation.[48]

These three political-cultural orientations do not by any means comprise the entire ideological map of Jewish Israeli society, and they are presented here only as ideal types in the Weberian sense of the term. Despite the gross differences between the three Israeli orientations in their perception of the "world," the cosmic order, and the nature of the relationship between Israel and the world, and the very different political conclusions they draw from these worldviews, there are salient common denominators among them, notably the centrality of military might to Israel's very survival and the perception of a real threat to the Israeli state as a Jewish settler society.

Thus, even the most eager "doves," who are ready to give up all the occupied territories in exchange for a minimal or limited peace settlement, and most of whom support the "two-state solution," seem to be among the strongest supporters of developing Israel's nuclear capabilities as an insurance policy in a "worst-case analysis."[49] This idea of the

47. That is, a sovereign and independent Palestinian state coexisting peacefully alongside the Israeli state.

48. See Feige, "Social Movements, Hegemony, and Political Myth." Yesh Gvul ("There Is a Limit"), "The Twenty-First Year," "Women in Black," etc., were very small protest groups, outside of the Zionist consensus, inasmuch as they violate the major "sacred cow" of Israeli culture: unconditional military service. Women have formed the overwhelming majority in most of the protest movements (that are to the left of the "Peace Now" movement) against the 1982 war of Lebanon and Israeli occupation of the Palestinian territories, and some protest groups are exclusively female. Thus two kinds of marginal protest issues are intermingled in the Israeli society—peace and gender. See Sasson-Levy, "Problem of Gender in Israeli Protest Movements"; Chazan, "Israeli Women and Peace Activism."

49. A small minority of radical leftists are the exception. Right-wingers committed to "territorial-securitism"—the argument that only territorial depth can provide "real security"—are also suspicious of the nuclear argument, believing that basing security on nuclear arms ("nuclear securitism") diminishes the territorial factors for "defense" and could weaken their "pragmatic" securitist argument for keeping the occupied territories.

"worst case" is a central ingredient of the powerful militaristic meta-cultural code to which the entire spectrum of the Jewish polity reacts. This is an additional reason why the boundaries of the securitist-oriented group are very vague, ideologically as well as socially.[50] In fact, this group includes some elements of the other two orientations, and there are internal contradictions. This is precisely its strength, however, because it represents the large coalition that makes up the "Jewish national consensus." Socially, it crosses almost every stratum of Jewish Israeli society. The mixture of the three orientations forms the special pattern of militarism I have defined here as "civilian militarism," using Alfred Vagts's term.[51]

CONCLUSIONS

Not all of Israeli society is molded by the impact of war and conflict. An important aim of social research is to discover, isolate, and analyze areas and institutions not influenced by the conflict, and to explain why and how this occurred. Despite its centrality and the high esteem accorded it,[52] the Israeli military is mainly professional and does not seek to intervene in social or political issues and processes. From this point of view, the military is not much more "militaristic" than any military in any democratic country; rather, considerable portions of Israeli civilian society have become highly militarized. The militarization of Israeli culture is expressed mainly by the use of excessive power in solving social and political problems, by the "military-mindedness" of large parts of the civilian population and political leadership, and by the high expectancy that the military will solve nonmilitary problems. Severe political instability could lead segments of the population to call for an implicitly or explicitly "strong" military regime, which would undermine the Israeli parliamentary regime.

Moreover, preparation for war and war-making overlap with all the

50. See also Mann, "Roots and Contradictions of Modern Militarism."

51. The term "civilian militarism" was originally coined by Vagts, History of Militarism. For the other patterns of militarism and their relations to civilian militarism, see Kimmerling, "Patterns of Militarism in Israel." See also Speier, "Militarism in the Eighteenth Century."

52. In the 1990s, despite huge numbers of reserve officers and its poor performance in the 1973 war, the 1982 war in Lebanon, and suppressing the Intifada, the military was one of the most trusted institutions in Israel, along with the High Court of Justice and "professors." Politicians and members of Knesset were far behind. See Yuchtman-Yaar and Peres, Between Consent and Dissent.

processes of state- and society-building, that is, Israeli irredentism.[53] This is commonly the case with immigrant settler states. In this sense, "statist logic" includes war-making and power-oriented practices, including trials of territorial expansion. However, the same statist logic also includes peace-making, as a complement of war-making.[54] After acquisition of control over a territory perceived as a "national territory," the state must consolidate its gains during periods of peace through a combination of a civilian presence, in the shape of settlements, often established under the pretext that they are necessary for security, and a military presence to defend those settlements.

However, in order to finalize the state-building process, consolidation must mean the legitimate acceptance, both by its own subjects and citizens and mainly by its immediate and broader international environment, of the state within determined boundaries and as having a given national and ethnic composition. Otherwise, the state wastes its human and material resources in unnecessary wars and conflicts until it reaches the point of self-destruction. No state or society, however, possesses self-regulating mechanisms of war- and peace-making; thus, both options are always subject to internal political and cultural controversies.

In the course of the state's crystallization, Israeli immigrant settlers developed war- and conflict-oriented as well as compromise-oriented values and groups, with their accompanying rhetoric. Owing to the routinization of war and conflict, however, an all-embracing militaristic metacultural code developed to blur the distinctions between peace and war, and between rational military and ideological religious "reasons" for keeping the occupied territories.[55] The first "peace in exchange for territory" agreement with Egypt was made in order to increase control over the components of Eretz Israel dubbed "Judea and Samaria" and was immediately followed by the 1982 war in Lebanon, fought for the same reason.[56] The Oslo Accords with the Palestinians were agreed to by Israel primarily in order to shed responsibility for densely Arab-populated areas by establishing indirect control using Arafat's

53. See Tilly, "War Making and State Making as Organized Crime"; Giddens, *Nation-State and Violence;* Marwick, *War and Social Change in the Twentieth Century.*

54. For a survey of long-term trends in Israeli opinion, see Arian, *Security Threatened,* pp. 54–90.

55. Another major distortion of the political culture and ideological map deriving from this situation is the identification of the "left" alone with compromise-oriented groups, while the "right" is equated with conflict-oriented groups. Both terms completely lose their original social and economic ideological context.

56. In Kimmerling, "Power-Oriented Settlement," pp. 223–53.

Palestinian Authority as subcontractor, but without giving up "overall security responsibility" for any part of Eretz Israel. This came about only after political and military elites had reached the conclusion that there was no acceptable military solution to the Palestinian problem (not all Israeli Jews were, however, in agreement). The making of de facto peace with the Hashemite kingdom of Jordan was aimed at weakening Palestinian political and military strength.

The existential anxiety built into Israeli collective identity and collective memory simultaneously fuels civilian militarism and reinforces "military militarism" and the military-cultural complex, creating a vicious circle that always leads to self-fulfilling "worst case" prophecies. Even the main motives for peace-making are driven either by xenophobic feelings of separateness or instrumental manipulation of improved control over "the other side" and preservation of "our" ultimate military might.

Conclusions

Modern Israeli or Hebrew identity and nationalism were originally created by the veteran pre-state Jewish community's political and cultural leadership as a part of a sociopolitical and monocultural control system over the unselective immigration that was flooding the country when the state was established. In light of the very fast, deep, and wide-ranging demographic and cultural changes that were occurring in the population as a result of unselective immigration and the 1948 war, it was perceived as an unquestionable necessity.

The veteran population regarded the new Jewish populations from Europe, Asia, and North Africa both compassionately and suspiciously as Holocaust survivors with a "Diaspora mentality" and as "wrecked people." Slowly, after the passing of about two generations, these newcomers transformed their suffering and the Israelification imposed on them into points of anger against veteran Israelis and state institutions and values. With this, they began to wage something very like cultural war. Some of them, mainly immigrants from North Africa, preserved and reinvented a subaltern cultural heritage and collective memories within their family frameworks, which were relatively impermeable by the state and its agencies. Later, when the hegemonic situation broke down, these stifled cultures, beliefs, and memories resurfaced and became the infrastructure for newly created cultures and invented identities.

Veteran Israelis were no longer able to rely on their heroic nation-building efforts for maintenance of their monopoly on state power and the continued imposition of their original culture. The mass immigration of non-European Jews had the potential to fundamentally change the system through "Levantinization," and, from the perspective of the European veterans, to downgrade it to the "low quality" of the surrounding Arab states and societies. In stereotypical terms, these immigrants were perceived as possessing a certain premodern biblical Jewish authenticity, although at the same time seen as aggressive, alcoholic, cunning, immoral, lazy, noisy, and unhygienic.

The newly invented "Israeli identity" and state incorporated some ingredients of the political-cultural "bubble" of Jewish communal identity in colonial Palestine, or Yishuv. Its blatant secularism and paternalism coercively promoted Hebrew language and culture and aspired toward the constitution of a "new muscular Jewish man"—the so-called "pioneer"—who would be both a warrior and a physical worker in agriculture and construction. In substitution for the Arab, a glorified new native species was invented—the sabra.

The state's citizenship boundaries formed a new sociopolitical community, the Israeli polity. Membership in the state was based on quasi-legal rationalistic criteria of formal and universalistic relationships, as opposed to the semi-voluntary and ascriptive membership conditions in the Yishuv community. Although this was not the intended purpose of the universalistic allocation of at least quasi-equal citizen rights to all subjects of the state, the remaining Arabs managed to use their citizenship and Israeliness to gradually improve their material conditions and political rights within the Jewish nation-state. Nonetheless, the rights of Jews in Israel are still defined personally and collectively, while the rights of Arabs are only defined personally. That is, they lack rights to common goods of the collectivity such as land, water, collective symbols, holidays, anniversaries, and commemorations. This differentiation between private and collective rights is precarious, however, and makes Israel an ethnocracy rather than the "Jewish and democratic" society it proclaims itself to be.

Another factor in the creation of Israel was the imperative need to locate the state, its institutions and agents—symbolically, ideologically, and politically—at the center of Israeliness. The original idea was that the establishment of a modern secular Israeli state was the fulfillment and the only and ultimate possible implementation not only of Zionist ideology but also of the theological aims of Judaism. The state was declared as "belonging" to all of world Jewry, but not unequivocally to all the state's citizens if they were not defined in various ways as Jewish. The inevitable internal contradiction of Israeliness and the main cause of its later fragmentation, its partial overlap with Judaism, was thus built in from the start.

The most blatant legal expression of this duality was the registration of nationality in legal documents (i.e., identity cards and population registers) as "Jewish," "Muslim," "Christian," "Druse," and so on, rather than as "Israeli."[1] A mixture of explicit and implicit legal, political, and cultural assumptions equated Judaic religion with Jewish secular nationalism, excluding the possibility of the legal existence of Jewish Muslims or Jewish Christians (and even Jewish Jews), as equivalent to American Christians or American Jews.

Indeed, it was not by chance that the first counterculture that was created and succeeded in rising above the hegemonic Israeli monoculture was a militant national religious culture in the form of the Gush Emunim movement. In the 1970s and 1980s, the territorial infrastructure was created for a "new [Jewish] society" of national religious settlers in "Judea and Samaria" (the occupied West Bank). This settler society was established through a national political mission of conquest, occupation, and confiscation of "homeland" territories and the expansion of the boundaries of the Israeli state to congruence with those of the "Land of Israel." Its establishment also laid the infrastructure for the establishment of a complete moral community, run according to Orthodox Jewish religious law and the judgments of rabbis.

Gush Emunim religious political fundamentalism threatened to conquer the mountainous heartland of Eretz Israel both geographically and symbolically, substituting itself for the secular Zionist sabra-kibbutznik-fighter-and-settler ethos. From "Judea and Samaria," the message was supposed to spread over the entire Land of Israel. Driven by burning faith, the national religious revolutionaries would establish a modern national Jewish (i.e., religious) state representative of the perceived collective interest, based on the re-creation of the "true and pure Jew."

The success of this revolution of faith seemed assured, especially given the absence of any truly attractive competing ideology that could

---

1. Some have argued that identities were registered as "Jewish," rather than as "Israeli," because of the need to single out Arab citizens for security reasons. After 1948, Arabs remaining in Israel were granted citizenship, but they were confined to their own localities by a harsh military government.

provide an answer to the political and social situation created in the aftermath of 1967 war. In this regard, the settlements and the settlers in the occupied territories were just the tip of the iceberg. "Judaism" as a mixture of religion and secular chauvinism was widespread among the population. Even many who had not "settled" and were not partners of, or even were opposed to, Gush Emunim espoused the sublime ethnocentric aspiration to transform the Israeli state into a "Jewish state."

The pioneering spirit and renewed settlement-security activism also charmed elite, even secular, groups, whose great ideological crises, especially among the socialists, had caused deep rifts among them (see chapter 4). In addition, by opening the frontier and acquiring control over the totality of the land that was the original objective of Zionist colonization, they reawakened dormant codes of the immigrant settler political culture that had lost most of their validity after 1948. Thus, some mainstream secular elite groups found that they, too, could empathize selectively with theocracy and especially with Gush Emunim and its version of Zionism.

The appearance of a national religious activism that challenged the secular socialist political hegemony was preceded by a slow and relative decrease in the perceived power, prestige, efficiency, and stability of state institutions such as the military, and hence a decrease in the centrality of the idea of the state ("stateness"). This was particularly so in the aftermath of the 1973 war. The power of the Gush Emunim idea was concealed in its promise to restore state power. Gush Emunim sanctified the state and assigned itself as the agent of Israel's interests, according to its interpretation of them.

The preliminary success of the religious revolution had two unintentional consequences, however, which essentially put an end to, or at least moderated, the Gush Emunim revolution. First, routinization of the revolution cultivated a new, essentially individualistic, younger generation who turned their backs on the revolution, preferring individual achievements and careers. Second, the Palestinian uprising proved that it was not possible to distinguish between control of the territories and control of their population without creating a de facto binational apartheid-style state, in which one nationality possesses all the rights and the other nothing. These two results also demonstrated that utopia has its own constraints and limitations.

It was also revealed that the religious and national foundations of the Gush Emunim version of messianism are as contradictory as they are complementary. More than once, contradictions were revealed between the national and religious elements, which the Orthodox segments embodied in pure form. As the latter began to dominate in parts of the Gush Emunim community, a convergence between the national religious and the Haredim began. The Haredim also discovered that there is no need to be a Zionist, to don a knitted skullcap,[2] to settle in the "Land of Israel," or to adopt various statist symbols in order to augment one's share in the allotment of the collective resources and even to participate in determining the character of the state.

What Orthodoxy discovered at the beginning of the 1990s, Jews from Arab lands had known from early on. So, while the Gush Emunim revolution encountered crisis and deadlock in the face of political changes and its own internal contradictions, a young, Orthodox Mizrahi elite educated in the very heart of Ashkenazi ultra-Orthodoxy took form and grew. In the face of galling feelings of discrimination in the Ashkenazic Orthodox world, this elite managed to hoist the banner of rebellion. Some of these young people were outstanding scholars according to the criteria of the Lithuanian-type Yeshiva "society of learners" in which they had been raised, yet they were prevented from marrying into families of the Haredi Ashkenazi nobility and were not granted appointments to prestigious rabbinical positions. Rebellion broke out when they realized that they were considered second-class.

They possessed two crucial advantages: a charismatic leader in the figure of Rabbi Ovadiah Yossef and a very large potential constituency (a quarter of the state's Jewish population), which had previously lacked leadership and an authentic focus for identification. The cultural-ideological revolution of the "Sephardic Torah Guardians" (the Shas party) included the revival—or more accurately the invention—of a new social identity. This identity not only bound together ethnicity, class, and religion but found its primary strength in the bestowal of legitimacy upon selective observance of religious commandments, almost according to the convenience and interpretation of the individual and the family, without threat of hellfire or, even worse, excommunication from the community.

By moving to the center of the social arena, national religious Judaism succeeded in breaking the secular socialist nationalist hegemony and also unintentionally paved the way for the establishment of other autonomous cultures, with varying degrees of separatism, within the Israeli state. It also made possible the increased autonomy and participation of

2. The skullcap is the symbol of new (or modern) Zionist orthodoxy.

Arab citizens in the state. Thus, the way was paved for institutions from different cultures and cultural markets to evolve without the development of an ideology that legitimized multiculturalism. Concurrently, however, the formation of these cultures did not undo, and perhaps even strengthened, a sense of common primordial identity among extensive segments of the Jewish population.

Any possible doubt was erased by the 1996 and 1999 elections. The new electoral method revealed the existence of the autonomous cultures and the internal tensions: secular versus religious, Russians versus Mizrahim, Russians versus Arabs, and so on. It also politically strengthened central sectors of these cultures to the extent that it emphasized the Jewish commonality, expressed to different degrees and in different ways in each of the Jewish cultures. Before one's very eyes, two seemingly opposite, but actually complementary movements are occurring in Israel, one centrifugal and the other centripetal.

Chapter 5 examined two latecomer cultural-political segments of the Israeli immigrant settler population, the Russians and the Ethiopians. The argument is not only that the collapse of secular Zionist hegemony made possible the creation of Russian and Ethiopian subcultures or subsocieties in Israel, but that they are likely to exist much longer than Zionist hegemony did—perhaps forever—because the "melting pot" mechanisms that served the hegemonic culture are losing their efficacy. Traditional sociological research asked how best to "resocialize" immigrants and "Israelify" them so that they could be absorbed into Israeli society. Under the present circumstances, the most proper question is the reverse. That is, how are earlier and latecomer immigrant groups each contributing to the changes presently occurring in the Israeli state and society? What seems almost obvious is that these population groups gave impetus to the trend of cultural segmentation and the transition from a monocultural hegemonic system toward a plurality of cultures.

Nonetheless, the existence of a pluralistic cultural system is not a multicultural situation—although it may be an intermediate stage. The state and the veteran and dominant elites still hold on to a monoculturalist vision of society, and the mechanism of the melting pot is still implicitly at work. Thus, the Israeli state is still far from granting legitimacy, recognition, and legal and institutional frameworks to this pluralistic situation.

Yet the desire of some of the abovementioned cultures is, in fact, to replace the previous hegemony with a new one by achieving political and cultural dominance, and either to force their own rules of the game and versions of collective identity on all the other sociocultural segments or to exclude them from the collectivity. The strategy of the other segments is to preserve or gain, if not hegemony, then at least a more or less dominant position, or—as the Arabs and Ethiopians aim to do—to participate in a culturally or politically dominant coalition. This social strategy is mainly available for most of the weakest minority Jewish groups and for the Arabs. Finally, there are the options of territorial or cultural separatism (labeled "cultural autonomy") or, conversely, a Jewish-Arab binational state within the boundaries of historical Palestine.[3]

Although they are engaged in sharpening their own identities, the boundaries around these identities, and their institutional and political infrastructures, Israel's diverse ethnic, religious, racial, and religious cultures are not ready to give up the common denominator of their claim to partnership and share-holding in the Israeli state. All of them aspire to remain "Israelis" politically and Jews (or Arabs) ethnically or nationally. Nevertheless, the meaning of this Israeliness is very different from its original monocultural and hegemonic content and definition. Every cultural segment provides its own particularistic meaning of "being Israeli" or "Jewish" in accordance with its symbolic and material interests, as the Jewish traditionalist, Russian, and Ethiopian cases clearly demonstrate. Everyone desires to share the common goods, but on their own terms and in their own interests.

While all other components of the hegemonic culture have collapsed, the value and the idea of the state, or stateness, has remained a very central component of the collectivity and is the main factor that binds together all the diverse political-cultural segments. Two major roles of the state have actually increased with the collapse of the secular Zionist hegemony—the extractive-redistributive role and the security-supplying role. The role of the state as a welfare state has become more salient, because the diverse political-cultural segments are continuously demanding redistribution of wealth and greater shares in the common goods of an economy that is simultaneously becoming more profit-oriented and privatized.

In the course of its crystallization, the Israeli immigrant settler state developed war- and conflict-oriented as well as complementary peace-oriented values, symbols, and institutions, along with their accompa-

3. A binational state within the boundaries of historical Palestine has recently been proposed by some Palestinian intellectuals, like Edward Said, to challenge both the Zionist and Palestinian exclusionary nationalisms and oppressive regimes.

nying rhetoric. Nonetheless, as a result of the routinization of war and conflict, an all-embracing dominant military-cultural complex developed to blur the distinctions between peace and war and between rational military and ideological religious "reasons" for keeping or giving up the occupied territories. Even the main initial motives for "peacemaking" were driven either by xenophobic feelings of "separation" or by instrumental manipulation to improve control over "the other side" and to ensure Israeli military might.

As noted in chapter 7, the first "peace in exchange for territory" agreement with Egypt was made in order to increase control over "Judea and Samaria" and was immediately followed by the 1982 war in Lebanon for the very same reason. The Oslo Accords with the Palestinians were made chiefly in order to shed responsibility for densely Arab-populated areas and to establish indirect control over the Palestinians without giving up "overall security responsibility" for any part of the "Land of Israel." This came about only after the political and military elite had reached the conclusion that there could be no acceptable military solution to the Palestinian problem. The formalization of the de facto tacit alliance with the Hashemite kingdom of Jordan was clearly aimed at weakening Palestinian political and military strength.

Even if a conclusive agreement is reached with the Palestinians,[4] peace is made with Syria, and arrangements and "normalization" are arrived at with the "outer circle" hostile Arab and Muslim states (e.g., Iraq, Libya, and Iran), the objective and subjective situation of the Israeli state will hardly be altered from the external security point of view. The existential anxiety built into the collective identity and memory, which fuels expressions of the military-cultural complex, will continue to exist. A demonic worldview that always leads to self-fulfilling "worst-case" prophecies (as demonstrated in chapter 7) will persist for at least another generation. Armed conflict will be reshaped into an "armed peace," frequently shackled by local clashes and mutual terror attacks initiated by peripheral but salient fundamentalist groups, which will continue to exist.

4. The author is very doubtful about the possibility of reaching a conclusive agreement with the Palestinians at this stage. Taking into account the geographical dispersal of the Jewish settlements in the Palestinian core territories, separation without dismantlement of most settlements is almost impossible. Apart from this, other problems, such as the return of Palestinian refugees, compensation for their vast properties, free passage between the Gaza Strip and the main Palestinian territory (without Israeli control), joint rule over Jerusalem, etc., seem to be insuperable obstacles to a solution within the present cognitive paradigms of each side.

Thus, the most central role of the state, aside from the regulation of resources and welfare, objectively and subjectively is still and will continue to be providing security. The social and cultural strata that make up the rank and file of the military will continue to dominate the Israeli state both in political and symbolic terms, but will be forced to share more power and material resources with the other segments.

The initial era of hegemony, as described in chapter 3, is over. The Israeli state is divided among seven major cultures challenging one another for control of the basic rules of the game, access to and criteria for resource distribution, and the identity of the polity. Six of them are bound together under the additional umbrella of Jewishness and militarism—two ambiguous but powerfully interlinked metacultural codes. Thus, some ingredients of the original hegemonic system have not only persisted but also actually increased in centrality and importance, albeit in a very different context. Because of the centrifugal movement and the fragmentation of the cultural system and the collective identity, the state and its bureaucratic institutions have become the most effective tool for coordination among old and new Israelis. Israeliness is now in the course of becoming a loose federation of identities—a prefix for other identities, as well as a legal and political concept of citizenship granted by the state to different segments of society.

Works Cited

Abrahamson, B. *Military Professionalization and Political Powers*. Beverly Hills, Calif.: Sage Publications, 1972.

Adamson, W. L. *Hegemony and Revolution: A Study of Antonio Gramsci's Political and Cultural Theory*. Berkeley and Los Angeles: University of California Press, 1980.

Aharoni, Y. *The Political Economy of Israel*. Tel Aviv: Am Oved and Eshkol Institute, Hebrew University, 1991. In Hebrew.

———. *State-Owned Enterprises in Israel and Abroad*. Tel Aviv: Ts'erikover, 1979. In Hebrew.

Alford, R. A. "Paradigms of Relations between State and Society." In *Stress and Contradiction in Modern Capitalism: Public Policy and the Theory of the State*, ed. Leon N. Lindeberg, R. Alford, C. Crouch, and C. Offe. Lexington, Mass.: Lexington Books, 1975.

Al-Haj, Majid. *Education, Empowerment, and Control: The Case of the Arabs in Israel*. Albany: State University of New York Press, 1995.

———. "Soviet Immigration as Viewed by Jews and Arabs: Divided Attitudes in a Divided Country." In *Population and Social Change in Israel*, ed. C. Goldscheider, pp. 90–108. Boulder, Colo.: Westview Press, 1992.

Almog, Oz. *The Sabra: A Portrait*. Tel Aviv: Am Oved, 1997. In Hebrew. English version forthcoming.

Anderson, Benedict R. O'G. *Imagined Communities: Reflections on the Origin and Spread of Nationalism*. New York: Verso, 1991.

Antonovsky, A. "Sociopolitical Attitudes in Israel." *Amot* 6 (1963): 11–22. In Hebrew.

Aran, G. "The Beginning of the Road from Religious Zionism to Zionist Religion." In *Studies in Contemporary Jewry*, vol. 2. Bloomington: Indiana University Press, 1985.

Arian, Asher. *Politics in Israel: The Second Generation*. Rev. ed. London: Chatham House, 1985.

————. *Security Threatened: Surveying Israeli Opinion on Peace and War.* Jaffe Center for Strategic Studies. Cambridge: Cambridge University Press, 1995.

Arian, Asher, I. Talmud, and T. Herman. *National Security and Public Opinion in Israel.* Boulder, Colo.: Westview Press for Jaffe Center for Strategic Studies, Tel Aviv University, 1988.

Aronson, S. *Israel's Nuclear Programme: The Six-Day War and Its Ramifications.* London: King's College London Mediterranean Studies, 1999.

Aschheim, E. S. *Brothers and Strangers: The East European Jew in German and German Jewish Consciousness, 1800–1923.* Madison: University of Wisconsin Press, 1982.

Avigur, Shaul, Yitzhak Ben-Zvi, Eliezer Galili, and Yehuda Szlutzky, *The History of the Hagana.* Tel Aviv: Am Oved, 1954. In Hebrew.

Avineri, Shlomo. *The Making of Modern Zionism: The Intellectual Origins of the Jewish State.* London: Weidenfeld & Nicolson, 1981.

————. "The Zionist and the Jewish Religious Tradition: The Dialectics of Redemption and Secularization." In *Zionism and Religion,* ed. S. Almog, J. Reinharz, and A. Shapira, pp. 9–20. Jerusalem: Zalman Schazar Center, 1994. In Hebrew.

Azarya, Victor, and Naomi Chazan. "Disengagement from the State in Africa: Reflections on the Experiences of Ghana and Guinea." *Comparative Studies in Society and History,* 29, 1 (1987): 106–31.

Azaryahu, M. *State Cults: Celebrating Independence and Commemorating The Fallen in Israel, 1948–1956.* Beersheba: Ben-Gurion University of the Negev Press, 1995. In Hebrew.

Bank of Israel. *Annual Report, 1997.* Jerusalem: Government Printer, 1998.

Bar Gal, Y. *Moledet and Geography during a Hundred Years of Zionist Education.* Tel Aviv: Am Oved, 1993. In Hebrew.

Bar-Lev, M. "Graduates of the High-School Yeshivoth in Eretz-Israel: Between Tradition and Innovation." Ph.D. thesis, Bar Ilan University, 1986. In Hebrew.

Barnett, Michael N. *Confronting the Cost of War: Military Power, State and Society in Egypt and Israel.* Princeton: Princeton University Press, 1992.

Bar-Tal, D. *The Rocky Roads toward Peace: Societal Beliefs in Times of Intractable Conflict—The Israeli Case.* Jerusalem: Hebrew University, Institute for Enrichment in Education, 1996

Bar-Yosef, R. "De-Socialization and Re-Socialization: The Process of Adaptation of New Immigrants in Israel." *International Migration Review* 2, 3 (1966): 27–45.

————. "The Moroccans: The Background to the Problem." *Molad* 17 (1959): 381–91. In Hebrew.

Barzilai, G. "The Argument of 'National Security' in Politics and Jurisprudence." In *Security Concerns: Insights from the Israeli Experience,* ed. Daniel Bar-Tal, Dan Jacobson, and Aharon Klieman, pp. 243–66. Stamford, Conn.: JAI Press, 1998.

Beckford, J. A. *Religion and Advanced Industrial Society.* London: Routledge, 1992.

Begin, Menachem. "War of No Choice and War by Choice." *Yedioth Acharonot* [Hebrew Daily], 20 August 1982.

Bellah, R. N. *Beyond Belief: Essays on Religion in a Post-Traditional World.* New York: Harper & Row, 1970. Reprint. Berkeley and Los Angeles: University of California Press, 1991.

———. "Civil Religion in America." *Daedalus* 1 (1967): 1–26.

Ben-Ari, E., and Y. Bilu. "Saints' Sanctuaries in Israeli Development Towns: On a Mechanism of Urban Transformation." *Urban Anthropology* 16 (1987): 243–72.

Ben-Eliezer, Uri. *The Making of Israeli Militarism.* Bloomington: Indiana University Press, 1998.

Benita, E., and G. Noam. "Absorption of Ethiopian Immigrants in Israel: Selected Findings from Local Surveys." In *Ethiopian Jews in the Limelight,* ed. Shalva Weil, *Israel Social Science Research* 1 (1997): 58–98.

Benita, E., G. Noam, and R. Levy. *Local Surveys of Ethiopian Immigrants: Findings from Afula, Netanya and Kiryat Gat.* Jerusalem: Brookdale Institute, 1994. In Hebrew.

Ben-Porat, A. *The Bourgeoisie: The History of Israeli Bourgeoisie.* Jerusalem: Eshkol Library, Magnes Press, 1999. In Hebrew.

Ben-Yehuda, Nachman. *The Masada Myth: Collective Memory and Mythmaking in Israel.* Madison: University of Wisconsin Press, 1995.

———. "The Social Meanings of Alternative Systems: Some Exploratory Notes." In *The Israeli-State and Society: Boundaries and Frontiers,* ed. Baruch Kimmerling, pp. 152–64. Albany: State University of New York Press, 1989.

Benziman, U., and A. Mansour. *Subtenants: The Arabs of Israel.* Jerusalem: Keter, 1992. In Hebrew.

Berkovitch, Nitza. "Motherhood as a National Mission: The Construction of Womanhood in the Legal Discourse of Israel." *Women's Studies International Forum* 20, 5–6 (1997): 605–19.

Bernstein, D. "The Black Panthers: Conflict and Protest in Israeli Society." *Megamot* 25 (1980): 65–79. In Hebrew.

———. "Immigrant Transit Camps: The Formation of Dependent Relations in Israeli Society." *Ethnic and Racial Studies* 11, 3 (1981): 26–43.

Beyer, G. A. "The Evolving United States Response to Soviet-Jewish Emigration." In *Soviet-Jewish Emigration and Resettlement in the 1990s,* ed. T. Basok and R. Brym, pp. 141–58. Toronto: York Lines Press, 1991.

Biale, D. *Power and Powerlessness in Jewish History.* New York: Schocken Books, 1986.

Bichler, S. "The Political Economy of Military Spending in Israel." Ph.D. thesis. Hebrew University, Jerusalem, Department of Political Sciences, 1991. In Hebrew.

Birnbaum, Pierre. *States and Collective Action: The European Experience.* New York: Cambridge University Press, 1988.

Bishara, Azmi. "On the Palestinian Minority in Israel." *Theoriya U'bikort* 3 (1993): 7–20. In Hebrew.

Bocock, Robert. *Hegemony.* New York: Tavistock Publications, 1986.

Bonacich, Edna, and Richard P. Appelbaum, with Ku-Sup Chin et al. *Behind the Label: Inequality in the Los Angeles Apparel Industry*. Berkeley and Los Angeles: University of California Press, 2000.

Bonacich, Edna, and John Modell. *The Economic Basis of Ethnic Solidarity : A Study of Japanese Americans*. Berkeley and Los Angeles: University of California Press, 1980.

Brown, C. G. "A Revisionist Approach to Religious Changes." In *Religion and Modernization: Sociologists and Historians Debate the Secularization Thesis*, ed. Steven Bruce, pp. 31–216. Oxford: Oxford University Press, 1992.

Brym, R. J., and R. Ryvkina. *The Jews of Moscow, Kiev and Minsk: Identity, Antisemitism and Emigration*. London: Macmillan, 1994.

Campbell, C. D. *Toward a Sociology of Irreligion*. New York: Cambridge University Press, 1971.

Chazan, N. "Israeli Women and Peace Activism." In *Calling the Equality Bluff*, ed. B. Swirski and M. Safir, pp. 152–61. New York: Pergamon, 1992.

Cohen, R. "Israel's Problematic Absorption of Soviet Jews." In *Soviet-Jewish Emigration and Resettlement in the 1990s*, ed. T. Basok and R. Brym, pp. 67–90. Toronto: York Lines Press, 1991.

Cohen, S. A. "The Peace Process and the Impact on the Development of a 'Slimmer and Smarter' Israeli Defence Force." *Israel Affairs* 1, 4 (1995): 1–21.

Cohen, Yinon. "War and Social Integration: The Effects of the Israeli-Arab Conflict on Jewish Emigration from Israel." *American Sociological Review* 53 (December 1988): 908–18.

Collier, D., and S. Levitsky. "Democracy with Adjectives: Conceptual Innovation in Comparative Research." *World Politics* 49 (1997): 430–51.

Cordova, A. "The Institutionalization of a [Jewish] Cultural Center in Palestine: The Case of the Writers' Association." *Jewish Social Studies* 42 (1980): 37–62.

Corinald, M. *Ethiopian Jewry: Tradition and Identity*. Jerusalem: Reuven Mass Publishers, 1988. In Hebrew.

Coser, Lewis A. *The Functions of Social Conflict*. New York: Free Press, 1956.

Cuddihy, J. M. *The Ordeal of Civility: Freud, Marx, Lévi-Strauss, and the Jewish Struggle with Modernity*. New York: Basic Books, 1974.

Davie, M. R. *World Immigration: With Special Reference to the United States*. New York: Macmillan, 1946.

Dawisha, K. "Democratization and Political Participation: Research Concepts and Methodologies." In *The Consolidation of Democracy in East-Central Europe*, ed. id. and B. Parrott, 1: 40–65. Cambridge: Cambridge University Press, 1997.

Deshen, Shlomo. "The Judaism of Middle-Eastern Immigrants." *Jerusalem Quarterly* 13 (1979): 98–110.

Dominguez, V. R. *People as Subject, People as Object—Selfhood and Peoplehood in Contemporary Israel*. Madison: University of Wisconsin Press, 1989.

Dowty, Alan. *The Jewish State: A Century Later*. Berkeley and Los Angeles: University of California Press, 1998.

————. "The Use of Emergency Powers in Israel." *Middle East Review* 30, 1 (1988): 34–46.

Dubnow, Simon [Semen Markovich]. *History of the Jews*. Translated from the Russian by Moshe Spiegel. 5 vols. South Brunswick, N.J.: Thomas Yoseloff, 1967–73.

Efroni, L. "Trends in the Israeli Payment System." In *Women, the Rising Power — Promotion of Women at Work — Shattering the Glass Ceiling,* ed. A. Maor, pp. 45–49. Tel Aviv: Sifriyat Poalim, 1997. In Hebrew.

Eisenstadt, S. N. *Israeli Society*. New York: Basic Books, 1967.

————. *The Transformation of Israeli Society: An Essay in Interpretation*. London: Weidenfeld & Nicolson, 1985.

Etzioni-Halevy, Eva, with Rina Shapira. *Political Culture in Israel: Cleavage and Integration among Israeli Jews*. New York: Praeger, 1977

Evans, Peter B., Dietrich Rueschemeyer, and Theda Skocpol. "On the Road toward a More Adequate Understanding of the State." In *Bringing the State Back In*, ed. id., pp. 347–66. Berkeley and Los Angeles: University of California Press, 1985.

Ezrahi, Y., and R. Gal. *High-School Student Worldview and Attitudes towards Society, Security and Peace*. Report. Rishon LeZion: Carmel Social Research Center, 1995. In Hebrew.

Fackenheim, E. L. *The Jewish Return to History: Reflections in the Age of Auschwitz and a New Jerusalem*. New York: Schocken Books, 1978.

Feige, M. "Social Movements, Hegemony, and Political Myth: A Comparative Study of Gush Emunim and Peace Now Ideologies." Ph.D. thesis, Hebrew University, Jerusalem, 1995. In Hebrew.

Fein, A. *The Immigrants of the CIS: Survey on Their Exposure to Communication Media, 1994*. Jerusalem: Tazpit Institute, 1994. In Hebrew.

Feiner, S. *Haskalah and History: The Emergence of a Modern Jewish Awareness of the Past*. Jerusalem: Zalman Shazar Center for Jewish History, 1995. In Hebrew.

Firer, R. *The Agents of Jewish Education*. Tel Aviv: Sifriyat Poalim, 1985. In Hebrew.

Friedman, Menachem. "The Haredim and the Holocaust." *Jerusalem Quarterly* 5 (1973): 84–114.

————. *Orthodox Society: Sources, Trends, and Processes*. Jerusalem: Jerusalem Institute of Study of Israel, 1991. In Hebrew.

————. *Society and Religion: The Non-Zionist Orthodox in Eretz-Israel — 1918–1936*. Jerusalem: Yad Ben Zvi, 1977. In Hebrew.

————. "The State of Israel as a Theological Dilemma." In *The Israeli State and Society: Boundaries and Frontiers*, ed. Baruch Kimmerling, pp. 163–215. Albany: State University of New York Press, 1989.

Friedmann, D. "The Case of the Falas Mura." In *The Beta Israel in Ethiopia and Israel: Studies on Ethiopian Jews*, ed. Tudor Parfitt and Emanuela Trevisan Semi, pp. 70–80. Surrey, Eng.: Curzon Press, 1999.

Gal, R. "A Portrait of the Israeli Soldier." In *Contributions in Military Studies*, No. 52. New York: Greenwood Press, 1986.

Galnoor, Itzhak. *The Partition of Palestine: Decision Crossroads in the Zionist Movement*. Albany: State University of New York Press, 1995.

—————. *Steering Politics: Communication and Politics in Israel.* Beverly Hills, Calif.: Sage Publications, 1992.

Gellner, Ernest. *Nations and Nationalism.* Ithaca, N.Y.: Cornell University Press, 1983.

Gertz, N. "The Security Narrative in Israeli Literature and Cinema." In *Security Concerns: Insights from the Israeli Experience,* ed. Daniel Bar-Tal, Dan Jacobson, and Aharon Klieman, pp. 193–214. Stamford, Conn.: JAI Press, 1998.

Giddens, A. *The Nation-State and Violence: A Contemporary Critique of Historical Materialism.* Berkeley and Los Angeles: University of California Press, 1985.

Glazer, Nathan, and Daniel Patrick Moynihan. *Beyond the Melting Pot: The Negroes, Puerto Ricans, Jews, Italians, and Irish of New York City.* Cambridge, Mass.: MIT Press, 1963.

Goldberg, A., and A. Kirchenbaum. "Black Newcomers to Israel: Contact Situation and Social Distance." *Sociology and Social Research* 74, 1 (1989): 52–57.

Gonen, A. "Population Spread in the Course of Passing from Yishuv to State." In *The Passing from Yishuv to State,* ed. S. Pilovski. Haifa: Haifa University, 1968. In Hebrew.

Gordon, Aharon David. "Our Account with Religion." In *The Writings of A. D. Gordon,* vol. 1. Jerusalem: World Zionist Organization, 1925. In Hebrew.

Goren, D. *Secrecy and the Right to Know.* Ramat Gan: Turtledove Publishers, 1979.

Graetz, Heinrich. *History of the Jews.* 6 vols. Philadelphia: Jewish Publication Society of America, 1891–98.

Greenberg, Stanley. *Legitimating the Illegitimate: State, Markets, and Resistance in South Africa.* Berkeley and Los Angeles: University of California Press, 1987.

Grinberg, L. L. "The Political Economy of the Dismantlement of the Old Histadrut." *Economic Quarterly* 1 (April 1995): 69–72.

—————. *Split Corporatism in Israel.* Albany: State University of New York Press, 1991.

Grossman, D. *Present Absentees.* Tel Aviv: Dvir, 1992. In Hebrew.

Gurr, B. "Between Immigration and Remaining." In *Soviet Union Jews in Transition,* ed. D. Prita, pp. 39–49. Jerusalem: Magnes Press, 1995. In Hebrew.

Hacohen, D. *The "Direct Absorption" System and Its Implications: Sociocultural Absorption of Immigrants from the CIS at the Beginning of the 1990s.* Jerusalem: Jerusalem Institute for Israel Research, 1994. In Hebrew.

Handelman, D., and L. Shamgar-Handelman, "Shaping Time: The Choice of the National Emblem of Israel." In *Culture and History: New Directions,* ed. E. Ohnuki-Tierney, pp. 193–216. Stanford: Stanford University Press, 1990.

Harkabi, Yehoshafat. *The Bar Kokhba Syndrome: Risk and Realism in International Politics.* Translated by Max D. Ticktin. Edited by David Altshuler. Chappaqua, N.Y.: Rossel Books, 1983.

———. *Israel's Fateful Decisions*. London: I. B. Tauris, 1988.

Harshav, B. *Language in Time of Revolution*. Berkeley and Los Angeles: University of California Press, 1993.

Hasson, S. *Urban Social Movements in Jerusalem: The Protest of the Second Generation*. Albany, N.Y.: State University of New York Press, 1993.

Hattis, S. *The Bi-National Idea in Palestine during Mandatory Times*. Haifa: Shikmona Publishing Co., 1970.

Hazony, Y. *The Jewish State: The Struggle for Israel's Souls*. New York: Basic Books, 2000.

Hechter, Michael. *Internal Colonialism: The Celtic Fringe in British National Development, 1536–1966*. Berkeley and Los Angeles: University of California Press, 1975.

Hegel, G. W. F. *Grundlinien der Philosophie des Rechts*. 1833. Hamburg: F. Meiner, 1955.

Helman, Sara. "Conscientious Objection to Military Service as an Attempt to Redefine the Contents of Citizenship." Ph.D. thesis, Hebrew University, Jerusalem, Department of Sociology, 1993. In Hebrew.

Herzog, E. *The Bureaucracy and Ethiopian Immigrants: Dependency Relationships in an Absorption Center*. Tel Aviv: Cherikower Publishers, 1998. In Hebrew.

———. "The Bureaucratic Absorption of Ethiopian Immigrants in Israel." In *Between Africa and Zion*, ed. S. Kaplan, T. Parfitt, and E. Trevisian Semi, pp. 189–222. Jerusalem: Ben-Zvi Institute, 1995. In Hebrew.

Herzog, H. "Women's Status in the Shadow of Security." In *Security Concerns: Insights from the Israeli Experience*, ed. Daniel Bar-Tal, Dan Jacobson, and Aharon Klieman, pp. 329–46. Stamford, Conn.: JAI Press, 1998.

Hirschberg, H. J. "The Oriental Jewish Communities." In *Religion in the Middle East: Three Religions in Concord and Conflict*, ed. A. J. Arberry, 1: 119–225. London: Cambridge University Press, 1969.

Hodge, R. W. "Toward a Theory of Racial Differences in Employment." *Social Forces* 52 (1973): 18–51.

Hofnung, M. *Law, Democracy and National Security in Israel*. Aldershot, Eng.: Dartmouth Publishing Co., 1997.

Holt, D. "The Culture Cluster: A Comparative Perspective on Ethiopian Jewish Problems in Israel." In *Ethiopian Jews in the Limelight*, ed. Shalva Weil, *Israel Social Science Research* 1 (1995): 97–116.

Horowitz, D., and B. Kimmerling. "Some Social Implications of Military Service and Reserve System in Israel." *Archives européennes de sociologie* 15 (1974): 262–76.

Horowitz, Dan, and Moshe Lissak. *Origins of the Israeli Polity: Palestine under the Mandate*. Translated from the Hebrew by Charles Hoffman. Chicago: University of Chicago Press, 1978.

———. *Trouble in Utopia: The Overburdened Polity of Israel*. Albany: State University of New York Press, 1989.

Horowitz, T. *Between Three Political Cultures: The Immigrants from the Former Soviet Union in Israel*. Jerusalem: Hebrew University, Davis Institute, 1996. In Hebrew.

Horowitz, T., and H. Frenkel. "Immigrants in an Absorption Center." Research Report, No. 185. Jerusalem: Szold Institute, 1975. In Hebrew.

Huntington, S. P. *The Soldier and the State: The Theory and Politics of Civil-Military Relations.* Cambridge, Mass.: Harvard University Press, Belknap Press, 1957.

Israel. Ministry of Foreign Affairs and Ministry of Justice. Second report of the State of Israel concerning the implementation of the United Nations Convention on the Elimination of all Forms of Discrimination against Women (CEDAW). Report submitted in 1997 to the UN Committee on the Elimination of Discrimination against Women. Cited in footnotes as CEDAW report.

Israeli Women's Network. "The Status of Women in Israeli Law." In *Women in Israel — Information, Statistics, and Analysis,* 1996, pp. 14–15. Israeli Women's Network Information Bulletin (Tel Aviv). In Hebrew.

Izraeli, D. N. "Gender in the Labor World," In *Sex, Gender, Politics: Women in Israel,* ed. id. et al., pp. 167–216. Tel Aviv: Ha'kibbutz Ha'meuchad, 1999. In Hebrew.

Jacobson, D. *Rights across Borders: Immigration and the Decline of Citizenship.* Baltimore: Johns Hopkins University Press, 1996.

Janowitz, M. *The Professional Soldier.* New York: Free Press, 1960.

Jiryis, Sabri. *The Arabs in Israel.* Haifa: Al-Itihad, 1966. Translated from Arabic by Inea Bushnaq. New York: Monthly Review Press, 1976. In Hebrew.

Johnson, J. J. *The Military and Society in Latin America.* Stanford: Stanford University Press, 1964.

Kahane, R., and T. Rapoport. *The Origins of Postmodern Youth: Informal Youth Movements in Comparative Perspective.* Berlin and New York: Walter de Gruyter, 1997.

Kaplan, Steven. *The Beta Israel (Falasha) in Ethiopia: From Earliest Times to the Twentieth Century.* New York: New York University Press, 1992.

———. "History, Halakha and Identity: Beta-Israel and World Jewry." In *Ethiopian Jews in the Limelight,* ed. Shalva Weil, *Israel Social Science Research* 1 (1997): 58–98.

Karsh, E., and I. Karsh. *Empires of Sand: The Struggle for Mastery of the Middle East, 1789–1923.* Cambridge, Mass.: Harvard University Press, 1999.

Katz, E., and M. Gurevitch, *The Secularization of Leisure: Culture and Communication in Israel.* London: Faber & Faber, 1976.

Katz, J. *Jewish Nationalism.* Jerusalem: World Zionist Organization, 1983.

Keane, J. *Democracy and Civil Society.* London: Verso, 1988.

Keren, M. *Ben-Gurion and the Intellectuals: Power, Knowledge and Charisma.* Dekalb: Northern Illinois University Press, 1983.

———. "Israel's Security Intellectuals." In *Security Concerns: Insights from the Israeli Experience,* ed. Daniel Bar-Tal, Dan Jacobson, and Aharon Klieman, pp. 181–92. Stamford, Conn.: JAI Press, 1998.

Kessler, D. *The Falashas: A Short History of the Ethiopian Jews.* London: Frank Cass, 1996.

Kimmerling, Baruch. "Academic History Caught in the Cross Fire: The Case of Israeli-Jewish Historiography." *History and Memory* 7, 4 (1995): 41–65.

———. "Anomie and Integration in Israeli Society and the Salience of the Arab Israeli Conflict." *Studies in Comparative International Development* 9, 3 (1974): 64–89.

———. "Between 'Alexandria-on-Hudson' and Zion." In *Israeli State and Society*, ed. id., pp. 224–57.

———. "Between Hegemony and Dormant *Kulturkampf* in Israel." *Israel Affairs* 4, 3–4 (1998): 49–72.

———. "Between the Primordial and the Civil Definitions of the Collective Identity." In *Comparative Social Dynamics*, ed. E. Cohen, M. Lissak, and U. Almagor, pp. 262–83. Boulder, Colo.: Westview Press, 1985.

———. "Boundaries and Frontiers of the Israeli Control System." In *The Israeli State and Society: Boundaries and Frontiers*, ed. id., pp. 265–84. Albany: State University of New York Press, 1989.

———. "Change and Continuity in Zionist Territorial Orientations and Politics." *Comparative Politics* 14, 2 (1982): 191–210.

———. "Determination of the Boundaries and the Frameworks of Conscription: Two Dimensions of Civil-Military Relations in Israel." *Studies in Comparative International Development* 14 (1979): 24–41.

———. "Elections as a Battleground over Collective Identity." In *Elections in Israel, 1996*, ed. A. Arian and M. Shamir, pp. 27–44. Albany: New York State University Press, 1999.

———. "Elites and Civil Societies in the Middle East." In *Elites, Minorities and Economic Growth*, ed. E. S. Brezis and P. Temin, pp. 55–64. Rotterdam: Elsevier, 1999.

———. "The Israeli Civil Guard." In *Supplementary Military Forces: Reserves, Militias, and Auxiliaries*, ed. L. A. Zurcher and G. Harries-Jenkins, pp. 107–25. Beverly Hills, Calif.: Sage Publications, 1978.

———. "Legislation and Jurisprudence in the Immigrant Settler State." Forthcoming in *Mekarey Mishpat* (Bar Ilan University Faculty of Law, Ramat-Gan) 16, 1, 2001. In Hebrew.

———. "The Most Important War." *Ha'aretz* [Hebrew Daily], 1 August 1982.

———. "The New Israelis: Plurality of Cultures without Multiculturalism." *Alpayim* 16 (1998): 264–308. In Hebrew.

———. "Patterns of Militarism in Israel." *Archives européennes de sociologie* 2 (1993): 1–28.

———. "Peace for Territories: A Macro-Sociological Analysis of the Concept of Peace in Zionist Ideology." *Journal of Applied Behavioral Science* 23, 3 (1987): 13–34.

———. "Political Subcultures and Civilian Militarism in a Settler-Immigrant Society." In *Security Concerns: Insights from the Israeli Experience*, ed. Daniel Bar-Tal, Dan Jacobson, and Aharon Klieman, 395–416. Stamford, Conn.: JAI Press, 1998.

———. "The Power-Oriented Settlement: Bargaining between Israelis and Palestinians." In *The PLO and Israel: From the Road to the Oslo Agreement and Back?* ed. M. Ma'oz and A. Sela, pp. 223–51. New York: St. Martin's Press, 1997.

———. "Process of Formation of Palestinian Collective Identities: The Ottoman and Colonial Periods." *Middle Eastern Studies* 36, 2 (April 2000): 48–81.

———. "Religion, Nationalism and Democracy in Israel." *Constellations* 6, 3 (1999): 339–63.

———. "The Social Construction of Israel's National Security." In *Democratic Societies and Their Armed Forces: Israel in Comparative Context*, ed. Stuart A. Cohen, pp. 215–52. London: Frank Cass, 2000.

———. "Sociology, Ideology and Nation-Building: The Palestinians and Their Meaning in Israeli Sociology." *American Sociological Review* 57 (1992): 446–60.

———. "State Building, State Autonomy, and the Identity of Society: The Case of the Israeli State." *Journal of Historical Sociology* 6, 4 (1993): 397–429.

———. "Yes, Back to the Family." *Politika* 40 (1993): 40–45. In Hebrew.

———. *Zionism and Economy.* Cambridge: Schenkman, 1983.

———. *Zionism and Territory: The Socioterritorial Dimension of Zionist Politics.* Berkeley: Institute of International Studies, University of California, 1983.

———, ed. *The Israeli State and Society: Boundaries and Frontiers.* Albany, N.Y. : State University of New York Press, 1989.

Kimmerling, Baruch, and Irit Backer. *The Interrupted System: Israeli Civilians in War and Routine Times.* New Brunswick, N.J.: Transaction Books, 1985.

Kimmerling, Baruch, and Joel S. Migdal. *Palestinians: The Making of a People.* New York: Free Press, 1993. Cambridge, Mass.: Harvard University Press, 1994.

Kimmerling, Baruch, and D. Moore. "Collective Identity as Agency, and Structuration of Society: Tested by the Israeli Case." *International Review of Sociology* 7, 1 (1997): 25–50.

Kook, A. I. *Abraham Isaac Kook: The Lights of Penitence; The Moral Principles; Lights of Holiness: Essays, Letters and Poems.* Translated by Ben Zion Bokser. New York: Paulist Press, 1978.

Krasner, S. D. "Approaches to the State: Alternative Conceptions and Historical Dynamics." *Comparative Politics* 16 (1984): 223–46.

Kretzmer, D. *The Legal Status of the Arabs in Israel.* Boulder, Colo.: Westview Press, 1990.

Lahav, Pnina. "When the 'Palliative' Just Spoils Things: The Parliamentary Debate in the Equal Rights Law." *Zemanim,* nos. 46–47 (1993): 151. In Hebrew.

Laitin, D. D. *Identity in Formation: The Russian-Speaking Populations in the Near Abroad.* Ithaca, N.Y.: Cornell University Press, 1998.

Landau, J. M. *The Arabs in Israel: A Political Study.* New York: Oxford University Press, 1969.

Laor, Yitzhak. *Narratives without Natives: Essays on Israeli Literature.* Tel Aviv: Ha'kibbutz Ha'meuchad, 1995. In Hebrew.

Laqueur, W. *A History of Zionism.* London: Weidenfeld & Nicolson, 1972.

Leibowitz, Y. *Judaism, Human Values and the Jewish State.* Translated and edited by E. Goldman. Cambridge, Mass.: Harvard University Press, 1992.

Leshem, E. "The Israeli Population and Its Attitude to the Immigrants of the 1990s." *Social Security* 40 (1993): 54–73. In Hebrew.

———. "Jewishness, Lifestyle and Opinions toward State and Religion among the Immigrants from the Former Soviet Union." In *Yearbook of Religion and State, 1993–1994,* ed. T. Horowitz. Tel Aviv: Center for a Plural Society and Ha'kibbutz Ha'meuchad, 1994. In Hebrew.

Levy, Y. *Trial and Error: Israel's Route from War to De-Escalation.* Albany: New York State University Press, 1997.

Lieberson, S. *A Piece of Pie: Black and White Immigrants since 1880.* Berkeley and Los Angeles: University of California Press, 1980.

Lieblich, A. *Transition to Adulthood during Military Service: The Israeli Case.* Albany: State University of New York Press, 1989.

Liebman, C. S. "In Search of a Status: The Israeli Government and the Zionist Movement." *Forum* 28/29 (1978): 39–56.

Liebman, C. S., and Eliezer Don-Yehiya. *Civil Religion in Israel: Traditional Judaism and Political Culture in the Jewish State.* Berkeley and Los Angeles: University of California Press, 1983.

Lijphart, A. *Democracies in Plural Societies: A Comparative Exploration.* New Haven: Yale University Press, 1977.

Lincoln, B. *Discourse and the Construction of Society: Comparative Studies of Myth, Rituals, and Classification.* New York: Oxford University Press, 1989.

Lissak, Moshe. "The Absorption Policy toward the Immigrants from the Soviet Union: A Sociohistorical Perspective." *Soviet Union Jewry,* 1992 36: 5–25. In Hebrew.

———. *Immigrants from the Commonwealth of Independent States between Segregation and Integration.* Jerusalem: Social Policy Research Center, 1995. In Hebrew.

———. "The Intifada and Israeli Society: Historical and Sociological Perspectives." In *The Effects of the Intifada on Israeli Society: Data, Evaluation, and Predictions,* ed. R. Gal, pp. 16–18. Zichron Yaacov: Israeli Institute for Military Studies, 1990. In Hebrew.

———. "The Israel Defense Forces as an Agent of Socialization and Education: A Research in Role in a Democratic Society." In *The Perceived Role of the Military,* ed. M. R. van Gils, pp. 325–40. Rotterdam: Rotterdam University Press, 1971.

———. *The Mass Immigration of the Fifties: The Failure of the Melting-Pot Policy.* Jerusalem: Bialik Institute, 1999. In Hebrew.

Lomsky-Feder, E. "Youth in the Shadow of War, War in the Light of Youth: Life-Stories of Israeli Veterans." In *Adolescence, Careers, and Culture,* ed. W. Meeus et al., pp. 393–408. Berlin: Walter de Gruyter, 1992.

London, Y. "The Quilt of the Left." *Politika* 4 (1985): 8–13.

Luckmann, Thomas. *The Invisible Religion: The Problem of Religion in Modern Society.* New York: Macmillan, 1967.

———. "The New and the Old in Religion." In *Social Theory for a Changing Society,* ed. Pierre Bourdieu and James S. Coleman, pp. 166–82. Boulder, Colo.: Westview Press; New York: Russell Sage Foundation, 1991.

Lukes, Steven. *Power: A Radical View.* London: Macmillan, 1974.

Lustick, I. *Arabs in a Jewish State: Israel's Control of a National Minority.*
Austin: University of Texas Press, 1980.

———. *For the Land and the Lord: Jewish Fundamentalism in Israel.* New
York: Council of Foreign Relations, 1988.

———. *Unsettled States / Disputed Lands: Britain and Ireland, France and Algeria, Israel and the West Bank–Gaza.* Ithaca, N.Y.: Cornell University Press,
1993.

Luz, E. *Parallels Meet: Religion and Nationalism in the Early Zionist Movement.* Philadelphia: Jewish Publication Society, 1988.

Maman, D. "The Social Organization of the Israeli Economy: A Comparative
Analysis." *Israel Affairs* 5, 2 and 3 (1999): 87–102.

Mann, Michael. "The Autonomous Power of State: Its Origins, Mechanisms
and Results." In *States in History,* ed. J. H. Hall. Oxford: Basil Blackwell,
1987.

———. "The Roots and Contradictions of Modern Militarism." *New Left Review* 162 (1987): 34.

Mapu, Abraham. *The Shepherd-Prince, Ahavat Tsiyon: A Historical Romance
of the Days of Isaiah.* 1845. Translated from the Hebrew by Benjamin A.
M. Schapiro. Rev. ed. New York: Brookside Publishing Co., 1937.

Mar'i, Sami Khalil. *Arab Education in Israel.* Syracuse, N.Y.: Syracuse University Press, 1978.

Margolis, H., and N. Singer. *What You See from There You Can't See from Here
. . . Factors That Influence Inclinations to Emigrate from the Commonwealth of Independent States.* Rechovot: Center for Development Studies,
1993. In Hebrew.

Martin, D. *The Breaking of the Image: A Sociology of Christian Theory and
Practice.* London: Basil Blackwell, 1980.

———. *The Religious and the Secular: Studies in Secularization.* London: Routledge & Kegan Paul, 1969.

Marwick, A. *War and Social Change in the Twentieth Century.* London: Macmillan, 1977.

Matras, J. *Social Change in Israel.* Chicago: Aldine, 1965.

Medding, P. *Mapai in Israel.* Cambridge: Cambridge University Press, 1972.

Memmi, A. *Who Is an Arab Jew?* Jerusalem: Academic Committee on the Middle East, 1975.

Metzer, J. *The Divided Economy of Mandatory Palestine.* Cambridge: Cambridge University Press, 1998.

Migdal, Joel S. "The Crystallization of the State and the Struggle over Rule-
making: Israel in Comparative Perspective." In *The Israeli State and Society:
Boundaries and Frontiers,* ed. Baruch Kimmerling, pp. 1–27. Albany: State
University of New York Press, 1989.

———. "State Making and Rule Making in Israel." In *The Israeli State and
Society: Boundaries and Frontiers,* ed. B. Kimmerling, pp. 1–23. Albany:
State University of New York Press, 1989.

———. *Strong Societies and Weak States: State-Society Relations and State Capabilities in the Third World.* Princeton: Princeton University Press, 1985,
1988

Miller, Y. N. *Government and Society in Rural Palestine, 1948.* Austin: University of Texas Press, 1985.

Mintz, A. "The Military Industrial Complex—The Israeli Case." *Journal of Strategic Studies* 6, 3 (1983): 103–27.

———. "Military-Industrial Linkages in Israel." *Armed Forces and Society* 12, 1 (1985): 9–27.

Mintz, A., and M. D. Ward, "The Political Economy of Military Spending in Israel." *American Political Science Review* 82 (1989): 521–33.

Mirski, Julia. "Psychological Adaptation of Students from the Former Soviet Union: Psychodynamic Aspects." Ph.D. thesis, Hebrew University, Jerusalem, 1983. In Hebrew.

Mirski, J., and L. Brawer. *To Make Aliyah as an Adolescent, to Become Adult as an Oleh: Immigrant Youth from the Former Soviet Union in Israel.* Jerusalem: Van Leer Institute, 1992. In Hebrew.

Mitchell, T. "The Limits of the State: Beyond Statist Approaches and Their Critics." *American Political Review* 85, 1 (1991): 77–96.

Moore, D., and B. Kimmerling. "Individual Strategies for Adopting Collective Identities." *International Sociology* 4 (1995): 387–408.

Morris, Benny. *The Birth of the Palestinian Refugee Problem, 1947–1949.* Cambridge: Cambridge University Press, 1988.

———. *Righteous Victims: A History of Zionist-Arab Conflict, 1881–1999.* New York: Knopf, 1999.

Mouffe, C. "Hegemony and Ideology in Gramsci." In *Gramsci and Marxist Theory,* ed. id., pp. 168–204. London: Routledge & Kegan Paul, 1979.

Nettl, J. P. "The State as a Conceptual Variable." *World Politics* 29 (1968): 552–59.

Nini, Y. *Kinneret's Yemenites: Their Settlement and Removal from the Land, 1912–1930.* Tel Aviv: Am Oved, 1996. In Hebrew.

Nordlinger, E. *The Autonomy of the Democratic State.* Cambridge, Mass.: Harvard University Press, 1981.

Panikkar, Raimundo. *Worship and Secular Man: An Essay on the Liturgical Nature of Man, Considering Secularization as a Major Phenomenon of Our Time and Worship as an Apparent Fact of All Times. A Study towards an Integral Anthropology.* London: Darton, Longman & Todd; Maryknoll, N.Y., Orbis Books, 1973.

Pankhurst, D. L. "Beta Esra'el (Falashas) in Their Ethiopian Setting." In *Ethiopian Jews in the Limelight,* ed. Shalva Weil, *Israel Social Science Research* 10 (1996): 1–12.

Parfitt, Tudor. *Operation Moses: The Story of the Exodus of the Falasha Jews from Ethiopia.* London: Weidenfeld & Nicolson, 1985.

Peled, Yoav. *Class and Ethnicity in the Pale: The Political Economy of Jewish Workers' Nationalism Late Imperial Russia.* New York: St. Martin's Press, 1989.

———. "Ethnic Democracy and the Legal Construction of Citizenship: Arab Citizens of the Jewish State." *American Political Science Review* 86, 2 (1992): 432–43.

Peleg, I., and O. Selikter, eds. *The Emergence of Bi-National Israel: The Second Republic in Making.* Boulder, Colo.: Westview Press, 1989,

Peri, Y., and A. Neubach. *Israeli Military-Industrial Complex.* Tel Aviv: International Center for Peace in the Middle East, 1984.

Porath, Y. *The Emergence of the Palestinian National Movement, 1917–1929.* London: Frank Cass, 1974.

———. *The Palestinian National Movement: From Riots to Rebellion.* London: Frank Cass, 1977.

Pratt, V. *Religion and Secularization.* London: Macmillan, 1970.

Quirin, A. *The Evolution of Ethiopian Jews: A History of the Beta Israel Falasha to 1920.* Philadelphia: University of Pennsylvania Press, 1992.

Rabinowitz, D. *Overlooking Nazareth: The Ethnography of Exclusion in a Mixed Town in Galilee.* New York: Cambridge University Press, 1996.

Raday, F. "On Equality." In *Women's Status in Israeli Law and Society,* ed. F. Raday, C. Shalev, and M. Liban-Kooby. Jerusalem: Schocken Publishing House, 1995. In Hebrew.

———. "Religion, Multiculturalism and Equality: The Israeli Case." *Israel Yearbook on Human Rights* 25 (1996): 195–241.

Radhakrishnan, R. "Toward an Effective Intellectual: Foucault or Gramsci?" In *Intellectuals: Aesthetics, Politics, Academics,* ed. B. Robbins, pp. 57–100. Minneapolis: University of Minnesota Press, 1990.

Ram, Uri. *The Changing Agenda of Israeli Sociology: Theory, Ideology and Identity.* Albany: State University of New York Press, 1995.

Ramon, Hayim. "A New Histadrut on Strong Pillars." *Economic Quarterly* 1 (April 1995): 9–16. In Hebrew.

Ravikowitz, Dahlia. "There Is No Secular Culture in This Country." *Globes,* December 22, 1995. In Hebrew.

Ravitzky, Aviezer. *Messianism, Zionism, and Jewish Religious Radicalism.* Translated by Michael Swirsky and Jonathan Chipman. Chicago: University of Chicago Press, 1996.

Reches, E. *The Arab Israeli Minority between Communism and Nationalism, 1965–1991.* Tel Aviv: Ha'Kibbutz Ha'Meuchad, 1993. In Hebrew.

Reisel, R., and E. Reisel. *A Secular Attachment to Judaism.* Tel Aviv: R. Reisel and E. Reisel, 1994.

Rejwan, Nissim. "The Two Israels: A Study in Europocentrism." *Judaism* 16, 1 (1967): 96–108.

Reuveny, J. *The Administration of Palestine under the British Mandate, 1920–1948: An Institutional Analysis.* Ramat Gan: Bar Ilan University, 1993. In Hebrew.

Rosenfeld, H., and S. Carmi, "The Privatization of Public Means, the State-Made Middle Class, and the Realization of Family Values in Israel." In *Kinship and Modernization in Mediterranean Society,* ed. J. G. Peristiany. Rome: American University Field Staff, 1976.

Roumani, M. M. *From Immigrants to Citizens: The Contribution of the Army to National Integration in Israel—The Case of Oriental Jews.* The Hague: Foundation for Studies of Plural Societies, 1979.

Rozenhek, Z. "Migration Regimes, Intra-State Conflicts, and the Policy of Exclusion and Inclusion: Migrant Workers in the Israeli State." *Social Problems* 47, 1 (2000): 49–67.

Said, Edward W. *Peace and Its Discontents: Essays on Palestine in the Middle East Peace Process.* New York: Vintage Books, 1996.

Salamon, Hagar. "Between Ethnicity and Religiosity—Internal Group Aspects of Conversion among Beta Israel in Ethiopia." *Pe'amim* 58 (1994): 104–99. In Hebrew.

———. "Slavery among the 'Beta-Israel' in Ethiopia." *Slavery and Abolition* 14 (1994): 72–88.

Sasson-Levy, O. "The Problem of Gender in Israeli Protest Movements: A Case Study," Paper presented at the Annual Meeting of the Association for Israel Studies, Milwaukee, Wisconsin, May 24–25, 1992.

Schweid, Eliezer. *The Idea of Judaism as a Culture.* Tel Aviv: Am Oved, 1986. In Hebrew.

———. *Israel at the Crossroads.* Philadelphia: Jewish Publication Society of America, 1973.

Segev, Tom. *The Seventh Million: The Israelis and the Holocaust.* Translated by Haim Watzman. New York: Hill & Wang, 1993.

Semyonov, Moshe, and Noah Lewin-Epstein. *The Arab Minority in Israel's Economy: Patterns of Ethnic Inequality.* Boulder, Colo.: Westview Press, 1993.

———. *Hewers of Wood and Drawers of Water: Noncitizen Arabs in the Israeli Labor Market.* Ithaca, N.Y.: Cornell University School of Industrial and Labor Relations, 1987.

Shabtay, M. "Identity Construction among Soldiers Immigrated from Ethiopia: Process of Interpretation and Struggle." Ph.D. thesis, Ben-Gurion University, Beersheva, 1995. In Hebrew.

Shafir, Gershon. *Land, Labor, and the Origins of the Israeli-Palestinian Conflict, 1882–1914.* New York: Cambridge University Press, 1989. Rev. ed. Berkeley and Los Angeles: University of California Press, 1996.

Shafir, Gershon, and Yoav Peled. "Citizenship and Stratification in an Ethnic Democracy." *Ethnic and Racial Studies* 21 (1998): 408–27.

Shalev, Michael. "Labor, State and Crisis: An Israeli Case Study." *Industrial Relations* 23, 3 (1984): 362–86.

———. *Labour and the Political Economy of Israel.* New York: Oxford University Press, 1992.

Shammas, Anton. *Arabesques.* Translated by Vivian Eden. New York: Harper & Row, 1988.

———. "Kitsch-22: On the Problems of the Relation between Majority and Minority Cultures in Israel." *Tikkun* 2 (1987): 22–26.

———. "A New Year for the Jews." *Kol Ha'Ir,* September 13, 1985. In Hebrew.

Shapira, Anita. "The Labor Movement and the Hebrew University." In *The History of the Hebrew University: Roots and Beginnings,* ed. S. Katz and M. Heyd, 1: 677–89. Jerusalem: Magnes Press, 1997. In Hebrew.

———. *Land and Power: The Zionist Resort to Force, 1881–1948.* Translated by William Templer. New York: Oxford University Press, 1992.

Shapiro, Yonathan. *Democracy in Israel.* Ramat Gan: Masada, 1977. In Hebrew.

———. "The End of the Dominant Party System." In *Elections in Israel,* ed. A. Arian. Jerusalem: Academic Press, 1980.

———. *The Formative Years of the Israeli Labor Party: The Organization of Power, 1919–1930.* London: Sage Publications, 1976.

Shavit, Z., ed. *The History of the Jewish Community in Eretz-Israel Since 1882: The Construction of Hebrew Culture in Eretz-Israel.* Jerusalem: Israeli Academy of Sciences and Humanities and Bialik Institute, 1998. In Hebrew.

Shehadeh, R. *The Third Way: A Journal of Life in the West Bank.* London: Quartet Books, 1982.

Shokeid, M. "Precepts vs. Tradition: Religious Trends among Middle Eastern Jews." *Megamot* 2–3 (1984): 250–64. In Hebrew.

Silberstein, Laurence J. *The Postzionism Debates: Knowledge and Power in Israeli Culture.* New York: Routledge, 1999.

Sivan, E. "The Intifada and Decolonization." *Middle East Review* 22 (1988–89): 1–12.

Smith, Anthony D. *The Ethnic Origins of Nations.* New York: Blackwell, 1986.

———. "The Myth of the 'Modern Nation' and the Myths of Nations." *Ethnic and Racial Studies* 1 (1988): 1–26.

———. "Zionism and Diaspora Nationalism," *Israel Affairs* 2 (1995): 1–19.

Smooha, Sammy. *Israel: Pluralism and Conflict.* Berkeley and Los Angeles: University of California Press, 1978.

———. "Minority Status in an Ethnic Democracy: The Status of the Arab Minority in Israel." *Ethnic and Racial Relations* 3, 3 (1990): 389–413.

Soysal, Y. *Limits of Citizenship: Migrants and Postnational Membership in Europe.* Chicago: University of Chicago Press, 1994.

Speier, H. "Militarism in the Eighteenth Century." In *Social Order and the Risks of War: Papers in Political Sociology,* pp. 230–52. Cambridge, Mass.: MIT Press, 1953.

Spilerman, S., and J. Habib. "Development Towns in Israel: The Role of Community in Creating Ethnic Disparities in Labor Force Characteristics." *American Journal of Sociology* 4 (1976): 781–812.

Sprinzak, E. *The Ascendance of Israel's Radical Right.* New York: Oxford University Press, 1978.

Stark, R., and W. Bainbridge, *The Future of Religion: Secularization, Revival and Cult Formation.* Berkeley and Los Angeles: University of California Press, 1985.

Swirski, S. *Israel: The Oriental Majority.* London: Zed Books, 1989.

———. *University, State, and Society in Israel.* Jerusalem: Mifras, 1982. In Hebrew.

Tamarin, G. R. *The Israeli Dilemma: Essays on a Warfare State.* Rotterdam: Rotterdam University Press, 1973.

Taylor, Charles. "Modes of Civil Society." *Public Culture* 3, 1 (1990): 95–132.

Teveth, S. *Moshe Dayan.* London: Weidenfeld & Nicolson, 1972.

Thompson, T. L. *The Mythic Past: Biblical Archaeology and the Myth of Israel.* New York: Basic Books, 1999.

Tilly, Ch. "War Making and State Making as Organized Crime." In *Bringing the State Back In,* ed. P. Evans, D. Rueschemeyer, and T. Skocpol, pp. 169–92. Cambridge: Cambridge University Press, 1988.

Turner, B. S. *Religion and Social Theory: A Materialist Perspective.* London: Heinemann, 1983.

United Kingdom. Royal Commission on Palestine. *Report.* Cmd. 5479. Presented by the Secretary of State for the Colonies to Parliament by Command of His Majesty. London: HMSO, 1937.

Vagts, Alfred. *A History of Militarism: Civilian and Military.* New York: Free Press, 1959 [1937].

Vital, D. *The Origins of Zionism.* New York: Oxford University Press, Clarendon Press, 1975.

Weber, Max. *The Theory of Social and Economic Organization.* Edited by Talcott Parsons. New York: Free Press, 1964.

Weil, Shalva. "Collective Denominations and Collective Identities among Ethiopian Jews." In *Ethiopian Jews in the Limelight,* ed. id., *Israel Social Science Research* 1 (1977): 58–98.

Weintraub, D., M. Lissak, and Y. Azmon. *Moshava, Kibbutz and Moshav: Patterns of Rural Settlement and Development in Palestine.* Ithaca, N.Y.: Cornell University Press, 1969.

Weisel, R., E. Leshem, and B. Adler. "Emigration Trends from Russia and Ukraine." Jerusalem: Jewish Agency, Department of Absorption, 1996. In Hebrew.

Wertburg, M. "Russian-Language Press in Israel." *Soviet Union Jews in Transition* 1, 16 (1994): 159–67.

Willis, A. P. "Sepharadic Torah Guardian: Ritual and the Politics of Piety." Ph.D. thesis, Department of Anthropology, Princeton University, 1993.

———. "Shas—The Sepharadic Torah Guardians: Religious Movement and Political Power." In *The Elections in Israel, 1992,* ed. A. Arian and M. Shamir, pp. 121–40. Albany: State University of New York Press, 1995.

Willner, D. *Nation Building and Community in Israel.* Princeton: Princeton University Press, 1969.

Wilson, Bryan. *Religion in a Secular Society: A Sociological Comment.* London: Watts, 1966.

Yannait, Rachel (Ben Zvi). *We are Ascending: Chapters of Life.* Tel Aviv: Am Oved, 1969. In Hebrew.

Yariv, A. "Wars by Choice—Wars by No Choice." In *Wars by Choice,* ed. J. Alpert, pp. 9–30. Tel Aviv: Jaffe Center for Strategic Studies, University of Tel Aviv, Ha'kibbutz Ha'meuchad, 1985. In Hebrew.

Yiftachel, Oren. "Israeli Society and Jewish-Palestinian Reconciliation: 'Ethnocracy' and Its Territorial Contradictions." *Middle East Journal* 51, 4 (1997): 505–19.

Yuchtman-Yaar, E., and Y. Peres. *Between Consent and Dissent: Democracy and Peace in the Israeli Mind.* Jerusalem: Israel Democracy Institute, 1998.

Yuval-Davis, N. *Gender and Nation.* London: Sage Publications, 1997.

Zakai, Dan. *The Economic Development in Judea and Samaria and Gaza Strip, 1985–1986.* Jerusalem: Research Division, Bank of Israel, 1988.

Zameret, Z. *Across a Narrow Bridge: Shaping the Education System during the Great Aliyah.* Shdeh Boker: Ben-Gurion Research Center, Ben-Gurion University, 1997. In Hebrew.

———. *The Melting Pot: The Frumkin Commission on the Education of Immigrant Children (1950).* Sdeh Boker: Ben-Gurion Research Center, Ben-Gurion University, 1993. In Hebrew.

Zemach, M., E. Leshem, and A. Weinger. "Survey on Adaptation of Immigrants from CIS." *Follow-Up Research,* No. 4. Tel Aviv: Dahaf Institute and the Jewish Agency, 1995. In Hebrew.

Zemach, M., and R. Weisel. "Adaptation of Immigrants from CIS (1990–1995) in Israel." *Follow-Up Research,* No. 5. Tel Aviv: Dahaf Institute and the Jewish Agency, 1996. In Hebrew.

Zerubavel, Yael. *Recovered Roots: Collective Memory and the Making of Israeli National Tradition.* Chicago: University of Chicago Press, 1995.

Zilberfarb, B. "Estimate of the Black Market in Israel and Abroad." *Economic Quarterly* 122 (1984): 319–22. In Hebrew.

Zloczover, A., and S. N. Eisenstadt, eds. *The Integration of Immigrants from Different Countries of Origin in Israel.* A Symposium held at the Hebrew University on October 25–26, 1966. Jerusalem: Magnes Press, 1969.

Zuckerman, M. *Shoah in the Sealed Room: The "Holocaust" in the Israeli Press during the Gulf War.* Tel Aviv: M. Zuckerman, 1993.

Zuriek, E. T. *The Palestinians in Israel: A Study in Internal Colonialism.* London: Routledge & Kegan Paul, 1979.

Index

Abu Bakr, caliph, as conqueror of Fertile Crescent and Middle East, 19
Abdullah ibn Hussein (king of Jordan), 40–41
absorption centers for new immigrants, 159–60
Achad Ha'am. *See* Ginsberg, Asher Hirsh
agency routinized, 100–102
Agranat, Judge Shimon, 200
agriculturization of Jews and Zionist project, 98
Agudat Israel party, 66, 105, 126; agreement with Jewish Agency, 198; foundation of, 188. *See also* Orthodoxy
AIDS, 157, 161–63
Alford, Robert, 58n
Algeria, French, 11, 45, 81n
aliyah, notion of, 187
Alliance Israélite universelle, 22
"Allon [Yigal] Plan," 46–47
Almog, Oz, 97
Aloni, Shulamit, 201n
Altneuland (Herzl), 25
America: and expansion of Hebrew cultural market, 118; immigration to, 189–200; North, 11, 44; South, 11, 44–45
Americanization of Israeli culture, 77n
American Jewish Joint Distribution Committee (AJJDC), activity in Ethiopia of, 154, 157
American Jewry, 203
American Revolution, 20
Amharization of ethnic groups in Ethiopia, 154
Am Oved (publishing house), 66

Anderson, Benedict, 100n
Anglo-American Committee of Inquiry, proposals of, 38
anti-Semitism, 22
Antonovsky, Aaron, 114n
"anxiety-arousing" tactics, 50
Aqaba, Gulf of, 41
al-Aqsa intifada, 171–72
Al-Aqsa Mosque, 32. *See also* Haram al-Sharif
Argentina, Jewish emigration to, 189
Arabization of Middle East, 19–20
Arab, "abandoned," property, 98
Arab Executive Committee, Palestinian, 29
Arab intellectuals in Israel, 135
Arab Jews, 94. *See also* Mizrahim
Arab Legion, 40–41
"Arab Liberation Army," 39
Arab parties in Israel, 53
Arabs in Israel: and boycott of 2001 elections, 172; cultural autonomy demanded by, 135n; as deprived of autonomous school system, 106; exclusion of, from Israeliness, 97, 171, 230; exclusion of, from peace camp, 244; formal citizenship of, 70; infiltration of, into middle class, 170–71; and solidarity with Palestinians of occupied territories, 171–72; and symbols of participation, 79; remnants of, after War of 1948, 94, 133–36; as threatened by Russian immigration, 142, 148; vote of, as "illegitimate," 185. *See also* Palestinians

Compositor: Binghamton Valley Composition, LLC
      Text: 10/13 Sabon
   Display: Sabon